ENDORSEMENTS

"I am deeply impressed on how some books can bring God's great plan for humankind together in a beautiful, unified historical story, which has not ended, but is still flowing like a great river: sometimes branching to become pools, awaiting more rain, and sometimes directly adding to the rushing current of Spiritual energy, but always flowing toward the ocean of life. *The Man Who Sent the Magi* is one such book opening up the exploration of a stream that I had never explored before. Zarathustra, I now see, was one who contributed greatly to religious thought. It certainly made me think."
– Shirlie Burriston, Member of the Baha'i Faith, Concord, CA

"Zarathustra's teaching that one of the main purposes for the creation of humankind was for Man to assume the position of Steward of His Earth is as appropriate today as in His time." – The Rev. Lori Sawdon, Pastor of Lafayette Methodist Church, Lafayette, CA

"This is a thought-provoking work worthy of your time. Of special interest to me was the table entitled 'Comparison of Religions' to be found on pages 242 to 250 with its amazing similarities between the Faith of Zarathustra and those of the Roman Catholic Church. Coincidence?" – Christoph Nauer, Pastoral Associate at St. Perpetua Catholic Church, Lafayette, CA

"This is one man's journey beyond the crossroads where Matthew's birth narrative and the three Persian visitors meet. It is a journey that leads the reader into a lost story that seems strangely familiar. This is clearly a work of dedication and commitment to the ongoing legacy of Zarathustra and the good life that continues to call the best out of humanity. Doug finds much in this legacy lingering in the construction of the Christ myth and percolating beneath the folds of history." – Rev. Dan Senter, ELCA Pastor of Our Saviour's Lutheran Church , Lafayette, CA

THE MAN
WHO SENT THE
MAGI

A RELIGIOUS ROSETTA STONE

by DOUGLAS ROPER KROTZ

Intermedia Publishing Group

The Man Who Sent The Magi

Published by:
Intermedia Publishing Group, Inc.
P.O. Box 2825
Peoria, Arizona 85380
www.intermediapub.com

ISBN 978-1-935529-87-3

CONTENTS

Chapter 3
Zarathustra – The Religion, Teachings, Ethics and Prophecies

Chapter 4
Zarathustra – The Nature of God   83

Chapter 5
Religion and Ministry of Jesus

Chapter 6
Parallels and Differences Between Jesus and Zarathustra

FOREWORD

The following book is a work of love, enlightenment, and gentle provocation. Douglas Krotz, whom I count as a friend, is a man who has roamed the religious landscape, and has found much to admire therein. He currently, and for many years now, finds himself in the Baha'i community. But from there, he has a wide and benevolent vista. As he writes in this book, "it should not be a surprise that all religions are full of tremendous similarities."

We are treated here to an explication of the religion of Zarathustra, whom the western world has come to know as Zoroaster. I am a Lutheran minister, whom Doug would be quick to point out means that I am a follower of Jesus first, and Martin Luther and other reformers second. My previous sum total knowledge of Zarathustra has been confined to his conception of a divine cosmic battle between good and evil (that was thought to underlie Christianity), and his cooptation by Nietzsche and Ricard Strauss, in their book and symphonic fanfare.

I am now much more appreciative of the scope and depth of Zarathustra's revelation and teaching. And I am deeply struck by the "tremendous similarities" between his and my religions, and am willing to consider that Jesus drank consciously or unconsciously of Zarathustrian waters. Otherwise, what to make of coinciding concepts of sin and evil, a coming judgment, life after death, temptation, salvation, prayer and the like?

One could argue that all of the good religious ideas have always been in the air, probably inherently so within the fabric of creation. And thus Jesus and Zarathustra and Moses and Mohammed and Buddha might have been tapping into the same source. But that just reinforces the idea that we will tend to share doctrines, no matter who had them revealed to them first.

I am not so naïve as to think that all people believe the same things. There are indeed radical and perhaps irreconcilable differences between people of faith, evidenced in the religious and so-called "culture wars" foaming around us. And we are far from being in agreement about what constitutes right thought and action and speech.

Nevertheless, I am impressed by Doug Krotz's encouragement, in the last chapter, to become an ethical and moral people. One might call the chapter, as in a subset of the Christian tradition, an "altar call." And the altar upon which he would ask us to kneel is the thought and insights of Zarathustra, as revealed by the very Ahura Mazda. And in this call back to Zarathustrian thought, and even to one's very self, I hear echoes of Buddhism, Islam, Taoism, Judaism, Sikhism, and yes, Christianity in general.

The human race is broad and protean. We have been created, as Doug suggests, with the capacity for free will. We are also the striving race, the technological race, and the uniquely creative race. . As a result, we are frequently the warring race. Doug's book, besides being that effort of enlightenment, as mentioned above, also has the purpose of peacemaking. I wish him well in that goal, as I commend this book to you, kind reader.

Rev. Brian Stein-Webber
Executive Director, Interfaith Council of Contra Costa County
August 21, 2010

ACKNOWLEDGEMENTS

For their encouraging attitude and patience with my odd hours on the computer, I offer my sincere appreciation to those family members with whom I share my home; my wife, Diana, my daughters Katie and Sarah, and my sister-in law, Pamela Carr, and further, my mother-in-law and sounding board, Nancy Carr. I am grateful for the interest and support of the members of the Lamorinda Interfaith Ministerial Association, and to one member thereof, for his kind foreword, the Reverend Brian Stein-Webber, director of the Interfaith Council of Contra Costa County and Pastor of Trinity Lutheran Church, Oakland, California. I say God Bless and thank you.

A special nod of thanks goes to Larry Davis and Terry Whalin of Intermedia Publishing Group. It is with their assistance this book will get published.

For using a part of her summer vacation from the University of California, to complete editing, formatting and final typing, THANK YOU, sweet daughter SARAH.

To Mary T. Nett, a long-time friend, I owe TO YOU a huge DEBT OF GRATITUDE for your several years of research and for your excellent editing skills.

An acknowledgement with deepest gratitude to my lovely daughter Christine Tonkin and her wonderful husband, Scotty "Bon Scot" Tonkin for never ceasing, even if sometimes rather insistent support from about day three through manuscript completion. THANK YOU GUYS.

Lastly, for encouraging and endorsing the out-of-the-box thinking that nudged me out of my comfort zone into doing the additional research and the actual writing, a sincere thank you to Kenneth Rairden.

INTRODUCTION

FOOD FOR THOUGHT

Quite often, religious beliefs are primarily based upon what you were taught as a youth by your parents, and in Catechism or Sunday school. If your religious views are as they have been for most of your life, it might be a good time to see how certain of those beliefs you are! How much of that religious training was received during your grade school days? Have many years gone by with a subsequent blurring of memory? Is there a chance that what you were taught was simplified to make it age appropriate?

With secular knowledge learned in school, there is a constant building upon the previous years' knowledge with this years' learning dependent upon the preceding. Knowledge gained in the second grade was built upon that learned in the first, the eighth grade upon the seventh and the accumulations of the preceding years, and so on. Through this process, the wealth of information grew and continued to become more challenging with each higher grade level.

It would have been wonderful if the same had been true with our studies of God and the Bible. However, with most spiritual instruction, the actual learning of religion, its history, significance and practical application was basically completed between the ages of eight to fifteen. In my case, I had barely put the Easter Bunny and the Tooth Fairy in their proper place when the real spiritual education ceased.

The writing of this book has assisted me in analyzing my spiritual lessons and in giving me a new focus. It is meant to help you do the same. Come join me on a journey of discovery. We will look at what it is that the Bible actually says, and, just as importantly, what it does not say. You should find that this book will change some perspectives, and possibly some of your long-held religious conclusions.

While looking at the life of Jesus, much of what was said and done by Him should take on beautiful new meanings especially as we look at another special man of God, Zoroaster, the Man who sent the Magi by his prophesy made centuries before the birth of Jesus. Zoroaster introduced the concept of a single deity. His teachings were supportive of the monotheistic view of Creation, but since most of the world believed otherwise, he had to teach with compassion and understanding. In order to have peoples with differing religious opinions listen to Him, he would listen very closely to theirs. It was not enough to merely listen, it was necessary for him to actually hear and understand their beliefs.

How will reading about a man who lived thousands of years ago assist in the adjustment of our religious perspectives? It may seem impossible in these days of rapid changes in technology, facts and fads. Remember, while technology has progressed immensely in the recent past, the basic mind, body and soul of man has remained essentially unchanged. Consider as you look at the early Romans, Egyptians, Sumerians, and Greeks that some of their accomplishments in architecture, art, mathematics, philosophy and many other areas of expertise, you should be aware, as Zoroaster was, that often these people credited the accomplishments to their many gods for aid in the processes, which brought new ideas to fruition. Were they wrong for so doing? Were they wrong for looking to and praying for guidance from what they believed was the correct spiritual path? The results from this guidance are still admired for their magnificence! Should the belief systems of these peoples be a reason for us to lessen our appreciation of their accomplishments in any way? Zoroaster, who we shall be calling by His Persian name, Zarathustra, from this point on, would have said NO!!

It is hoped that the journey of discovery upon which you are about to embark will bring to you a sense of astonishment and wonder similar to that which I have experienced in writing this book. **So come, let us make a spiritual journey of discovery together!**

❧ CHAPTER 1 ❧

THE BIRTH AND EARLY LIFE OF JESUS

THE IMPORTANCE OF THE STORY OF THE MAGI

Since childhood, I have been fascinated by the Magi, those three beautifully dressed Wise Men who came to Israel bearing gifts of great value for Jesus, the Christ Child. To me, as a seven-year-old, the whole episode seemed so magical. First, the Magi met with the evil King Herod and told him of a special new star. They followed the star again to Bethlehem, and knelt at a manger to worship an infant, but not his parents. Finally, they gave to the parents extremely expensive gifts, which they had brought from so far away. To me, there seemed to be a great significance to this biblical story. To my frustration, I found there seemed to be far less importance to the story and its wonderful details in the eyes of many that I queried.

Some sixty years later, I feel even stronger about the importance of these majestic individuals in the Nativity story of the New Testament. Join me in this journey, and see if you, too, feel that there should be far more, and a different, emphasis placed upon this story than there presently is, from Christian and other religions.

Who were the Magi? Why had they come over a thousand miles to visit a child? Were they really Kings? I was told by the minister in the small community church of my parents that these were unimportant questions, and that I should not waste time or energy on them. After all, was it not enough that Jesus was born? I made the mistake of asking this truly fine man of the cloth that, if the Magi and the story were so unimportant, why the early biblical placement and the tremendous detail? I received a roughly ten minute sermon on respect of the holy and what is meant by the phrase "to have Faith." It was a very nice personal sermon, but it neither answered my questions, nor made them go away. Over the years since then, to my similar questions, priests and pastors of various churches and denominations have been uniformly dismissive in their answers. While researching these questions, I discovered that there was indeed a sender of the Magi, which only reinforced what I had often wondered. The Magi's journey was the result of a prophecy made many hundreds of years before the birth of Jesus, which made me even more curious.

Wait! I'm sounding again like that curious seven-year-old! Let's investigate some of the recorded history of the time and circumstances into which the Magi came.

Herod the Great was a member of the dynasty who ruled parts or all of Palestine (Israel) from 55 BC to approximately 93 AD, at the behest of the Roman Empire. Herod had been of service to Rome during years of Palestinian unrest, and had been appointed Governor of Judea in 37 BC. He was appointed King in 30 BC, and would continue his reign until approximately 4 BC.[1]

In many ways, the Jewish population benefited from Herod's rule. He was successful at keeping the peace during difficult times, and he remitted the taxes due Rome as required and in timely fashion. In addition, he was responsible for the expansion of the Temple of Solomon in Jerusalem.[2] However, Herod was a man whose life was full of melodrama, due in part to his temperamental flare-ups, but also due to the palace intrigues among his ten wives. He is said to have been responsible for the murder of his wife, Mariamne, her grandfather and brother, and even some of his own children, because of alleged plots on his life.[3]

And what about the Magi? Who or what were they? The term "Magi" is derived from the Old Persian term "moγu," in the Zarathustrian Scriptures "The Avesta."[4] The term moγu was used to refer to the Zarathustrian priest caste who, in most cases, were directly related to Zarathustra, its prophet-founder. At the time of the Nativity, the mandates of their office required the Magi to be the guardians and interpreters of the religion, and, as such, they were very aware of its teachings and prophecies. They traveled to Bethlehem because of a very special prophecy, which stated that there would be a return of the spirit that had been within Zarathustra many hundreds of years earlier.[5] The Zarathustrian Pahlavi Rivayat (48:1-6) says of the Messiah (Aushedar):

48:1   "After that time, when Zarathushtra came to a consultation with Ohrmazd [i.e., God], and 1500 years after the time of Zarathushtra, when it is the millennium of Religion, Aushedar will come into consultation with Ohrmazd for 50 years.

48:2   On the same day Mihr Yazad, that is, the sun, will stand at mid-day, for ten days and nights it will stand at the zenith of Heavens.

48:3   For three years, whatever plants are not needed (i.e. not harvested), they will not wither then.

48:4   He will purify the religion, he will bring [the ritual precepts of] Hadamansar into use, and men will act according to Hadamansar.

48:5   The (members of the) wolf species will all go to one place, and in one place they will be merged, and there will be one wolf whose breadth (will be) 415 paces and length 433 paces.

48:6   And on the authority of Aushedar they will muster an army, and they will go to battle with that wolf. First they will perform the yasna [i.e., oblation], and through their yasna (it will) not (be) possible to withstand [them]."[6]

Another prophecy of the Messiah [Soshyans] is provided in the Zand of Vahman Yasht, Chapter 9:

9:1-2   "As regards Ushedar,... at thirty years of age he will come to a conference with me, Ohrmazd, and receive the Religion.

When he departs from the conference, he will call to the swift-horsed sun: 'Stand still!'"[7]

Zarathustra prophesied that, in that return, there would be a different man, a newborn child.[8] The child would have its own physical body, and what would be returning was the Spirit of God that had been within Zarathustra Himself. He went on to say that the ministry of the child would not commence until He was thirty years of age.[9]

In the King James Version of the Bible, Matthew describes the visit of the Magi:

Matthew 2:1 "Now when Jesus was born in Bethlehem of Judaea in the days of Herod the King, behold there came wise men from the east to Jerusalem,

Matthew 2:2 Saying, Where is he that is born King of the Jews? for we have seen his star in the east, and are come to worship him.

Matthew 2:3 When Herod the king had heard these things, he was troubled, and all Jerusalem with him.

Matthew 2:4 And when he had gathered all the chief priests and scribes of the people together, he demanded of them where Christ should be born.

Matthew 2:5 And they said unto him, In Bethlehem in Judaea: for thus it is written by the prophet,

Matthew 2:6 And thou Bethlehem, in the land of Juda, art not the least among the princes of Juda: for out of thee shall come a Governor, that shall rule my people Israel.

Matthew 2:7 Then Herod, when he had privily called the wise men, inquired of them diligently what time the star appeared.

Matthew 2:8 And he sent them to Bethlehem, and said, Go and search diligently for the young child; and when ye have found him, bring me word again, that I may come and worship him also.

Matthew 2:9 When they had heard the king, they departed; and lo, the star, which they saw in the east, went before them, till it came and stood over where the young child was.

Matthew 2:10 When they saw the star, they rejoiced with exceeding great joy.

Matthew 2:11 And when they were come into the house, they saw the young child with Mary his Mother, and fell down, and worshipped him: and when they had opened their treasures, they presented unto him gifts; gold, and frankincense and myrrh.

Matthew 2:12 And being warned of God in a dream that they should not return to Herod, they departed into their own country another way."[10]

Let's think a bit about the implications of the visit of the Magi.

1. The visit validated the visions and dreams of Joseph and Mary, with respect to the special nature of Jesus.

Matthew 1:18 "Now the birth of Jesus Christ was on this wise: When as his mother Mary was espoused to Joseph, before they came together, she was found with the child of the Holy Ghost.

Matthew 1:19 Then Joseph her husband, being a just man, and not willing to make her a publick example, was minded to put her away privily.

Matthew 1:20 But while he thought on these things, behold, the angel of the Lord appeared unto him in a dream, saying, Joseph, thou son of David, fear not to take unto thee Mary thy wife" for that which is conceived in her is of the Holy Ghost.

Matthew 1:21 And she shall bring forth a son, and thou shalt call his name Jesus: for he shall save his people from their sins.

Matthew 1:22 Now all this was done, that it might be fulfilled which was spoken of the Lord by the prophet, saying,

Matthew 1:23 Behold, a virgin shall be with child, and shall bring forth a son, and they shall call his name Emmanuel, which being interpreted is, God with us."[11]

Luke 1:26 "And in the sixth month the angel Gabriel was sent from God unto a city of Galilee, named Nazareth,

Luke 1:27 To a virgin espoused to a man whose name was Joseph, of the house of David; and the virgin's name was Mary.

Luke 1:28 And the angel came in unto her, and said, Hail, thou that art highly favoured, the Lord is with thee: blessed are thou among women.

Luke 1:29 And when she saw him, she was troubled at his saying, and cast in her mind what manner of salutation this should be.

Luke 1:30 And the angel said unto her, Fear not, Mary: for thou hast found favor with God.

Luke 1:31 And behold, thou shalt conceive in thy womb, and bring forth a son, and shalt call his name Jesus.

Luke 1:32 He shall be great, and shall be called the Son of the Highest: and the Lord God shall give unto him the throne of his father David:

Luke 1:33 And he shall reign over the house of Jacob for ever; and of his kingdom there shall be no end."[12]

It would have been rare to have such important men come to the birth place of a commoner to honor, worship and offer valuable gifts to a newborn. What would be the impact today if you, as a new parent, should receive such a visit from world leaders and holy men, even though they could fly in from anywhere on earth in less than forty-eight hours? How much more amazing in the case of the Magi? Theirs was a journey of many weeks of arduous and dangerous land travel.

What would you ask of these men [and women] during their visit?

How would this incident affect your parenting and subsequent decisions for your child?

2. The Magi offered gifts appropriate for a child of royal and possibly prophetic birth.

The Jewish prophet Isaiah foretold the coming of the Messiah, and that Gentiles and kings would become aware of, and attracted by, His light. He prophesied that they would gather together, come from afar by camel, and bring gifts of gold and incense:

Isaiah 60:1 "Arise, shine; for thy light is come, and the glory of the Lord is risen upon thee.

Isaiah 60:2 For, behold, the darkness shall cover the earth, and gross darkness the people: but the Lord shall arise upon thee, and his glory shall be seen upon thee.

Isaiah 60:3 And the Gentiles shall come to thy light, and kings to the brightness of thy rising.

Isaiah 60:4 Lift up thine eyes round about, and see: all they gather themselves together, they come to thee: thy sons shall come from afar, and thy daughters shall be nursed at thy side.

Isaiah 60:5 Then thou shalt see, and flow together, and thine heart shall fear, and be enlarged; because the abundance of the sea shall be converted unto thee, the forces of the Gentiles shall come unto thee.

Isaiah 60:6   The multitude of camels shall cover thee, the dromedaries of Midian and Ephah; all they from Sheba shall come: they shall bring gold and incense; and they shall shew forth the praises of the Lord."[13]

The Magi's gifts were all appropriate for a king. The meaning of the gold is fairly obvious; in the ancient world, myrrh was used as an anointing oil, and frankincense as a perfume.

As prophetic symbols, it is said that gold is a symbol of kingship on earth, frankincense is a symbol of the priesthood, and myrrh is a symbol of death, in that it is an embalming oil.[14]

3. Though the Magi initially met with King Herod, they were warned by God in a dream not to return to him following their visit to the child Jesus in Bethlehem:

Matthew 2:12   "And being warned of God in a dream that they should not return to Herod, they departed into their own country another way."[15]

It seems logical that the Magi would have been able to warn Mary and Joseph of the potential for repercussions on the part of Herod, and could have assisted them in seeing that baby Jesus was not harmed. The Bible records that Herod did, in fact, subsequently order the mass slaying of hundreds, if not thousands, of infants under the age of two:

Matthew 2:16   "Then Herod, when he saw that he was mocked of the wise men, was exceeding wroth, and sent forth, and slew all the children that were in Bethlehem, and in all the coasts thereof, from two years old and under, according to the time when he had diligently enquired of the wise men."[16]

I was amazed to discover, while writing this book, that the King James Version of the Bible states that Herod's edict concerned all infants, not just males, under the age of two years. Is this not what you remembered, too?

4. It seems likely that the Magi would have introduced themselves to Mary and Joseph, and explained the reason for their visit.

After all, they were men of culture and good breeding. From the nature of their discourse with King Herod (Matt. 2:1-9)[17], we can infer that they must also have offered a detailed explanation to Mary and Joseph of why they had come and why they had bowed down to worship the infant in the manger.

5. The journey of the Magi would have taken many weeks, and possibly as long as four months.

Tradition states that their journey originated in their separate homelands of modern day Iraq, Iran and Ethiopia. Travel to Bethlehem would be in excess of 900 to 1300 miles if the trip had been by air; since the Magi traveled an overland route, they probably traveled at least twenty percent further. And since they journeyed by either camel or horseback, and the average daily distance that could have been traveled by either mode is approximately twenty-five miles, the total journey might easily have taken several months.[18]

6. The size of the traveling party would have had to be sufficient to ensure the safety and comfort of the Magi, without posing a visible threat to Herod or the Roman Empire.

For all practical purposes, the Magi had traveled into enemy territory, passing through lands which harbored roving bands of highwaymen and bandits, and crossing over borders guarded by foreign soldiers.

Over the years, estimates from theological scholars, both Christian and Zarathustrian, have placed the number in the party at between twenty and seventy-five, including the Magi themselves. This number is logical in that they would need a compliment of soldiers, guides, animal handlers, cooks and equipment managers, but their party would have to be small enough so as not to be a threat to the armies of Rome.

7. The Magi would have been aware of diplomatic protocol, and benefited from their regal status.

Since they were indeed "wise men," the Magi would likely have investigated the state of affairs in the country to which they traveled. They would have sent an emissary to inform King Herod, and thus the Roman soldiers, of their impending visit, so that they might have safe passage, as well as a respectful, prompt audience with the king.

In the Nativity story of Matthew, we are told that the Magi chose to return home by a different route from the one by which they had arrived.[19] Might they not, as a courtesy, have sent a message to the King regarding their change in plans? Remember, the Roman soldiers at the border could have stopped them if Herod chose to end any diplomatic immunity they might have enjoyed.

And if they indeed were afforded a form of diplomatic immunity, might they not have included Mary, Joseph and the baby Jesus in their party for at least part of the journey from Bethlehem? It is even possible that the Magi might have escorted the Holy Family all of the way to Egypt, which was not yet a part of the Roman Empire,[20] and was therefore a logical place of refuge.

8. The "Star of Bethlehem" which guided the Magi was an astronomical phenomenon which seems to have been noticed by almost no one else.[21]

As part of their clerical duties, the Magi paid particular attention to the stars. They had, in fact, gained an international reputation in astrology and astronomy, which was a highly regarded science in the ancient world.[22]

If the star had been not only visible, but obvious, to the Magi for the months of their journey, it should have been a source of much speculation and wonderment throughout the world of that day. This was a time when the stars were not blotted out by city lights, a time when people were familiar with the night skies.

A pamphlet from the Hayden Planetarium in New York, entitled "The Christmas Star,"[23] suggests several possibilities for the Star: a) a bright meteor, although meteors are too transient to have lighted the sky for so long a journey; b) a comet; Halley's Comet appeared in 11 BC, and another comet appeared in 4 BC; c) a nova, not a new star, but perhaps an old one which suddenly burst into exceptional brilliance; d) a conjunction of stars and planets, but, again, this phenomenon would not have continued for the time necessary for the journey.

An interesting side story, which is not a part of the rendition found in Matthew, concerns what has become known in the Holy Land as "the Well of the Star." It is an old, stone-curbed drinking place still to be found, and still working, on the northern outskirts of Bethlehem. Today, that well is still the resting and refreshment place for cameleers and shepherds. It has beside it a low stone basin or "cup" into which travelers can pour water from the well for their thirsty animals. Ancient legend[24] says that the Magi, en route from Herod's palace in Jerusalem to Bethlehem, temporarily lost their guiding star, but found it in the reflection of this unfailing well.

9. The Magi were descendents of the once powerful Persian Empire, whose relations with the Jewish people had always been friendly and compassionate.

Their interactions, however, had consistently been from the stance of the powerful interacting with the weak. The Jews had required the military and financial assistance of the Persian Emperors Cyrus the Great and Darius I to escape their bondage in Babylon and to reconstruct the Temple of Solomon in Jerusalem.[25]

Why should it be so important for these Persians to honor the birth of this peasant child, whom they termed "King of the Jews"[26]? Even should Jesus have been able to assume the role of earthly king, He would have remained subservient to the Roman Empire.

Various Aspects of the Visit of the Magi

How might history have been different, without the visit by the Magi?

1. Herod might not have executed the children under the age of two in Bethlehem and the surrounding coastal regions, since he would not have been aware of Jesus' birth and the perceived threat to his throne. This might have reduced Jesus' visibility in later years, when He would have been surrounded by many more people of His own age.

2. Mary and Joseph might not have taken Jesus to Egypt for His important early childhood development years, thus altering His experience and education.

3. If Mary and Joseph had not taken Jesus to Egypt, the biblical prophecy foretelling God's calling of His son out of Egypt would have gone unfulfilled.

Hosea 11:1   "And Israel was a child, then I loved him, and called my son out of Egypt."[27]

4. Without the gifts "of great value," things might have been very different for Mary, Joseph and the child Jesus. Their ability to undertake major life changes such as the journey to, and the stay in, Egypt would have been vastly reduced.

Now take a look at some other things not addressed in the biblical story of the Magi, according to St. Matthew. How important might their visit have really been?

For yourself, try re-asking this question inserting:

"...for Mary?"

"...for Joseph?"

"...for Jesus, especially as it related to His later life?"

"...for each of the Wise Men?"

"...for the rest of the people in the world, then and now?"

Jesus' Early Years

The Bible has very little to say about the infancy and childhood of Jesus. The gospel of Luke describes the presentation of the baby Jesus at the Temple in Jerusalem for His circumcision in accordance with the laws of Moses, and the recognition of his status as the Messiah by Simeon and Anna:

Luke 2:21   "And when eight days were accomplished for the circumcising of the child, his name was called JESUS, which was so named of the angel before he was conceived in the womb.

Luke 2:22   And when the days of her purification according to the law of Moses were accomplished, they brought him to Jerusalem, to present him to the Lord;

Luke 2:23   (As it is written in the law of the Lord, Every male that openeth the womb shall be called holy to the Lord;)

Luke 2:24   And to offer a sacrifice according to that which is said in the law of the Lord, A pair of turtledoves, or two young pigeons.

Luke 2:25   And, behold, there was a man in Jerusalem, whose name was Simeon; and the same man was just and devout, waiting for the consolation of Israel: and the Holy Ghost was upon him.

Luke 2:26   And it was revealed unto him by the Holy Ghost, that he should not see death, before he had seen the Lord's Christ.

Luke 2:27   And he came by the Spirit into the temple: and when the parents brought in the child Jesus, to do for him after the custom of the law,

Luke 2:28   Then took he him up in his arms, and blessed God, and said,

Luke 2:29   Lord, now lettest thou thy servant depart in peace, according to thy word:

Luke 3:30   For mine eyes have seen thy salvation,

Luke 2:31   Which thou hast prepared before the face of all people;

Luke 2:32   A light to lighten the Gentiles, and the glory of thy people Israel.

Luke 2:33   And Joseph and his mother marvelled at those things which were spoken of him.

Luke 2:34   And Simeon blessed them, and said unto Mary his mother, Behold, this child is set for the fall and rising again of many in Israel; and for a sign which shall be spoken against;

Luke 2:35   (Yea, a sword shall pierce through thy own soul also,) that the thoughts of many hearts may be revealed.

Luke 2:36   And there was one Anna, a prophetess, the daughter of Phanuel, of the tribe of Aser: she was of a great age, and had lived with an husband seven years from her virginity;

Luke 2:37   And she was a widow of about fourscore and four years, which departed not from the temple, but served God with fastings and prayers night and day.

Luke 2:38   And she coming in that instant gave thanks likewise unto the Lord, and spake of him to all them that looked for redemption in Jerusalem.

Luke 2:39   And when they had performed all things according to the law of the Lord, they returned into Galilee, to their own city Nazareth.

Luke 2:40   And the child grew, and waxed strong in spirit, filled with wisdom: and the grace of God was upon him."[28]

In the balance of the second chapter of Matthew, we are told of the vision of Joseph in a dream that he should take Mary and Jesus at night and depart for Egypt, where they stayed until they became aware of the death of Herod.[29] Jesus is said to have been eight years of age when His family returned to Israel.

Matthew 2:13   "And when they were departed, behold, the angel of the Lord appeareth to Joseph in a dream, saying, Arise, and take the young child and his mother, and flee into Egypt, and be thou there until I bring thee word: for Herod will seek the young child to destroy him.

Matthew 2:14   When he arose, he took the young child and his mother by night, and departed into Egypt:

Matthew 2:15   And was there until the death of Herod: that it might be fulfilled which was spoken of the Lord by the prophet, saying, Out of Egypt have I called my son."[30]

When they returned to Israel, they settled in Nazareth.

Matthew 2:19   "But when Herod was dead, behold, an angel of the Lord appeared in a dream to Joseph in Egypt,

Matthew 2:20   Saying, Arise, and take the young child and his mother, and go into the land of Israel: for they are dead which sought the young child's life.

Matthew 2:21   And he arose, and took the young child and his mother, and came into the land of Israel.

Matthew 2:22   But when he heard that Archelaus did reign in Judea in the room of his father Herod, he was afraid to go thither: notwithstanding, being warned of God in a dream, he turned aside into the parts of Galilee:

Matthew 2:23   And he came and dwelt in a city called Nazareth: that it might be fulfilled which was spoken by the prophets, He shall be called a Nazarene."[31]

Sadly, there is no history of Jesus' education while in Egypt. He must have received an extensive education there, as evidenced by the surprise of His parents over the knowledge He displayed at the age of twelve, when the family visited Jerusalem for the Passover. Jesus was somehow left behind when Mary and Joseph left to return to Nazareth. The couple returned when they became aware of His absence, and discovered Him sitting in the Temple, in the midst of the doctors and other learned men, both listening to them and asking them questions. "And all that heard him were astonished at his understanding and answers."[32]

Is the importance of this incident, and thus, its inclusion in Luke, to bring to light the education Jesus received in Egypt, or His very special nature and innate knowledge, or both?   Since there is no way of knowing the answer, we must leave these questions for later discussion.

Jesus returned from Jerusalem with His parents, and entered into what biblical theologians refer to as "the Years of Silence."[33] There is no history of these years in the Gospels of Matthew, Mark, Luke and John. Christian tradition states that this was the period in which He learned the trade of His earthly father, Joseph, first as an apprentice, and finally, as a full-fledged carpenter.[34]

The Methodology of Piece by Piece Analysis

So far in this chapter, we have analyzed the short biblical story of the Magi in the same way a youth would take his grandfather's pocket watch apart, piece by piece. As each piece came out, it was cleaned and carefully put aside in a logical order, so that the watch could be put back together later. There was a wonderment on the part of the youth at the beautifully crafted little pieces, not only at how precise they were, but how, when they were put back together correctly, the watch would again work. Despite the age of the watch, it seemed to the youth to be a marvel of science.

It is a real shame if you did not actually experience as a youth what was just described. I did, and for me, it was a real eye-opener regarding the intrinsic beauty of old things, and how, in olden times, there was much that is not appreciated today. If you did not have the watch experience as a youngster, it is not suggested that you actually attempt to have it as an adult. This is most likely an experience that should be pursued only by youth, in that the patience required, not to mention the manual dexterity, is a physical attribute that I, at least, no longer have.

The purpose of the example is not to turn you into a watchmaker, but to encourage you to look at the various parts of the Magi story, or any other item that we will be analyzing, and to put it back together in a way that works for you, at your present age and maturity. Too often, we seek the first obviously correct answer and treat it as the total truth, without stopping to see if there is more to the question at hand. I believe that this may be the cause of much of the misunderstanding in the world today.

Another lesson from the watch exercise is that all of the parts need to fit back together in the correct order, and that there can be no leftover parts. Yet another lesson is that, after seeing how the watch works, you must find the adjustment mechanism that allows you to adjust the speeds of the hands of the watch. It is not enough that the watch now works and keeps time; it must also be adjusted so that the time showing on the watch face will continue to correspond to the actual passage of time. In a similar way, we must realize that no part of the Nativity story, or any other event in life, should be considered as isolated by itself. The following table entitled "The Chronology of Modern Man" contains information from new discoveries in Archeology, Paleogeology and other sciences, some of which may be found less than complete. The inclusion is for the purpose of assisting you to open up to new possibilities and to question traditional history, such as man leaving his caves and life as a hunter/gather and suddenly appearing well-dressed, and building cities and pyramids. Peruse the table and open your mind up enough to enjoy the contents. Consider the idea that since the appearance of Modern Man there has been the ability to question, investigate and create with capacities not allowed to other members of the animal kingdom.

The Next Chapter

Let us now look at the source of the inspiration for the journey of the Magi, Zarathustra Spitama, the man who, by His prophecies made so many years ago, was the journey's motivating factor. We will return to discussion of the life and ministry of Jesus, but we will now jump back in history to Zarathustra, founder of the religion bearing His name, which has become widely known as the "Ethical Religion"[35] and the "Religion of the Good Life."[36]

Chronology of Modern Man (MM)

General History	Persian/ Zarathustrian History	Date	Judeo- Christian History	Other Religious History
MM travels as hunter-gatherers throughout Africa, Asia and Europe		160,000-74,000 BC		
Eruption of Mt. Toba causes a six year nuclear winter and instant 1000 year Ice Age		74,000 BC		
Dramatic warming allows movement again through the Fertile Crescent and into Europe and Asia		72,000-50,000 BC		
Groups from Central Asian continent move north into the Arctic Circle; Birth of cave art		50,000-22,000 BC		
Start of a new Ice Age; Native Americans cross into North American continent	Aryans (Indo-Europeans) forced South	22,000-18,000 BC		
Egypt: first cultivate cereals		18,000-9,000 BC		
Final collapse of Ice Age; Paleolithic Era ends	Iran/Iraq: agriculture and pottery, copper centers	9,000-7000 BC	Palestine: agriculture and pottery, copper centers	
First Neolithic cultures in the Fertile Crescent		7,000-5000 BC		

General History	Persian/ Zarathustrian History	Date	Judeo- Christian History	Other Religious History
Bronze Age emerges; Unification of Upper and Lower Kingdoms of Egypt; Use of papyrus; Beginning of pyramid construction	Middle East: use of lost wax process (bronze molds), gold, silver, lead; Domestication of Horses on south Russian Steppes; Iron war chariots	5,000-2,000 BC	Israel: bronze, use of plow; Sumer: casting of copper, first cities; Sinai: copper mines, copper trade with Egypt	First year of the Mayan Calendar; Systematic astronomy in Egypt, Babylon, India and China
Babylonian King Hammurabi develops oldest existing code of laws	Birth of Zarathustra. Reign of King Vishtaspa in greater Iran. Composition of the Gathas, Yasna	2,000-1,500 BC	Sumeria: first iron and steel; Sumeria/ Northern Israel "caravans bring the tin to Hazor"	Birth of Abraham(1840 BC) Abraham moves to Egypt as an advisor; The Hebrews migrate to Egypt, beginning a 450 year sojourn
New Kingdom period begins in Egypt. Fall of the city of Troy	Haptanghaiti and other Old Avestan literature.	1,500-1,300 BC	Israel: first alphabets.	
The Iron Age in the ancient Near East		1,300-1,200 BC	Moses, the Hebrew lawgiver and prophet, reveals the Torah; The Jews emigrate from Egypt to Palestine (1260)	
	Zarathustrianism spreads in eastern Iran	1,200-1,000 BC	Unification of the 12 tribes of Israel under Saul	Compilation of the Hindu Rig Veda
		1,000-800 BC	Solomon builds the Jerusalem temple; Hebrew elders begin to write the Old Testament books of the Bible.	
The first Olympiad; Romulus founds the city of Rome.	Empire of the Medes includes all of Iran; Zarathustrianism gains strength in western Iran	800-600 BC	Jewish prophets Amos, Hosea, Micah and Isaiah. Jonah, Nachym, Jeremiah, Zephaniah and Habakkuk	Birth of Lao Tse, Chinese philosopher and founder of Taoism

General History	Persian/ Zarathustrian History	Date	Judeo-Christian History	Other Religious History
	Birth of Cyrus II	600-550 BC	Babylonian King Nebuchadnezzar destroys Jerusalem, begins the captivity of the Jews; Jewish prophet Ezekiel	Birth of Buddha; Birth of Confucius; Birth of Mahavira, the founder of Jainism.
Persian Period I begins in Egypt; Development of stable weights and measures, currency, written laws, efficient mailing system	Reigns of: Cyrus II, 550-530; Darius the Great, 522-486; Xerxes, 486-465; Darius III, 336-330	550-500 BC	Cyrus II conquers Babylon, frees the Jews; Jewish prophets Zechariah and Haggai; Rebuilding of the Temple in Jerusalem, 520	
Beginning of the Golden Age of Greece	End of Graeco-Persian wars, Peace of Callias	500-450 BC	Ezra leads 5,000 Israelites from Babylon to Jerusalem, establishes definitive reading of the Torah, bans intermarriage	
Peloponnesian War ends when Athens surrenders to Sparta		450-400 BC	Jewish prophets Obadiah, Joel and Malachi	
Socrates is sentenced to death		400-350 BC	Pentateuch, the first five books of the Old Testament, in final form	
Persian Period II begins in Egypt.	Conquest of Iran by Alexander the Great, 321; Slaughter of Zarathustrian priests, leading to loss of much Avestan literature	350-300 BC	Conquest of Jerusalem by Alexander the Great, 336-323	
	Second (partial) Zarathustrian Arsacid Empire	250-200 BC		
		200-150 BC		Composition of the Hindu Bhagavad Gita

General History	Persian/ Zarathustrian History	Date	Judeo- Christian History	Other Religious History
	Empire of the Arsacid Parthians, including all Iran; Conversion of oral Avestan texts, and local Zands, possibly written.	150-100 BC		
Spartacus leads the revolt of the Roman gladiators		100-50 BC	Jerusalem: first glass blowing techniques; Roman General Pompey conquers Jerusalem, 63	.
Death of Julius Caesar; Cleopatra commits suicide; Egypt is annexed to Rome	Treaty between Rome and Persia (Parthians) fixes the boundary between the two empires along the Euphrates River (Iraq)	50 BC-1 AD	Herod becomes Roman Governor of Jerusalem, 37; Birth of Jesus, the founder of Christianity.	
		1-50 AD	Crucifixion and death of Jesus; Conversion and missionary Journeys of Paul the Apostle	
Nero sets fire to Rome and blames the Christians; Vesuvius erupts and destroys Pompei		50-100 AD	Writing of Matthew, Mark, and Luke; Peter, first bishop of Rome, dies; Roman persecution of Christians begins; Jews revolt against Rome, Jerusalem is destroyed, 70	
		100-150 AD	Final Diaspora (dispersion) of the Jews begins.	
		150-200 AD	Bishop Iranaeus selects gospels of Matthew, Mark, Luke and John as canon	

General History	Persian/ Zarathustrian History	Date	Judeo- Christian History	Other Religious History
	The Third Zarathustrian Sasanian Empire, including all of Iran; Ancient Zarathustrian texts finally compiled and written down	200-250 AD		
Classic Period of Mayan Civilization		250-313 AD	313AD Constantine converts to Christianity, which becomes official religion of Roman Empire	

❧ CHAPTER 2 ❧

ZARATHUSTRA

Background

To more fully understand Zarathustra and His circumstances, we travel back in time to a period over 50,000 years ago, when the earth underwent a global warming. The massive ice sheets from the preceding short-lived Ice Age had all but melted on every continent of the planet, and the population of Modern Man (*Homo sapiens*) was rapidly growing from the approximately 10,000 individuals world-wide after the Massive eruption of Mt. Topa in Sumatra, [See the Chronology of Modern Man table-page 29] in approximately 74,000 BC. The volcanically caused dust cloud resulted in a six year nuclear winter and a thousand year long Ice Age. It had taken a terrible toll on both animal and plant life. The remnant of modern man consisted of familial bands, or tribes of hunter/gatherers in the world that had been previously dominated by the much taller and stronger Neanderthal (and other pre-homo sapien species) people. The global warming which followed left much of the equatorial portion of Earth in a semi-desert condition. All of this, plus an expanding population, forced mankind to constantly move to find adequate food supplies.[1]

Ancient texts say that one tribe, the distant ancestors of Zarathustra, moved to a land above the Arctic Circle, which they called Airyana-Vaeja.[2] This land was described as having many mountains, valleys and pastures; it was rich in water with deep lakes and wide rivers.[3] During the interglacial period, the climate of this polar area was mild and temperate. The tribe turned one obstacle of the region into a major asset. That inconvenience was the long polar night which the tribe made use of by conceiving of and commencing farming and domestication of wild animals.[4] The animals were pleased to find food, love and shelter during the long winter. Soon the tribe was living as pastoralists herding their cattle over their vast grazing grounds.[5] They called themselves "The Aryas," and had adopted a single religion in which they worshipped one God, the god of Nature, whom they called Mazda.[6]

From time to time small family groups drifted away to Europe and Asia to new pastures and to start separate lives. At some point, the balance of the now large Indo-European tribe began to migrate south. This relocation might well have been precipitated by the advent of the final Ice Age, although tradition blames disputes which had developed in the Mazdayasnian religion concerning the rituals, dogma and the actual meanings of their belief.[7] The once cohesive group, which had spoken a single language, split in two. Today, both groups are known as an Aryan branch of the Caucasian race.[8] The larger group settled in what is now the Indian subcontinent, the ancestor of today's Indian and Pakistani populations. The ancestors of Zarathustra followed their leader, Jamshid, into the steppes of Russia and eventually on to Afghanistan, Iran and Iraq.[9]

It is believed that widespread migration of Aryan tribes into the Iranian plateau began between 6000 and 3000 BC. The tribesmen and their families slowly integrated with the indigenous peoples during the next several centuries. The Aryans eventually emerged as the dominant race in the region.[10] It was into this race that Zarathustra was born, at least 1600 years before the birth of Jesus.[11] Zarathustra has been all but forgotten by modern historians but, as we shall discover, He deserves to have a place among the giants of both political and religious history. The predominant focus of the ancient Mazdayasnian religion had been "from Nature to Nature's God," with an underlying belief in an omnipresent, omniscient, and omnipotent Creator of the Universe. The Indo-Iranians believed that religion grew out of nature, as a natural progression and as the result of man's thinking processes.[12] As pastoralists they probably had no temples, and worshipped mainly in the open, without altars or images. They offered hymns of praise and thanksgiving, and made daily offerings to the hearth fire and sources of pure water.[13]

By the time of Zarathustra's birth, the Mazdayasnian religion had degenerated from a beautiful monotheistic explanation of creation and guide to life into a religion of nature worship, loaded with superstition and the worship of spirits, many of whom were evil and needed to be appeased.[14] As Mazda worship lost ground to the worship of evil spirits, or "daeva," huge changes developed. The Mazdayasni virtues of honesty and not causing harm to others were replaced by dishonesty, greed, violence and lawlessness. The Shahnameh, the national epic of Iran, describes this period of religious conflict:

> "I've said preceding sovereigns worshipped God [Mazda]
> By whom their crowns were given
> To protect the people from oppressors.
> God they served, acknowledging God's goodness—
> For to God, the pure, unchangeable, the Holy One!
> They owed their greatness and their earthly power.
> But after times,
> Worship of God gave way to idolatry and pagan faith,
> And then Mazda's name was lost
> In adoration of created things."[15]

As had happened with prior ancient beliefs, a prophet or reformer came forward to restore the religion to its original purity.

The Life of the Man Who Sent the Magi

Zarathustra's birth has been reported to have occurred at a variety of different times, within the wide range of years from 300 BC to 10,500 BC. Some of the earliest classical Greek and Egyptian writers, whose own lives should have been a close parallel to His, often place His birth between 3000 and 10,000 BC. Some modern scholars place Zarathustra's birth approximately three to four centuries prior to the defeat of the Persian Emperor Darius III by Alexander the Great, in 331 BC.[16]

In attempting to fix the place of Zarathustra's birth, one also finds a mixture of myth and unproven history. Although some scholars say that He was born in Rae district of modern day Iran, others place his birth in the Iranian district of Urumiah,[17] or in Shiz, in Media Atropatene.[18]

The Conception and Birth of Zarathustra

Zarathustra's father, Pourushaspa, was a member of the Aryan warrior clan named Spitama. His mother, Dughdhova, was the daughter of a nobleman. Zarathustra, whose name has been variously translated as "high priest" and "the possessor of yellow colored camels," was the third of the couple's five sons.[19]

There was nothing normal about the pregnancy of Zarathustra's mother, nor of the circumstances of His birth. Legend says that, from shortly after conception, a glow emanated from the womb and face of His mother, and that this glow grew with the maturation of the fetus.[20] This story was chronicled not only in the legends of Zarathustra's own people, but became an oft-repeated story in the written histories of many other nations and societies.

The night of Zarathustra's birth was said to be dark and cold, except for the house in which He was born. It was said that the house actually glowed, and that the interior was extremely warm. The Roman historian Pliny the Elder wrote in his *Natural History*:

"Zoroaster was the only human being who ever laughed on the same day on which he was born. We hear, too, that his brain pulsated so strongly that it repelled the hand when laid upon it, as presage of his wisdom."[21]

These signs of impending greatness were said to have caused Zarathustra's father to foresee that his child would grow to become a great warrior like himself, or at the very least, an important member of the royal court. On the first count, His father was to be greatly disappointed. On the second count, what eventually occurred far exceeded the wildest bounds of His father's imagination.[22]

The childhood of Zarathustra is not well chronicled, despite His special birth story. The accounts of His early life vary greatly. What seems to be true, in that it occurs in all accounts,[23] is that Zarathustra was a disappointment to His father in both His studies and His interests as a young boy. He had little interest in learning to be either a warrior or a politician, nor was He the horseman that His father would have wished. He was far more interested in music, the stars and flowers than in swords and studies. His teachers were perturbed by His constant questioning, and reported that He tended to be argumentative concerning the prevailing knowledge.

Zarathustra's instructors knew that He was intelligent for many reasons, including His ability to learn languages, a skill at which He showed amazing aptitude. His formal education was cut short because of His attitude, lack of focus and disruptive behavior. He was sent home to be "homeschooled."[24] As a youth, Zoroaster was renowned for His numerous kind and holy deeds, His lofty virtues and devotion toward God and His fellow man. Worldly objects and pleasures lost all value for him and He generously provided food and clothing to the poor and needy of the community. He labored day and night in the service of all living beings, and vigorously defended what he believed was right and true.[25]

At a young age, between fifteen and twenty, which varies with the storyteller, Zarathustra left His home and withdrew from the world. He sought communion with what He considered to be His heavenly father. Where He wandered and what He might have suffered, neither history nor legend reveals. He spent several years in dreary and remote places in the wilderness. Zarathustra was alone with nature, alone with His own thoughts and reality, meditating deeply on the eternal riddles of the universe and the great mysteries of existence. In the vast nothingness to which He had retired, He raised His hands to the sky and prayed fervently, imploring God to meet with Him, if for but one moment, and to speak to Him by words of His own mouth about the mysteries of life. It is recorded that Zarathustra cried out to God from His isolation:

Yasna 44:3 "This I ask thee, tell me truly, O Lord: Who was the first generator and father of Asha (Law)? Who determined the path of the sun and stars? Who (has ordained) that the moon shall wax and wane? All this, O Wise One, and yet more, I wish to know.

Yasna 44:4 This I ask Thee, tell me truly, O Lord: Who upheld the earth beneath and the heavens (above) from falling? Who (created) water and plants? Who yoked the two horses to the wind and clouds? Who, O Wise One, is the creator of Vohu Manah [Good Mind]?

Yasna 44:5 This I ask Thee, tell me truly O Lord: Who created light and darkness? Who made sleep and waking? Who (created) morning, noon and night, that remind man of his duty?"[26]

At last, when the longing to see God and the thirst for "the vision divine" had consumed His every desire, Vohu Manah, the embodiment, or "angel," of the good mind, appeared to Zarathustra in a vision and led His soul in holy trance into the presence of God [Ahura Mazda]. Zarathustra prayed[27]:

Yasna 33:7 "Come hither to me, oh ye Best ones, hither, O Ahura Mazda, in thine own person and to the sight, Oh Right and Good Mind, and I may be heard beyond the limits of the people. Let the august duties be manifest to all of us and be clearly seen."[28]

The fulfillment of His prayer was recorded as follows:

Yasna 43:5 "And I recognized Thee as the Beneficent, O Wise Lord, when I saw Thee first at the creation of Life, that Thou wilt make the deed and words to be recompensed—evil for the evil and good for the good—through Thy generosity at the last turning-point of the Creation."[29]

Yasna 31:8 "When I first conceived of Thee, O Mazda, in my mind, I sincerely regarded Thee as the First Actor in the universe, as the Father of Reason [the Good Mind], as the true Originator of the Right Law [Righteousness], as the Governor over the actions of mankind."[30]

"Now is his mind illumined, his soul entranced and he feels more and more of Ahura Mazda within him and without. Suddenly now, thanks to this divine illumination; he can read sermons in stones and whole books in the running brooks. He sees all nature pulsating with the message of hope, traced with the hand of Ahura Mazda on plants and trees, pebbles and sands, banks of rivers and the summits of hills." "Now, indeed, the truth dawns on him, now is the enigma of life solved, and the herald of Ahura Mazda is ready to deliver his 'message of hope to mankind.'" Joyfully, he turns his steps towards his father's house, to embark on his mission of preaching the profound truth vouchsafed to him by the Lord, determined to make any sacrifice, to surrender his life, in the service of Ahura Mazda."[31]

"Ahura Mazda, as envisioned by Zarathustra, was neither a being nor could He be viewed as an abstraction. He was in fact a living active existence, that eternal being who could be perceived only in thought, but whose creation and governance over same is apparent, or should be to all. It was He who was ever to be served and adored. It was through Him that everything came into life and existence. He was older than the oldest in the universe, brighter than the brightest of creation. He knew no elder and had no equal. He was the first and the foremost. Immune from the limitations of time and space, He was the ever-the-same, the most perfect being. Absolutely everything came through Him and from Him, for He was truly the Lord of All."[32]

Zarathustra now clearly knew, because of the infusion of the Spirit of God, that Ahura Mazda was the father of all. He first created the invisible or spiritual universe, after which He created the corporeal or physical Universe. He had created the stars, the sun, the moon, the sea, the land, the sky, the vegetable kingdom and the animal kingdom, and lastly, the crowning act of His creation was the Righteous Man.[33]

Zarathustra had gone from the asking of truly simplistic questions, based on the knowledge of His day, to seeing with the knowledge and perspective of the Creator Himself. This, He explained, had occurred with the infusion of the Spirit of God. He stated that He not only envisioned the beginning of the universe, but far into the future. In addition, He could feel much of the "hows," "whens" and "whys" for all that was and would be.[34] Much of the information and power with which He was now endowed would be of unbelievable use, as long as He could make use of it in a way which could be accepted by people of His day. It was necessary that He become a positive force for that which was good and Godly, and not feed into the superstitious nature and the ungodliness that was currently prevalent throughout His country.

From the ancient Mazdayasnian religion, Zarathustra took the name of "Mazda" for God, and to this He prefixed the adjective "Ahura," thus making the combined form of Ahura Mazda, "the All Wise Lord."[35] Ahura Mazda was not only the Creator, but the Ever-Creating. Zarathustra alluded to the fact that the All-Knowing Ahura Mazda had given humankind freedom of choice, but that He could override this if He should so decide.

The Will of God Revealed

It was the desire of Ahura Mazda that His might, wisdom and goodness should be utilized in promoting the happiness and enjoyment of mankind in this world. His goal was to enable each human to play a meritorious part in the existence of the physical world, and thus to equip each to soar higher during his mortal life as an individual, so that he would enjoy more fully life in the next world. Thus it was that Ahura Mazda commenced the work of creation, for it was from that moment that the present cycle was commenced.[36]

For each man, the struggle within himself was a counterpoint to the struggle which he encountered in the outside world because of his freedom of choice. Ahura Mazda made it clear to Zarathustra that, to eliminate diseases and make the world more habitable, man must learn to fight and harness the elements. At the same time, he must diligently wage a crusade against the forces of superstition, ignorance, and bigotry for the emancipation of his reasoning faculty and intellectual progress. Man must fight against social wrongs and injustice as an individual for his social advancement. For his moral ascent, he must wage the greatest of all crusades—an incessant war against his inner self. Armed with this spiritual knowledge, Zarathustra headed in the direction of His father's home, bent upon changing the world.[37]

The Appearance of Temptation

The appearance of so gifted a seer and savior is said to have displeased the evil spirit, Angra Mainyu, a close aide and ally of Ahriman [the very essence of Satanic forces]. Zarathustra was offered riches beyond His comprehension, and after that, a house like a palace with the most beautiful and handsome women and men as servants and slaves. Zarathustra rejected the offers emphatically and exclaimed[38]:

Fargard 19:6 "Again to him said the Maker of the evil world, Angra Mainyu: 'Do not destroy my creatures, O holy Zarathustra! Thou are the son of Poursaspa; by thy mother I was invoked. Renounce the good Religion of the worshippers of Mazda, and thou shalt gain such a boon as Vadhaghna gained, the ruler of nations'.

Fargard 19:7 Spitama Zarathustra said in answer: 'No! never will I renounce the good Religion of the worshippers of Mazda, either for body or life, though they should tear away the breath!'

Fargard 19:8 Again to him said the Maker of the evil world, Angra Mainyu: 'By whose Word wilt thou strike, by whose Word wilt thou repel, by whose weapon will the good creatures (strike and repel) my creation, who am Angra Mainyu?'

Fargard 19:9 Spitama Zarathustra said in answer: 'The second mortar, the sacred cups, the Haoma, the Word taught by Mazda, these are my weapons, my best weapons! By this Word will I strike, by this Word will I repel, by this weapon will the good creatures [strike and repel thee], O evil-doer, Angra Mainya!'..."[39]

This confrontation was many-faceted, as was the encounter of Zarathustra with Ahura Mazda. However, thanks to the knowledge given to Him by the spirit of Ahura Mazda, which was now within him, He was totally resolved in His rejection.

If Zarathustra was expecting to make His father proud, or expecting that His new knowledge and awareness would be noticed by anyone in His home kingdom, He was mistaken. Legend has it that, for a very long time, possibly close to ten years, nobody paid heed to the Prophet or His message, not even His friends and kinsmen. He preached on the street corners and in the public square. He was the target of ridicule, and even physical abuse. He was denounced by the clergy as being either a heretic or a sorcerer. He went from door to door, only to have those doors slammed in His face. Totally alone, ignored by kinsmen, forsaken by friends, harassed by enemies, and persecuted by the minions of the evil spirit,[40] He turned to His heavenly friend within, and asked:

Yasna 46:1 "To what land shall I turn, whither shall I go, forsaken by kinsmen and nobles, am I; neither do my people like me, nor do the wicked rulers of the land. How then, shall I please Thee, Mazda Ahura?

Yasna 46:2 This I know Mazda, wherefore I fail, few are my flocks, and few my followers. In grief I cry to thee, Ahura, behold it. Help me even **as** friend unto friend, show me through righteousness the riches of the Good Mind."[41]

At last, and in answer to His prayer, Zarathustra found His first convert, His cousin Maidhyomah. But still, no one else listened to Him. His cousin observed that it was hopeless to approach the people in the kingdom into which He was born and grew up. His cousin suggested that until, and unless, Zarathustra was able to catch the ear of someone of great importance, the people of His own town, and very likely His whole nation, would not pay any attention. Therefore he suggested that Zarathustra travel to Bactria, a kingdom in what is now Turkistan, wherein ruled the kind and known to be very wise King Vishtaspa.[42]

To be received at the court of King Vishtaspa was not an easy matter, even for someone who had communed with God. Zarathustra waited patiently for the coveted audience in the courtyard of the palace for many days. At last, on one auspicious day, He was ushered into the presence of Vishtaspa. The king received Him cordially, and allowed Him to explain His creed to himself and the nobles, priests and learned ones of the court. What He said to Vishtaspa is known as "The Blessing of the Prophet Zarathustra"

Yast 23:1 "…And Zarathustra spake unto King Vistaspa, saying: 'I bless thee, O man! O lord of the country! with the living of a good life, of an exalted life, of a long life. May thy men live long! May thy women live long! May sons be born unto thee of thy own body!

Yast 23:2 'Mayest thou have a son like Gamaspa, and may he bless thee as (Gamaspa blessed) Vistaspa (the lord) of the country!

'Mayest thou be most beneficent, like Mazda!

'Mayest thou be fiend-smiting, like Thraetaona!

'Mayest thou be strong, like Gamaspa!

'Mayest thou be well-armed, like Takhma-Urupa!

Yast 23:3 'Mayest thou be glorious, like Yima Khshaeta, the good shepherd!

'Mayest thou be instructed with a thousand senses, like Azi Dahaka, of the evil law!

'Mayest thou be awful and most strong, like Keresaspa!

'Mayest thou be a wise chief of assemblies, like Urvakhshaya!

'Mayest thou be beautiful of body and without fault, like Syavarshana!

Yast 23:4 'Mayest thou be rich in cattle, like an Athwyanide!

'Mayest thou be rich in horses, like Pourusaspa!

'Mayest thou be holy, like Zarathustra Spitama!

'Mayest thou be able to reach the Rangha, whose shores lie afar, as Vafra Navaza was!

'Mayest thou be beloved by the gods and reverenced by men!

Yast 23:5 'May ten sons be born of you! In three of them mayest thou be an Athravan! In three of them mayest thou be a warrior! In three of them mayest thou be a tiller of the ground! And may one be like thyself, O Vistaspa!

Yast 23:6 'Mayest thou be swift-horsed, like the Sun!

'Mayest thou be resplendent, like the moon!

'Mayest thou be hot-burning, like fire!

'Mayest thou have piercing rays, like Mithra!

'Mayest thou be tall-formed and victorious, like the devout Sraosha!

Yast 23:7 'Mayest thou follow a law of truth, like Rashnu!

'Mayest thou be a conqueror of thy foes, like Verethraghna, made by Ahura!

'Mayest thou have fulness of welfare, like Rama Hvastra!

'Mayest thou be freed from sickness and death, like king Husravah!

Yast 23:8 'May it happen unto thee according to my blessing!

Let us embrace and propagate the good thoughts, good words and good deeds that have been done and that will be done here and elsewhere, that we may be in the number of the good."[43]

So impressed was the king by Zarathustra's words that he publicly embraced the new Faith, as did many in his court. However, some of the priests and nobles soon became jealous of the prophet's favor with the King. They declared Zarathustra to be a sorcerer, a charlatan and a heretic, and convinced Vishtaspa to withhold his allegiance until Zarathustra could somehow prove himself. The intensity of their arguments was such that Vishtaspa bent under the pressure, and temporarily withdrew his allegiance. Zarathustra was arrested and thrown into prison. Prison held no terror for Zarathustra, for surely He was not alone. Ahura Mazda dwelt within Him, and therefore nothing would harm Him and likewise, there could be nothing to depress Him. Zarathustra cheerfully went to jail.[44]

Legend has it, that, shortly thereafter, the favorite horse of Vishtaspa became extremely ill. After none of the physicians in the kingdom were able to cure the stallion, Zarathustra asked to be allowed to heal him. He was allowed to place His hand upon the forehead of the horse, and the fever and illness immediately disappeared. With this miracle accomplished, Zarathustra was again embraced by Vishtaspa, who publicly declared his belief in the new religion. Zarathustra soon became a political, as well as a religious, advisor to the King. He married the daughter of Frashaoshtra, a nobleman of the court, with whom He had several children. With the support of a royal patron, the new religion spread rapidly.

According to the Shahnameh, Vishtaspa's adoption of the religion of Zarathustra angered the monarch of a neighboring land, Kin Arjasp of Turan:

"But tidings concerning Zerdusht [Zarathustra] were come even unto Arjasp, who sat upon the throne of Afrasiyab, and he said unto himself, "This thing is vile". So he refused ear unto the faith, and he sent a writing unto (Vishtaspa), wherein he bade him return to the creed of his fathers. And he said, 'If thou turn thee not, make thee ready for combat; for verily I say unto thee, that unless thou cast our Zerdusht [Zarathustra], this man of guile, I will overthrow thy kingdom and seat me upon thy throne'."

"When (Vishtaspa heard the haughty words that Arjasp had spoken, he marveled within himself. Then he called before him a scribe, and sent back answer unto Arjasp. Then he said that he would deliver up to the sword whosoever swerved from the paths of Zerdusht [Zarathustra], and whosoever would not choose them, him also would he destroy."

Vishtaspa gave command of the army to his son, Isfendiyar, who battled the forces of Arjasp in Turan for fourteen days. The Shahnameh continues:

"And their rage was hot against one another, but in the end the might of Iran overcame, and Arjasp fled before the face of Isfendiyar. Then Isfendiyar returned him unto Iran, and presented himself before his father, and demanded a blessing at his hands. But (Vishtaspa) said, 'time is not yet come when thou shouldst mount the throne.' So he sent him forth yet again that he might turn all the lands unto the faith of Zerdusht [Zarathustra]."[45]

Under Vishtaspa, the boundaries of the kingdom quickly expanded to the north, east and west, often without military action. Zarathustra was allowed to preach His Faith almost unmolested, and Zoroastrianism became the religion of the Iranian Kingdom. In addition to suppressing sorcery and the worship of demons, he was reputed to have performed many miracles. He is given credit for ending a plague and removing other pestilences, and for averting national disasters. He cured disease, healed the sick, and restored sight to the blind. He always gave the credit for the healings to the power of Ahura Mazda, and would only accept credit as the vessel that allowed it to occur.[46]

Zarathustra chanted before the people the praises of Ahura Mazda and the hymns of the Good Spirit, imploring all within the hearing of His voice to choose that creed which would be best for themselves. They should choose what was "Right" by making use of their God-given mind and freedom of choice. During one of His addresses, He appealed to the good sense and understanding of His audience thusly; "Ye offspring of renowned ancestors, awaken to agree with us!"[47] He then earnestly asked His followers and even His disciples not to take any dogma or doctrine on trust or faith, and not to yield to a blind unreasoning submission to anything, but to invoke the assistance of both the sincere, well ordered mind as well as the assistance of Ahura Mazda in examining calmly all of the pros and cons of His teachings:

Yasna 30:2 "Hear with your ears the best, see with your minds the beliefs of your choice; every man or woman is to think for his or her own self."[48]

Yasna 31:11 "...O Mazda, in the beginning didst thou create the Individual and the Individuality, through Thy Spirit, and powers of understanding—when Thou didst make life clothed with the body, when (Thou madest) actions and teachings, whereby one may exercise one's convictions at one's free will."[49]

Not a New Religion?

Zarathustra did not claim to be the founder of a new religion, but a reformer of the ancient Mazdayasnian religion of His people. Whenever the ancient belief of God has been corrupted in this way, prophets or reformers, who should be called Saoshyants shall come or be brought forth to restore the religion to its pristine purity.[50]

The religion which Zarathustra founded was intrinsic to the development and direction of the Empire of the Medes, and later, the

Persian Empire. The paths which He chose not only had tremendous effect upon the world of His time, but also, very possibly, on humankind for centuries into our future. He is an excellent example that a person can have as much and even more lasting influence on society and history in the realm of religion and spirituality than in politics, education, science and war.

The original Avesta canon comprised twenty two books.[51] Pliny the Elder, writing in his Natural History about the scholar of Smyrna:

> "Hermippus, who wrote most painstakingly about the art of magic, and interpreted two million verses by Zarathustra, also added lists of contents; The subjects were said to have included healing, human behavior, medicine, nutrition, herbology, astronomy, mathematics, engineering, meteorology, architecture, the needed reverence and protection of nature, the proper use and care of precious stones, of proposed systems of governance and justice, hydrology, water purification, as well as astrology, farming practices, animal husbandry, human parenting, and the art and method of prognostication."[52]

Unfortunately, the majority of Zarathustra's books no longer exist, and we are left with only 83,000 words. The Parsi population has recovered the essence of His works from fragments of the oral tradition.[53] To a great extent, the content has remained basically the same since before 1500 BC.[54]

The writings of Zarathustra's religion are known as the Avesta, which translates as "the injunction" or "the praises." Its adjoining explanation is known as the Zend, which best translates as "commentary."[55] Included in the missing texts are many of Zarathustra's prophesies.[56] While there are allusions to them, it would be great to know how the Magi knew how to term the object of their search "the King of the Jews,"[57] that this object would be an infant, and to understand the many other mysteries around their journey. Were the Magi aware that Jesus would have to face Satanic temptation, or that by His own free will he would be able to choose to accept the call of God? If they had this additional knowledge, what portion of it would they or could they have shared with Mary and Joseph?

Zarathustra's Ministry

For over forty years, Zarathustra labored ceaselessly to expand and expound the positive message of Ahura Mazda. The number of His disciples and believers continued to grow. There has been an ethnic exclusion in membership of the Zarathustrian faith, for Aryans only, the reasons for which have been lost in time.[58] It could have been that Ahura Mazda felt that mankind was not yet ready in its social maturity to be joined together in one common Faith.

It should be noted that, throughout Zarathustra's teachings, the physical world was a battlefield wherein mankind was called to be the ally of the "Beneficent Spirit," Ahura Mazda, in combating evil in all its manifestations. His "Prescription" was that the followers must be the active and virile fighters in cooperation with the "Spirit of Good" in defeating all that was ungodly. It was definitely not enough to ignore or to be non-cooperative with evil. Man must abhor it wholeheartedly, and fight it vigorously. Thus "Resist Evil" was the Zarathustrian battle cry.[59]

Compassion and Understanding

There was room in this new Faith for compassion and understanding of the religions of others. Zarathustra did not say that these people were incorrect in their religious beliefs, and, in many cases, encouraged them to continue to believe as they had, especially if their religion emphasized good behavior.

Yasht II:20 "Ahura Mazda spake unto Spitama Zarathustra, saying: 'If in this material world, O Spitama Zarathustra! Thou happenest to come upon frightful roads, full of dangers and fears, O Zarathustra! And thou fearest for thyself, then do thou recite these words, then proclaim these fiend-smiting words, O Zarathustra!

Yasht II:21 "'I praise, I invoke, I meditate upon, and we sacrifice unto the good, strong, beneficent Fravashis [guardian angels] of the faithful. We worship the Fravashis of the masters of the houses, those of the lords of the boroughs, those of the lords of the towns, those of the lords of the countries, those of the Zarathustrotemas; the Fravashis of those that are, the Fravashis of those that have been, the Fravashis of those that will be; all the Fravashis of all nations, and most friendly the Fravashis of the friendly nations.'"[60]

Quite often, these friendly interactions resulted in the inclusion of portions of the knowledge of Zarathustra's faith without the name or rituals of Ahura Mazda. Because of this unusual tolerance of the beliefs of others there was respect for Zarathustra and His teachings. There was an acceptance of many of the beliefs of the Faith throughout the civilized world, even where the Zarathustrian religion could not be formally accepted.

Zarathustra was an extremely busy man. He was married three times, and a loving father to six children.[61] During His long ministry, He served as political and religious advisor to the crown. He oversaw the affairs of the Zarathustrian religion and its priests, and was the ultimate decision maker regarding the location and design of new temples and schools in newly acquired territories. His counsel was sought by the learned of nations throughout the known world. He had the time to question that "Spirit of God" within him, and, thus, to continue to be a source of revelation throughout the better part of the forty plus years of His ministry.

What Zarathustra accomplished during His life was immense and legendary, but receives little attention in the western world today.

Death of the Prophet

Zarathustra Spitama more than surpassed His father's hopes and dreams. Even the manner in which He died would have made his father proud in that, according to legend, He died a warrior's death. History records that Zarathustra was killed while defending a fire-temple in which He had been praying, a worthy end for the seventy-seven-year-old promoter and defender of the cause of God.[62]

❧ CHAPTER 3 ❧

ZARATHUSTRA

THE RELIGION, TEACHINGS, ETHICS AND PROPHECIES

Creation

In the beginning,

Bundahishn 1:3 "...is the explanation of both spirits together; one is he who is independent of unlimited time, because (Ahura Mazda) and the region, religion, and time of (Ahura Mazda) were and are and ever will be; while Ahriman in darkness, with backward understanding and desire for destruction, was in the abyss, and it is he who will not be; and the place of that destruction, and also of that darkness, is what they call the 'endlessly dark'.

Bundahishn 1:4 And between them was empty space, that is, what they call 'air' in which is now their meeting."[1]

Yasna 30:4 "And when these twain Spirits came together in the beginning, they created Life and Not-Life, and that at the Worst Existence shall be to the followers of the Lie, but the Best Existence to him that follows Right.

Yasna 30:5 Of these twain Spirits he that followed the Lie chose doing the worst things; the holiest Spirit chose Right, he that clothes him with the massy heavens as a garment. So likewise they that are fain to please Ahura Mazda by dutiful actions."[2]

The Avesta thus describes the existence of the primal spirits of good and evil at the beginning of time. They lived separately, in the light and the dark, respectively, for 3,000 years, during which time Ahura Mazda conceived the idea and spiritual essence of creation, and, in his omniscience, was aware of the need to first meet with his "twin," who had perceived the light, and sought to destroy it. After Ahriman's rejection of an offer of peace, Ahura Mazda uttered the Ahunwar, a sacred prayer, and the evil spirit was cast back into the abyss for another 3,000 years.

During the second 3,000 year period, Ahura Mazda created the Amesha Spentas, or holy immortals, and the Good Mind. The Gathas says:

Yasna 28:7 "About which he [Ahura Mazda] in the beginning thus thought, 'let the blessed realms be filled with Light', he it is that by his wisdom created Right. [Those realms] that the Best Thought shall possess those dost Thou exalt, O Mazda, through the Spirit, which, O Ahura, is ever the same."[3]

Ahura Mazda next created the physical universe and the world, in seven stages. The Greater Bundahishn describes:

"First, He created Sky, bright, visible, high, its bounds afar, made of shining metal. And He joined its to the Endless Light, and created all creation within the sky, like a castle or fort in which are stored all the weapons needed for a struggle. The Spirit of the Sky accepted it as a strong fortress against the Evil Spirit, so that he will not allow him to escape. Like a heroic warrior who has put on armour so that he may be fearlessly victorious in battle, so the Spirit of the Sky is clad in the sky. And to help the sky, He created joy. Now indeed in the Mixture creations abides through joy. "Second, He created Water. And to help Water He created wind and rain. Third, after Water He created Earth, round, very broad, without hill or dale..., set exactly in the middle of this sky. And He created in the Earth the substance of the mountains, which afterwards waxed and grew out of the earth. And to help Earth He created iron, copper, sulphur, borax, chalk, all the products of the hard earth. Beneath this Earth there is water everywhere. "Fourth, He created the Plant. At first it grew in the middle of this earth, several feet high, without branch or bark or thorn, moist and sweet. And it had in its essence the vital force of all plants. And to help the Plant He created water and fire, through their power it kept growing. Fifth, He fashioned the Uniquely-created Bull in Eranvej in the middle of the world, on the bank of the river Veh Daiti. It was white and bright like the moon, and it was three measured rods in height. And to help it He created water and plants, for in the Mixture its strength and growth are from these. Sixth, he created Gayomard, bright as the sun, and four measured rods in height, on the bank of the river Daiti, where is the middle of the world—Gayomard upon the left side, the Bull upon the right side. And to help him He created sleep, the giver of repose. "Seventh (He created) Fire, whose radiance is from the Endless Light, the place of Ahura Mazda. And He distributed Fire within the whole creation. And He commanded Fire to serve mankind during the Assault, preparing food and overcoming cold."[4]

Please note that to this point everything has been the creation of Ahura Mazda.

During the third 3,000 year period, Ahriman broke free from the abyss, and assaulted the material creations of Ahura Mazda. The sun, moon and stars, which had been fixed within the heavens, were shaken loose; after thirty years, the plant, the ox and the first man lay dead. Yet Ahriman's apparent victory was thwarted by the rain that Ahura Mazda sent to cleanse the earth of the evil that had assailed it. From the remains of the first plant and ox arose all the plants and animals of the modern world. From Gayomart's remains came forth the first human couple, Mashye and Mashyane, whose fifteen sets of twins repopulated the earth.

The Bundahishn describes the initial communication between Ahura Mazda and the first man and woman:

Bundahishn 15:6 "Ohrmazd spoke to Mashye and Mashyane thus: 'You are man, you are the ancestry of the world, and you are created perfect in devotion by me; perform devotedly the duty of the law, think good thoughts, speak good words, do good deeds, and worship no demons!

Bundahishn 15:7 Both of them first thought this, that one of them should please the other, as he is a man for him; and the first deed done by them was this, when they went out they washed themselves thoroughly; and the first words spoken by them were these, that Ohrmazd created the water and earth, plants and animals, the stars, moon, and sun, and all prosperity whose origin and effect are from the manifestation of righteousness.

Bundahishn 15:8 And, afterwards, antagonism rushed into their minds, and their minds were thoroughly corrupted, and they exclaimed that the evil spirit created the water and earth, plants and animals, and the other things as aforesaid."[5]

The Nature of Man

Ervad Sheriarji Dadabhai Bharucha, read from his essay at the 1893 World Congress meeting in Chicago:

"His physical parts are well known, such as 'tanu' the body, 'gaya' and 'ushtana' life, with their several subdivisions. Of his spiritual parts the principal is 'urvan' the soul, with his several faculties, such as 'manas' the mind, 'baodhas' consciousness, and so on. The body [tanu] is to the soul [urvan] what an instrument is to the worker, or the horse to the rider, or the house to its master. The body is formed in the womb of the mother and the soul, coming from the spiritual world along with the several faculties and senses, enters it and begins his sublunary career which lasts until death, when he returns to the spiritual world. The soul can best perform his duties if the body be in full health. And as the health of the body is affected by its physical and mental surroundings, Zoroastrianism enjoins the duty of preserving and maintaining the health of the body. The maxim *'mens sana in corpore sano'* may truly be said to be a distinctive feature of this renowned religion."[6]

Bharucha goes on to describe man's spiritual nature:

"Of the spiritual parts of man the most important are only two: (1) the Urvan and (2) the Fravashi. The Urvan or soul is responsible for his deeds. It is he who according to his acts receives reward or punishment after death. On the morning of the fourth day after his death, his actions having been judged and appraised, he enters the spiritual world and from that time all his connection with this material world ceases and is never afterwards allowed to return to it. Zoroastrianism does not teach the doctrine of Ghosts and Goblins, the soul hovering about the nether world 'Doomed for a certain time to walk the night, And for the day confined to fast in fires.' Nor does it profess metempsychosis [reincarnation]. In the Gathas of the prophet Zoroaster as well as in several other parts of the Avesta, all that is said as to the ultimate destination of the soul after the shuffling off of the mortal coil is that it enters heaven or hell according to the preponderance of his good or bad deeds."[7]

Yasna 31:11 "When thou, O Mazda, in the beginning didst create the Individual and the Individuality, through Thy Spirit, and powers of understanding—when Thou didst make life clothed with the body, when (Thou madest) actions and teaching, whereby one may exercise one's convictions at one's free will;...

Yasna 31:22 Clear it is to the man of understanding, as one who has realized it with his thought. He upholds Asha together with good Dominion by his word and deed. He will be, O Mazda Ahura, the most helpful helper to Thee." [8]

By providing man with free will, Ahura Mazda provided man with the responsibility for his own fate. Through his good deeds, words and thoughts and by continually keeping clean his body and soul, the righteous man earned both a temporal and an everlasting reward. It was therefore to man's benefit that he grow in knowledge of the "Spiritual Law." By placing his will in harmony with the laws of God, he would be able to withstand the assaults of wrong and falsehoods, while attaining the virtues of love, benevolence, righteousness and charity.

Man's freedom of choice is a cornerstone of the Zarathustrian Faith. Ahura Mazda set forward what was best for man, but created him with freedom in his determinations and his decisions. Zarathustra was the first prophet of God to teach the ideas of guilt and merit, and the doctrine of immortal life. In His religion, each act, word and thought of man's physical life was related to his existence after death. The tally of good versus evil was determined for each man according to his earthly performance and adherence to the Divine Law, and the soul was rewarded according to its tally.

Ahura Mazda's Purpose for the Creation of Man

Zarathustra taught that man's primary purpose was to know God [Ahura Mazda] and that which He willed, to glorify the Godhead and His creation, and to improve the fortunes of individual souls and all of the creation, male and female alike:

Bundahishn 15:6 "...'You are man, you are the ancestry of the world, and you are created perfect in devotion by me; perform devotedly the duty of the law, think good thoughts, speak good words, do good deeds, and worship no demons (daeva)!'"[9]

Good thoughts were important to man's spiritual journey, because they were the genesis of all else. Without them, man could not hope to become subject to the Divine Will of Ahura Mazda. Man must endeavor to speak the truth at all times, and to shun hypocrisy and duplicity. Of equal importance on the spiritual path was the performance of good deeds, including the chanting of ritual hymns and prayers, fulfilling the duty of worship of Ahura Mazda. Only thus was man able to impair the power of Ahriman, and to strengthen the power of the Divinity.

The Creed of Zarathustra dates to the earliest days of the religion, and was most likely intended by the prophet to be recited or chanted in open assembly:

Yasna 12:1 "I curse the Daevas. I declare myself a Mazda-worshipper, a supporter of Zarathustra, hostile to the Daevas, fond of Ahura's teaching, a praiser of the Amesha Spentas, a worshipper of the Amesha Spentas. I ascribe all good to Ahura Mazda, 'and all the best', Asha-endowed, splendid, xwarena-endowed, whose is the cow, whose is Asha, whose is the light, 'may whose blissful areas be filled with light'.

Yasna 12:2 I choose the good Spenta Armaiti for myself; let her be mine. I renounce the theft and robbery of the cow, and the damaging and plundering of the Mazdayasnian settlements.

Yasna 12:3 I want freedom of movement and freedom of dwelling for those with homesteads, to those who dwell upon this earth with their cattle. With reverence for Asha, and (offerings) offered up, I vow this: I shall nevermore damage or plunder the Mazdayasnian settlements, even if I have to risk life and limb.

Yasna 12:4 I reject the authority of the Daevas, the wicked, no-good, lawless, evil-knowing, the most druj-like of beings, the foulest of beings, the most damaging of beings. I reject the Daevas and their comrades, I reject the demons [yatu] and their comrades; I reject any who harm beings. I reject them with my thoughts, words and deeds. I reject them publicly."[10]

Yima

The story of a global flood or disaster is chronicled in nearly every culture. In the Zarathustrian religion, this story is interwoven with the record of Yima Kshaeta, the ancient king of the Aryans in Airyanam Vaejahi, their homeland above the Arctic Circle. Zarathustra questions Ahura Mazda regarding man's first opportunity to receive the religion of Mazda:

Fargard 2:1 "Zarathustra asked Ahura Mazda:

O Ahura Mazda, most beneficent Spirit, Maker of the material world, thou Holy One!

Who was the first mortal, before myself, Zarathustra, with whom thou, Ahura Mazda, didst converse, whom thou didst teach the Religion of Ahura, the Religion of Zarathustra?

Fargard 2:2 Ahura Mazda answered: The fair Yima, the good shepherd, O holy Zarathustra! he was the first mortal, before thee, Zarathustra, whom I taught the Religion of Ahura, the Religion of Zarathustra.

Fargard 2:3 Unto him O Zarathustra, I, Ahura Mazda, spake, saying: 'Well, fair Yima, son of Vivanghat, be thou the preacher and bearer of my Religion!' And the fair Yima, O Zarathustra, replied unto me, saying: 'I was not born, I was not taught to be the preacher and the bearer of thy Religion.'

Fargard 2:4 Then I, Ahura Mazda, said thus unto him, O Zarathustra: 'Since thou dost not consent to be the preacher and the bearer of my Religion, then make thou my world increase, make my world grow: consent thou to nourish, to rule, and to watch over my world.'

Fargard 2:5 And the fair Yima replied unto me, O Zarathustra, saying: 'Yes! I will make thy world increase, I will make thy world grow. Yes! I will nourish, and rule, and watch over thy world. There shall be, while I am king, neither cold wind nor hot wind, neither disease nor death.'

Fargard 2:6 Then I, Ahura Mazda, brought two implements unto him: a golden seal and a poniard inlaid with gold. Behold, here Yima bears the royal sway!

Fargard 2:22 And Ahura Mazda spake unto Yima, saying: 'O fair Yima, so of Vivanghat! Upon the material world the evil winters are about to fall, that shall bring the fierce, deadly frost; upon the material world the evil winters are about to fall, that shall make snowflakes fall thick, even an aredvi deep on the highest tops of mountains.

Fargard 2:23 And the beasts that live in the wilderness, and those that live on the tops of the mountains, and those that live in the bosom of the dale shall take shelter in underground abodes.

Fargard 2:24 And before that winter, the country would bear plenty of grass for cattle, before the waters had flooded it. Now after the melting of the snow, O Yima, a place wherein the footprint of a sheep may be seen will be a wonder in the world.

Fargard 2:31 Then Yima said within himself: 'How shall I manage to make that Vara which Ahura Mazda has commanded me to make?' And Ahura Mazda said unto Yima: 'O fair Yima, son of Vivanghat! Crush the earth with a stamp of thy heel, and then knead it with thy hands, as the potter does when kneading the potter's clay.'

Fargard 2:32 [And Yima did as Ahura Mazda wished; he crushed the earth with a stamp of his heel, he kneaded it with his hands, as the potter does when kneading the potter's clay.]

Fargard 2:33 And Yima made a Vara, long as a riding-ground on every side of the square. There he brought the seeds of sheep and oxen, of men, of dogs, of birds, and of red blazing fires. He made a Vara, long as a riding-ground on every side of the square, to be an abode for the men; a Vara, long as a riding-ground on every side of the square, for oxen and sheep.

Fargard 2:34 There he made waters flow in a bed a hathra long; there he settled birds, on the green that never fades, with food that never fails. There he established dwelling-places, consisting of a house with a balcony, a courtyard, and a gallery.

Fargard 2:35 There he brought the seeds of men and women, of the greatest, best, and finest on this earth; there he brought the seeds of every kind of cattle, of the greatest, best, and finest on this earth.

Fargard 2:36 There he brought the seeds of every kind of tree, of the highest of size and sweetest of odour on this earth; there he brought the seeds of every kind of fruit, the best of savour and sweetest of odour. All those seeds he brought, two of every kind, to be kept inexhaustible there, so long as those men shall stay in the Vara.

Fargard 2:37 And there were no humpbacked, none bulged forward there; no impotent, no lunatic; no one malicious, no liar; no one spiteful, none jealous; no one with decayed tooth, no leprous to be pent up, nor any of the brands wherewith Angra Mainyu stamps the bodies of mortals.

Fargard 2:38 In the largest part of the place he made nine streets, six in the middle part, three in the smallest. To the streets of the largest part he brought a thousand seeds of men and women; to the streets of the middle part, six hundred; to the streets of the smallest part, three hundred. That Vara he sealed up with the golden ring, and he made a door, and a window self-shining within.

Fargard 2:39 O Maker of the material world, thou Holy One! What are the lights that give light in the Vara which Yima made?

Fargard 2:40 Ahura Mazda answered: 'There are uncreated lights and created lights. The one thing missed there is the sight of the stars, the moon and the sun, and a year seems only as a day.

Fargard 2:41 'Every fortieth year, to every couple are born, a male and a female. And thus it is for every sort of cattle. And the men in the Vara which Yima made live the happiest life.'" [11]

Author's Note: Could this be another rendition of the story of Noah or even a different man chosen by God for the same purpose?

Man's Stewardship of the Earth

Ahura Mazda created man with both the right and the responsibility to rule over his creations.[12] The Pahlavi texts provide a list of man's duties on earth; the first five are provided below:

"Man's First (duty) on earth is to profess the religion and to practice and worship according to it; not to turn from it, but to have belief in the Good Religion of the Mazda-worshippers ever in mind; to distinguish profit from loss, sin from virtue, goodness from badness, light from darkness, Mazda-worship from daeva-worship. Second, he should take a wife and beget earthly progeny. He should be diligent in this and not neglectful of it. Third, he should turn the soil into ploughground and cultivate it. Fourth, he should treat domestic animals properly. Fifth, a third of his days and nights he should attend the priests' school and inquire after the wisdom of just men; a third of his days and nights he should work and create prosperity; and a third of his days and nights he should eat and take pleasure and rest."[13]

Ahura Mazda made it clear to Zarathustra that the righteous man was he who would find true happiness in this life and who would make use of, and not abuse, His creation. In every way, Zarathustra taught His followers to treat their environment as something holy and to include in their prayers the rendering of thanks to Ahura Mazda for letting them know how they could please him through better use of, as well as protection of, His creation. In the Vendidad, Zarathustra queried Ahura Mazda as to the source of happiness for the Earth:

Fargard III:2 "…Ahura Mazda answered: 'It is the place whereon one of the faithful erects a house with a priest within, with cattle, with a wife, with children, and good herds within; and wherein afterwards the cattle go on thriving, holiness is thriving,

Fargard III:3 fodder is thriving, the dog is thriving, the wife is thriving, the child is thriving, the fire is thriving, and every blessing of life is thriving.'"[14]

Zarathustra taught the importance of purity, not only of one's self, but "the four elements, fire, air, water and earth" were to be maintained in an undefiled state. He stressed the importance of agriculture[15]:

Fargard III:4 "O Maker of the material world, thou Holy One! Which is the third place where the Earth feels most happy?

Ahura Mazda answered: 'It is the place where one of the faithful cultivates most corn, grass and fruit, O Spitama Zarathustra! where he waters ground that is dry, or dries ground that is too wet.'

Fargard III:5 O Maker of the material world, thou Holy One! Which is the fourth place where the Earth feels most happy?

Ahura Mazda answered: 'It is the place where there is most increase of flocks and herds.'

Fargard III:6 O Maker of the material world, thou Holy One! Which is the fifth place where the Earth feels most happy?

Ahura Mazda answered: 'It is the place where flocks and herds yield most dung.'"[16]

Ahura Mazda offered detailed advice to ensure effective production of crops and herds. Once cleared and purified, the land was to be tilled and sown, then there was the need to tend to the crops grown so that they would be free of weeds and brambles, to protect them from wild foraging animals, to fertilize them early in the growing cycle, to keep them properly watered with the fresh and pure waters from the streams that flowed from the mountains, to harvest at the appropriate time, with the edible remains to be used as fodder for the domestic animals and further, that the best seeds were to be preserved for the next years' crops. So strongly did agriculture figure in the lives of the Zarathustrians, that it was revered as an act of worship[17]:

Fargard III:31 "'He who sows corn, sows holiness: he makes the law of Mazda grow higher and higher: he makes the law of Mazda as fat as he can with a hundred acts of adoration, a thousand oblations, ten thousand sacrifices.

Fargard III:32 'When barley is coming forth, the Daevas start up; when the corn is growing rank, then faint the Daevas' hearts; when the corn is being ground, the Daevas groan; when wheat is coming forth, the Daevas are destroyed. In that house they can no longer stay, from that house they are beaten away, wherein wheat is thus coming forth....'"[18]

Equally important to Zarathustra were the proper care and respect of both wild and domesticated animals. "Care for and maintenance of innocent and useful domestic animals, such as cows, goats, sheep and dogs, is a virtue specially inculcated by the Prophet of Iran." 'May we be one in spirit with the Behman Ameshaspend of good mind', prays the devout Zoroastrian, 'who spreads peace in the midst of good creation. Animals of all kinds in the world are under his protection.'"[19]

The Shayast-La-Shayast (c. XV, 10) enjoins upon the man who would propitiate the divine Good Mind, that he 'should keep them [the kine] in a warm place'; that 'in summer he should provide for them a store of straw and grain, to the end that it be not necessary to turn them out to graze in the winter'[20]; and that 'he should not separate them from their young nor bar their young from their udders; for they are the counterpart in the world of the divine Good Mind.'"[21] Next to the herd, the dog was of utmost importance to the people. Zarathustra enjoined the faithful as a prime duty to exercise of the Good Mind to provide benevolent care towards the dog. In the Vendidad, Ahura Mazda says to Zarathustra:

Fargard XIII:8 "Whosoever shall smite either a shepherd's dog, or a house dog, or a stray dog, or a hunting dog, his soul when passing to the other world, shall fly amid louder howling and fiercer pursuing than the sheep does when the wolf rushes upon it in the lofty forest."[22]

Zarathustra Refreshes the Faith and Brings New Laws

Zarathustra was told by God that His people had lost their spiritual way, and that He wished them to return to His true path. The Avesta records these words of Ahura Mazda:

Tahmuras' Fragments XLIV:99 "But at present in this world below, O Spitama Zarathustra! there is not one just man, not two, nor three, nor several.

Tahmuras' Fragments XLIV:100 They seek not after righteousness, they seek not to succour and maintain the poor follower of the Holy Law."[23]

Through Zarathustra, the Aryan people were intended to become an example to the people in all regions of the world as to what would make them most truly happy—to think, speak and do only that which was good. It was not enough just to know what was good and what was bad; the point was for man to choose what was right not out of fear, but because it was the correct thing to do. Zarathustra brought a return to a code of virtues and of morals so that His people would be known for their integrity and loftiness of character. Many of the societies and intellectuals of ancient times looked to the followers of Zarathustra for their obvious virtues and their happy dispositions as believers in the "Good Life." Zarathustra promised:

Yasna XLV:5   "Yea, thus will I declare that which the most bountiful One told me, that word which is the best to be heeded by mortals. They who therein grant me obedient attention, upon them cometh Weal to bless, and the Immortal being, and in the deeds of His Good Mind cometh the Lord."[24]

It became obvious to both friend and foe that the main mission of Zarathustra was to promote a new set of rules of behavior, which he asked Ahura Mazda for by saying, "Teach thou me, by mouth, how it will be."[25] As a confirmation he asked,

Fargard V:22   "O Maker of the material world, thou Holy One! This law, this fiend-destroying law of Zarathustra, by what greatness, goodness and fairness is it great, good, and fair above all other utterances?"

The answer was,

Fargard V:23   "… 'As much as above all other floods as is the sea, Vouru-kasha, so much above all other utterances in greatness, goodness, and fairness is this law, this fiend-destroying law of Zarathustra.

Fargard V:24   'As much as a great stream flows swifter than a slender rivulet, so much above all other utterances in greatness, goodness and fairness is this law, this fiend-destroying law of Zarathustra.

'As high as the great tree stands above the small plants it overshadows, so high above all other utterances in greatness, goodness and fairness is this law, this fiend-destroying law of Zarathustra.

Fargard V:25   'As high as heaven is above the earth that it compasses around, so high above all other utterances is this law, this fiend-destroying law of Mazda.'"[26]

That there is generally a direct connection between one's deeds and recompense was reflected in the following:

Yasna XLVI:13 "Yea, he who will propitiate Zarathustra Spitama with gifts midst men, this man is fitted for the proclamation, and to him Ahura Mazda will give the (prospered) life. And he will likewise cause the settlements to thrive in mental goodness. We think him, therefore, Your good companion to further and maintain Your Righteousness and meet for Your approach."[27]

The Equality of Men and Women

With the advent of Zarathustra and His renewal of the Mazdayasnian religion, the Aryan culture became a progressive proponent of human rights, and the social and spiritual equality of man and woman. Zarathustra generally made no distinction of gender in His teachings, and when He did, he addressed them to the sexes in no particular order of hierarchy.[28]

A verse from the Avesta, in which a priest calls the faithful to worship, beautifully illustrates this parity and shared purpose:

Yasna 39:2 "And we worship the souls of... the saints wherever they were born, both of men and of women, whose good consciences are conquering in the strife against the Daevas, or will conquer, or have conquered."[29]

Visperad 3:4   "We venerate the righteous woman who is good in thoughts, word and deeds, who is well-educated, is an authority on religious affairs, is progressively serene, and is like the women who belong to the Wise God. We venerate the righteous man who is good in thoughts, words and deeds, who knows well the religion he has chosen, and who does not know blind following."[30]

In this era, women shared with men the responsibility for their individual progress in this world and the next, as well as an equal standing in the areas of social and religious leadership. The Erpatistan of the Avesta clarifies this, and underscores the freedom of choice allowed to both men and women by Zarathustra:

Fargard I: "The Priest officiating out of his house.

Fargard I:1 Who is he in the house who shall officiate as priest?—He who longeth most after holiness,....

Fargard I:5 Which of the two shall officiate as priest, the mistress or the master of the house? And if either be fit to take charge of the estate, which shall go forth?

If the master of the house take charge of the estate, the woman shall go forth. If the woman takes charge of the estate, the master of the house shall go forth.

Fargard I:6 If a man should take with him as priest the wife of another, without (her husband's) leave, May the woman fulfil the holy office?—Yea, if she is willing; nay, if she is not willing...."[31]

Men and women also shared an equal responsibility to teach and propagate the faith of Zarathustra, and to provide the Aryan youth an education in worldly arts and in the sciences. In fact, Zarathustra taught that mothers were particularly important as the first promoters of knowledge and wisdom, as they typically spent more time with the children than did the father, whose other duties often kept him away from home. Obviously, this required that the mother be well-educated herself, so that she might aptly assume the role of teacher.[32]

The Promotion of Education

Zarathustra promoted education in all nations among both men and women, for in education the youth would find that knowledge which would assist them in distinguishing that which was right. They hold it unlawful to talk of anything which it is unlawful to do. The most disgraceful thing in the world, they think, is to tell a lie; the next worst is to owe a debt: because, among other reasons, the debtor is obliged to tell lies.[33]

The Persian laws, however, begin at the beginning and take care that from the first their citizens shall not be of such a character as to ever desire anything improper or immoral. All Zarathustrians may send their children to the common schools of justice, and those who are not so situated may be educated by the public teachers.[34]

While education, and through it, the advancement of civilization was of supreme importance, it was not to be without a spiritual balance. For the sake of the individual and the soul, education was for naught if it did not include the recognition of that which was truly righteous:

Yasna XLVIII:11 "Yea, when shall our perfected Piety appear together with Thy Righteousness? When shall she come, as having the amenities of home for us, and provided (like our land) with pastures (for the kine)? And who shall give us quiet from the cruel (men) of evil life and faith? To whom shall Thy Good Mind's sacred wisdom come [to guide them in their toil to rescue and avenge us?]

Yasna XLVIII:12 (To whom? The answer lieth near.) Such shall be the Saviours of the Provinces, and they who, through Thy Good Mind's grace, shall go on hand in hand with mental keenness (as it spreads among Thy saints) by the doing every deed of Thy commandment, O Ahura! through the help of, and in accordance with, Thy Holy Order; for such as these are set (for us), as steadfast foes of hate!"[35]

This was to encourage His believers, if not all of humankind, to be industrious, to seek education and in all things to pursue the life that would be pleasing to their Creator and in so doing they would find satisfaction in themselves and thus true happiness!

The Art of Healing

In the Gathas, Zarathustra clearly described His conversations with Ahura Mazda, and His all consuming thirst for knowledge. He brought many truths of science to mankind, including knowledge of medicine that was far superior to that known in the world at that time.

The Avesta records this conversation between Zarathustra and Ahura Mazda concerning medicine:

Fargard 19:1 "Zarathustra asked Ahura Mazda: 'Ahura Mazda, most beneficent Spirit, Maker of the material world, thou Holy One! Who was the first of the healers, of the wise, the happy, the wealthy, 'the glorious, the strong, the PARAHALAS (first Iranian dynasty), drove back sickness to sickness, drove back death to death, and first turned away the point of the sword and the fire of fever from the bodies of mortals?"

Fargard 19:2 Ahura Mazda answered: "Thrita it was who first of the healers, the wise, the happy, the wealthy, the glorious, the strong, the Paradhalas, drove back sickness to sickness, drove back death to death, and first turned away the point of the sword and the fire of the fever from the bodies of mortals.

Fargard 19:3 He asked for a source of remedies; he obtained it from Khahathra-Vairya. [Presiding over metals, i.e. a knife], to withstand sickness and to withstand death, to withstand pain and to withstand fever; to withstand Sarana and to withstand Sarastya [headache and cold fever]; to withstand Azana and to withstand Azahva; to withstand Kurugha and to withstand Azivaka, to withstand Duruka and to withstand Astairya, to withstand the evil eye, rottenness, and infection which (Ahriman) had created against the bodies of mortals.

Fargard 19:4 And I Ahura Mazda brought down the healing plants that, by many myriads, grow up all around the one Gaokerena [tree of eternal life].

Fargard 19:5 All this do we achieve; all this do we order; all these prayers do we utter, for the benefit of the bodies of mortals.

Fargard 19:6 "to withstand sickness and to withstand death; to withstand pain and to withstand fever; to withstand Sarana and to withstand Sarastya; to withstand Azana and to withstand Azahva, to withstand Kurugha [leprosy] and to withstand Azivaka [snake bite]; to withstand Duruka and to withstand Astairya [epidemic]; to withstand the evil eye, rottenness and infection which (Ahriman) had created against the bodies of mortals."[36]

The Magi, [Zarathustrian High Priests] were made the holders of this medical knowledge, and became renowned physicians and healers. They passed on their expertise and learning to their pupils for generation after generation, with the understanding that the provision of healing was not restricted by class, ethnicity, race, gender or religion. As a result, during the subsequent Median, Achaemenid and Sassnian Empires, scientists from Greece and various other countries came to Persia to study under them.[37]

The Avesta divided the medical disciplines into five branches:

1. The Health Physician—was responsible for overseeing the purity and cleanliness of the living environment; the city as well as that of the individual.

2. The Medical Examiner—performed autopsies examining the dead with a twofold purpose. After ascertaining the cause of death and seeking what preventive measures might be employed in the future, they were responsible for issuing permission for burial.

3. The Surgeon—was responsible for healing through the use of the knife.[38]

Fargard 7:36 "O Maker of the material world, thou Holy One! If a worshipper of Mazda wants to practice the art of healing, on whom shall he first prove his skill? On worshippers of Mazda or worshippers of the Daevas?

Fargard 7:37 Ahura Mazda answered: 'on worshippers of the Daevas shall he first prove himself, rather than worshippers of Mazda. If he treat with the knife a worshipper of the Daevas and he die; if he treat with the knife a second worshipper of the Daevas and he die; if he treat with the knife for the third time a worshipper of the Daevas and he die, he is unfit forever and ever.'

Fargard 7:38 let him therefore never attend any worshipper of Mazda, let him never treat with the knife and worshipper of Mazda, nor wound him with the knife. If he shall ever attend any worshipper of Mazda and wound him with the knife, he shall pay for his wound the penalty for wilful murder.

Fargard 7:39 If he treat with the knife a worshipper of the Daevas and he recover, if he treat with the knife a second worshipper of the Daevas and he recover; if for the third time he treat with the knife a worshipper of the Daevas and he recover; then he is fit for ever and ever.

Fargard 7:40 He may thenceforth at his will attend worshippers of Mazda; he may at his will treat with the knife worshippers of Mazda, and heal them with the knife."[39]

4. The Doctor of Herbal Medicine—whose art advanced with the advent of agriculture in ancient Persia. The Zarathustrian priests were among the first to utilize herbs to cure disease, and developed unique methods for the preparation of healing extracts. Contrary to many other ancient traditions, the Magi used only tender branches and parts so that the plants could regenerate themselves; they did not dry the herbs and generated only cold extracts, as heat might destroy some of the inherit healing and restorative components of the medicinal plants. Herbal remedies included the use of:

a. *Haoma*, the chief amongst the healing plants. Haoma was nourishing, improved stamina, imparted clear thinking, and contained spiritual properties that were of assistance to the dead. It is traditionally associated with the ephedra plant, and was used as a blood purifier, against colds and flu, and to treat cardiovascular and respiratory ailments.

b. *Tamarisk* which grew well in a salty and arid climate, and was used to treat headache, fever, ulcers and skin inflammations.

c. *Myrtle* was used to treat inflammation, prevent wound infection, as a pain reliever, astringent and decongestant.

d. *Laurel* was used as a pain reliever, to treat insect stings, to aid digestion, against seizures and convulsions, and to prevent insect contamination of grain stores.

e. *Pomegranate* was used to treat a wide range of diseases from dysentery to gum and mouth ailments.

f. *Jujube* was used to cool the body and to treat sleeplessness and mental fatigue.

g. *Willow* was used as a disinfectant and antiseptic, and to treat headache, fever, pain, arthritis, and inflammation.

h. *Juniper* was used to treat digestive ailments, colic, high blood pressure and as a preventative measure against the spread of infection.

i. The *Chenar* or *Plane tree* could be used to start a fire by rubbing together two dried pieces of wood; the smoke was useful in preventing the spread of airborne disease. Extracts were used to treat snake bites and scorpion stings and to reduce inflammation and bleeding.

j. *Camel Thorn* was used to ease gastric discomfort, to increase milk production in dairy animals, and to ward off the "evil eye."

k. *Garlic* was used to treat infections and reduce blood pressure.

l. *Rue* was used to treat earache, joint pain, and as a deterrent to fleas.

m. *Frankincense* was used for respiratory ailments

n. *Aloeswood* was used to treat heart ailments.

The Magi were also familiar with such herbs as *borage, fenugreek, sweet majoram* and *chiory*; and with *date palm.*[40]

5. The Psychiatrist or "Behavior Inducer"—practiced the healing arts with the understanding that mental disorder was a sickness of the body, mind and soul. He utilized conversation, prayer, music, and the recitation of the Gathas and other religious sources to calm and treat the patient. The Avesta was clear on the importance of prayer in the medical disciplines:

Fargard 7:44   "If several healers offer themselves together, O Spitama Zarathustra!   Namely, one who heals with the knife, one who heals with herbs, and one who heals with the Holy Word; he will best drive away sickness from the body of the faithful. [41]

Physicians' fees were to be based on the patient's income as detailed in the Avesta:

Fargard 7:41   "A healer shall heal a priest for a blessing of the just; he shall heal the master of a house for the value of an ox of low value; he shall heal the lord of a borough for the value of an ox of average value; he shall heal the lord of a town for the value of an ox of high value; he shall heal the lord of a province for the value of a chariot and

Fargard 7:42   He shall heal the wife of the master of a house for the value of a she-ass; he shall heal the wife of the lord of a borough for the value of a cow: he shall heal the wife of the lord of a town for the value of a mare: he shall heal the wife of the lord of a province for the value of a she-camel.

Fargard 7:43   He shall heal the heir of a great house for the value of an ox of high value: he shall heal an ox of high value for the value of an ox of average value: he shall heal an ox of average value for the value of an ox of low value: he shall heal an ox of low value for the value of a sheep: he shall heal a sheep for the value of a piece of meat."[42]

Admonition to Be the Source of Charity

To Zarathustra, Ahura Mazda gave "the Golden Rule" thusly:

Dadistan-I Dinik 94:5   "That nature alone is good which shall not do unto another whatever is not good for its own self…".

It was immediately followed by the affirming text:

Dadistan-I Dinik 94:6 "And this, too, was thus considered by them, that one is to become a friend of every one, and this is thy nature; also, bring them on into goodness, and this is thy wisdom; also, consider them as thine own, and this is thy religion; also, through them it shall produce happiness, and this is thy soul."[43]

The importance and rewards of education, compassion, and the daily practice of ethical values such as honesty, purity and good citizenship were underscored again and again in the religion of Zarathustra.

Dadistan-I Dinik 38:1 "As to the thirty-seventh question and reply, that which you ask is thus: The measure that they measure good works with being revealed, how is it then when there is more, or not, done by us?

Dadistan-I Dinik 38:2 The reply is this, that every thought, word, and deed whose result is joy, happiness, and commendable recompense—when a happy result is obtainable, and the exuberance (afzuno) of thought, word, and deed is important—is well-thought, well-said, and well-done."[44]

And further,

Dinkard:306 "Be it known that a man is saved from hell by his receiving from the doctors of the faith excellent education and instruction about the soul and purity. A man's body is protected in this world by philanthropy and by that good monarch who makes people happy. Philanthropic men are of three kinds as follows: First, the religious philanthropists who are such owing to their love of the religious reward. Second, the pure philanthropists who do good to their fellow-subjects through love. And third, the philanthropists to trustworthy persons who are so through zeal and love....."[45]

According to Zarathustra, the very essence of divinity called for the protection and loving care of the poor and less fortunate among people, animals and, in fact, all of creation. He added the admonition that these principles must be taught and fostered in conjunction with the education of the less fortunate, for only thus would poverty be eliminated.

Yasna XXX:9 "And may we be such as those who bring on this great renovation, and make this world progressive, (till its perfection shall have been reached)"[46]

Dinkard 3:414 "Be it known that the invisible feeling generosity is warm and passionate and that of avarice cold. The source of both is in the conscience of men. The heart and conscience of the generous man are warm and such a heart has the light of the holy fire. It is the warmth of this luster that indicates the presence of this feeling. The generous man is exalted among men."[47]

The promise of a happy fate, both on earth and in the afterlife, was promised to those who helped the needy.

Prayers and Worship

Prayer was a way of asking for guidance. It was the best way for man to communicate with that which was greater than himself, and for the beseecher to rid himself of his consternation and stress by trusting in Ahura Mazda.

Prayers, however, were totally different than thoughts, in that the supplicant focused his "Good Mind" with intensity and purpose. Prayers said with focus and intelligence had much more power than those said without much thought. To recite your prayer without appropriate focus or attention was a sign of disrespect to Ahura Mazda. Since the righteous man had the clearest conscience, his prayers and focus would be better than most, and therefore the most effective.

Zarathustra revealed numerous prayers of homage to Ahura Mazda through His Divine conversations within the Gathas, as well as prayers for use on liturgical and ceremonial occasions. He proclaimed that the duty of prayer was incumbent upon all, irrespective of social status or gender. Zarathustra taught that it was through the recitation or chanting of prayer that an individual would find daily affirmation of the values of self. From prayers of the righteous mind, one could find peace, joy, protection, healing, assistance and guidance in both the physical and spiritual worlds.

There were two types of Zarathustrian prayer—those for private recitation and those used in public liturgies. Personal prayers were recited at meal times, before significant undertakings, in the temple, and at major turning points in life such as birth, marriage and death. Prayer was the prescribed way to set one's mind on the path of "Good Thought." Hence, there were times of the day in which there was a special need for refocusing of one's thoughts with special prayers for protection and guidance. Every Zarathustrian was expected to recite the "kusti" prayers at least five times each day, after having first ensured a physical purity by washing.

Formal liturgies might be performed in the temple, or at home, according to their designation as "higher" or "lower" ceremonies. The former might be performed only in the most pure locations, such as a fire temple, by a priest. The latter might be performed in private homes, in worship before the household fire.[48]

The Names of God (revealed for special protection)

Ormazd Yasht:5 "Then Zarathustra said: 'Reveal unto me that name of thine, O Ahura Mazda! that is the greatest, the best, the fairest, the most effective, the most fiend-smiting, the best-healing, that destroyeth best the malice of Daevas and Men;

Ormazd Yasht:6 'That I may afflict all Daevas and Men; that I may afflict all Yatus and Pairikas; that neither Daevas nor Men may be able to afflict me; neither Yatus nor Pairikas."

Ormazd Yasht:7 Ahura Mazda replied unto him:

'My name is the One of whom questions are asked, O holy Zarathustra!

'My second name is the Herd-giver

'My third name is the Strong One

'My fourth name is Perfect Holiness.

'My fifth name is All good things created by Mazda, the offspring of the holy principle.

'My sixth name is Understanding;

'My seventh name is the One with understanding.

'My eighth name is Knowledge;

'My ninth name is the One with Knowledge.

Ormazd Yast:8 'My tenth name is Weal;

'My eleventh name is He who produces Weal.

'My twelfth name is AHURA (the Lord).

'My thirteenth name is the most Beneficent.

'My fourteenth name is He in whom there is no harm.

'My fifteenth name is the unconquerable One.

'My sixteenth name is He who makes the true account.

'My seventeenth name is the All-seeing One.

'My eighteenth name is the healing One.

'My nineteenth name is the Creator.

'My twentieth name is MAZDA (the All-Knowing One). '"[49]

Ormazd Yasht:9 "Worship me, O Zarathustra, by day and by night, with offerings of libations well accepted I will come unto thee for help and joy, I, Ahura Mazda; the good, holy Sraosha will come unto thee for help and joy; the waters, the plants, and the Fravashis of the holy ones will come unto thee for help and joy.'...[50]

Ormazd Yasht:16 ...'These are my names, And he who in this material world, O Spitama Zarathustra! shall recite and pronounce these names of mine either by day or by night;

Ormazd Yasht:17 'He who shall pronounce them, when he rises up or when he lays him down; when he lays him down or when he rises up; when he binds on the sacred girdle (kushti) or when he unbinds the sacred girdle; when he goes out of his dwelling-place, or when he goes out of his town, or when he goes out of his country and comes into another country:

Ormazd Yasht:18 'That man, neither in that day nor in that night, shall be wounded by the weapons of the foe who rushes Aeshma-like and is Druj-minded; not the knife, not the crossbow, not the arrow, not the sword, not the club, not the sling-stone shall reach and wound him.

Ormazd Yasht:19 'But those names shall come in to keep him from behind and to keep him in front, from the Druj unseen, from the female Varenya fiend, from the evil-doer bent on mischief, and from that fiend who is all death, Angra Mainyu. It will be as if there were a thousand men watching over one man.'"[51]

Ahuna Vairya (the most sacred prayer of Zarathustrianism, revealed by Ahura Mazda to the prophet Himself, upon the occasion of His temptation by the Evil Spirit. A single recitation earns for the worshipper merit equivalent to that of the singing of a hundred Gathas.[52]

"The will of the Lord is the will of righteousness.

The gifts of Vohu-mano to the deeds done in the world for Mazda.

He who relieves the poor makes Ahura king."[53]

Priesthood and Commitment to the Faith

Dinkard:410 "Be it known that among men it is the pious man who pleases the Creator most. That man pleases the Creator most who benefits His creation most. That man benefits the creation most who strengthens men's faith in the good God and makes them active and zealous in doing holy deeds. The priest of the good religion is considered wise among men; he keeps the Creator highly pleased and is most pious on account of his piety."[54]

The Indo-Aryan culture into which Zarathustra was born was based upon three cooperative professions: priests, warriors and "prospering settlers." The Gathas describes them in the following stanzas of invocation and dedication:

Yasna 13:2 "And I invoke the friendly and most helpful person's lord, the Fire of Ahura Mazda, and also the most energetic lords of holy men, those who are most strenuous in their care of cattle and the fields, and the chief of the thrifty tiller of the earth. And I invoke the steady settler of sanctity, (and) the chief of the charioteer."[55]

As a reformer of the Mazdayasnian religion, Zarathustra both acknowledged some of its existing structures, and strove to expand the consciousness of His believers through His doctrines of freedom of choice and personal responsibility. Consequently, although the priesthood of the Zarathustrian Faith was, to some degree, hereditary, an intellectually or spiritually gifted youth (male or female) might be encouraged to study for the priesthood. [56]

Zarathustrian priests were categorized by the tasks which they performed. The athravan class was responsible for the care of the ritual fire, both in the fire temples and in individual homes, and through their duties became well-acquainted with the members of the community. The priests of the magi class were renowned throughout the ancient world for their wisdom and unsurpassed knowledge of philosophy, history, geography, plants, medicine and astronomy. Collectively, the priests were responsible for teaching the religion and performing many functions of service for the faithful, including the conducting of marriage and funeral rites, ministry to the sick, and assuring that the sacred fire remained lit and the waters remained pure. They counseled the community regarding the faith's ethical and moral codes, and the more senior priests were sought as arbiters in resolving conflicts within the community.[57]

Traditionally, it was an early practice for the priests to do no work other than that of ministering to the community, for which they received gifts from the faithful, or were allowed to beg alms. There were exceptions for the priests who were not able to survive on gifts or alms alone[58]:

Dadistan-i-Denig 46:1 "The forty-fifth question is that which you ask thus: Is it allowable that those of the priesthood, when there is no daily livelihood for them from the life of the priesthood, should abandon the priesthood, and that other work be done, or not?

Dadistan-i-Denig 46:2 The reply is this, that there is no loss of reputation to priests from priestly duties, which are themselves the acquired knowledge that is accumulated by the priestly disposition, care for the soul, and the requisite good works.

Dadistan-i-Denig 46:3 And there is this advantage, that, through acquaintance with the religion of the sacred beings, and certainty as to the reward of the spirit, they make them become more contented in adversity, more intelligent as regards stability of character in difficulty and restriction, and more thorough knowledge the abode of hope for those saved.

Dadistan-i-Denig 46:4 So that it is not fit they should abandon the priesthood, which is both harmless and an employment with advantages that has required much trouble to learn.

Dadistan-i-Denig 46:5 But, indeed, when they do not obtain a daily livelihood from priestly duty, and the good do not give them chosen righteous gifts for it, and they do not let them obtain any from next of kin or the wicked even by begging, a livelihood may be requested from the paid performance of ceremonies, management of all religious rites (dino), and other priestly disciple's duty therein.

Dadistan-i-Denig 46:6 When even by that they do not obtain it, they are to seek a livelihood by agriculture, sheep-rearing, penmanship, or other proper employment among priests; when it is not possible for them to live even by these, they are to seek it by bearing arms, hunting, or other proper employment in the profession of a virtuous warrior.

Dadistan-i-Denig 46:7 And when even it is not possible for them to maintain their own bodies, which are in requisite control, by that which is cravingly digested, they are to beg a righteous gift authorisedly as an effectual remedy; by living idly, or not expending strength, their own bodies, which are in control, are without livelihood, but not authorisedly."[59]

Confession, Renunciation, Penance and Absolution

Much of the priest's time was consumed by believers wishing to confess and atone not only for their own errors and misdeeds, but also for those of their loved ones, both living and dead. There might be partial atonement through the working of meritorious deeds, partial atonement through the sacrifice of goods such as the payment of livestock or monies to the priest or to the temple. There likewise could be partial absolution through the chanting of special prayers by the priest, which would have generally required some form of compensation.

The process required a renunciation of certain wickedness through prayer and sacrifice, after the confession of same to the priest who would then prescribe acts of penance. The priest would base his prescription upon the perceived sincerity of both the confession and the renunciation. The Vendidad records this conversation with Ahura Mazda:

Fargard 3:41 "'The Religion of Mazda indeed, O Spitama Zarathustra! takes away from him who makes confession of it, the bonds of his sin; it takes away the breach of trust, it takes away (the sin of) murdering one of the faithful; it takes away (the sin of) burying a corpse; it takes away (the sin of) deeds for which there is no atonement; it takes away the worst sin of usury; it takes away any sin that may be sinned.

Fargard 3:42 'In the same way the Religion of Mazda, O Spitama Zarathustra! cleanses the faithful from every evil thought, word, and deed, as a swift-rushing mighty wind cleanses the plain. So let all the deeds he doeth be henceforth good, O Zarathushtra! a full atonement for his sin is effected by means of the Religion of Mazda.'"[60]

The Prophecies of Zarathustra

There were many prophecies attributed to Zarathustra, which is credible considering both His questioning nature and the length of His ministry. Tradition holds that these prophecies were extremely detailed, and touched on almost every subject. Unfortunately, many of the written records of these prophecies have disappeared, in large part due to the targeted cultural destructions of the Persian national libraries carried out by both Alexander the Great in 334 BC and others later on.

Most of Zarathustra's prophecies had to do with the Indo-Aryan believers, and greatly influenced the dynasties and global decisions of such Persian rulers as Cyrus the Great and Darius I. Many of the remainder had to do with the manifestation of future spiritual leaders or saoshyants, and the end of the physical world. These prophecies were recorded in the Avesta. In the Gathas, Zarathustra discusses His own mission, and that of future saviors (saoshyants) with Ahura Mazda:

Yasna 48:2 "Tell me, for thou art he that knows, O Ahura—shall the Righteous smite the Liar before the retributions come which thou has conceived? That were indeed a message to bless the world.

Yasna 48:3 For him that knows, that is the best of teachings which the beneficent Ahura teaches through the Right, he the holy one, even thyself, O Mazda, that knows the secret lore through the wisdom of Good Thought."…

Yasna 48:7 "Violence must be put down! against cruelty make a stand, ye who would make sure of the reward of Good Thought through Right, to whose company the holy man belongs. His dwelling place shall be in thy House, O Ahura.

Yasna 48:8 Is the possession of thy good Dominion, Mazda, is that of thy Destiny assured to me Ahura? Will thy manifestation, O thou Right, be welcome to the pious, even the weighing of actions by the Good Spirit?

Yasna 48:9 When shall I know whether ye have power, O Mazda and Right, over everyone whose destructiveness is a menace to me? Let the revelation of Good Thought be confirmed unto me; the future deliverer should know how his own destiny shall be."[61]

Zarathustra prophesied that He would be followed by three future manifestations, Aushedar, Aushedar-mah and Saoshyant, each born of a virgin mother. "…three times (Zarathustra) approached his wife, Hvovi. Each time his seed fell to the ground. The yazad Neryosang took all the light and power of that seed, and …it was consigned to Lake Kayansih, in the care of the Waters…. It is said that even now three lamps are seen shining at night in the depths of the lake. And for each, when his own time comes, it will be thus: a virgin will go to Lake Kayansih to bathe; and the Glory will enter her body, and she will become with child. And so, one by one, the (three) will be born thus, each at his own time."[62]

The Appearance of Aushedar, the first of the future "Saviors":

Zand-I Vohuman Yasht 3:13 "Ohrmazd (Ahura Mazda) spoke thus: 'O Zartosht the Spitaman! when the demon with disheveled hair of the race of Wrath comes into notice in the eastern quarter, first a black token becomes manifest, and Aushedar son of Zartosht is born on Lake Frazdan.

Zand-I Vohuman Yasht 3:14 It is when he comes to his conference with, me, Ohrmazd, O Zartosht the Spitaman!' that in the direction of Chinistan, it is said—some have said among the Hindus—'is born a prince (kai); it is his father, a prince of the Kayanian race, approaches the women, and a religious prince is born to him; he calls his name Warharan the Varjavand, some have said Shahpur.

Zand-I Vohuman Yasht 3:15 'That a sign may come to the earth, the night when that prince is born, a star falls from the sky; when that prince is born the star shows a signal.'"[63]

Zand-I Vohuman Yasht 3:43 …"Ohrmazd said to Zartosht the Spitaman: 'This is what I foretell, when it is the end of thy millennium it is the beginning of that of Aushedar.

Zand-I Vohuman Yasht 3:44 Regarding Aushedar it is declared that he will be born in 1600, and at thirty years of age he comes to a conference with me, Ohrmazd, and receives the religion.'"[64]

And from the Pahlavi Rivayat of the Avesta:

Pahlavi Rivayat 48:1 "After that time when Zarathustra came to a consultation with Ohrmazd [Ahura Mazda], and 1,500 years after the time of Zarathustra, when it is the millennium of Religion, Aushedar will come into consultation with Ohrmazd for 50 years.

Pahlavi Rivayat 48:2 On the same day Mihr Yazad, that is, the sun, will stand at mid-day, for ten days and nights it will stand at the zenith of Heavens.

Pahlavi Rivayat 48:3 For three years, whatever plants are not needed, they will not wither then.

Pahlavi Rivayat 48:4 He [i.e., Aushedar] will purify the religion, he will bring (the ritual precepts of Hadamansar into use, and men will act according to Hadamansar."[65]

To many scholars and theologians, these prophecies refer to Jesus of Nazareth. It was because of these prophecies that the Magi responded to an astronomical phenomenum [the guiding star] and sought "the King of the Jews" as an infant. This event was of so much importance to them that they secured some of the most extravagant items available and commenced their journey to worship the child in Bethlehem, despite the fact that Zarathustra stated that His mission would not commence until His thirtieth year.

The Avesta continues with descriptions of the second and third predicted world saviors, Aushedar-mah and Saoshayant:

Pahlavi Rivayat 48:22 "At the end of the millennium, Aushedar-mah will come in to consultation with Ohrmazd for 30 years.

Pahlavi Rivayat 48:23 The sun will stand at the zenith from that day for 20 days and nights.

Pahlavi Rivayat 48:24 And for six years, those plants which are not needed will not wither.

Pahlavi Rivayat 48:25 And he will bring (the legal precepts of) Dadig into use; people will act according to the law."[66]

Zand-I Vohuman Yasht 3:52 "And, afterwards, when the millennium of Aushedar-mah comes, through Aushedar-mah the creatures become more progressive, and he utterly destroys the fiend of serpent origin; and Peshotan son of Vishtasp becomes, in like manner, high priest and primate of the world.

Zand-I Vohuman Yasht 3:53 In that millennium of Aushedar-mah mankind become so versed in medicine, and keep and bring physic and remedies so much in use, that when they are confessedly at the point of death they do not thereupon die, nor when they smite and slay them with the sword and knife."[67]

Aushedar-mah would, like his predecessor, renew the religion of God. There would be a diminution of decay along with the extension of life. There would be an increase of humility and peace and the perfection of liberality. Man would not only live longer, but far more healthily. Herbs, flowers, and scents would become used for their healing properties as the words of Zarathustra recalled:

Bundahishn 9:3 "On the whole earth plants grew up like hair upon the heads of men.

Bundahishn 9:4 Ten thousand of them grew forth of one special description, for the keeping away the ten thousand species of disease which the evil spirit produced for creatures; and from those ten thousand, the one hundred thousand species of plants have grown forth."[68]

Towards the end of this millennium, owing to the tolerance of the believers of Aushedar-mah towards people of other beliefs, the spirit of evil [Ahriman] would once more attain power. He would be released from confinement on Mount Dimavand to work evil in the world until Ahura Mazda sent His angels to rouse Keresasp the Saman. Keresasp would arise from his trance and kill the doer of evil at the end of the millennium, thus making way for the next Apostle. At that time would be the coming of Saoshyant and the final resurrection. The Avesta says:

Pahlavi Rivayat 48:37 ..."After that, at the end of the millennium of Aushedar-mah, the Soshyans [Saoshyant] will come in to consultation with Ohrmazd for 30 years.

Pahlavi Rivayat 48:38 And (on) that day the sun will stand at the zenith for 30 days.

Pahlavi Rivayat 48:94 ..."Ohrmazd will stand up with Srosh the righteous, and Srosh's righteousness will smite Greed.

Pahlavi Rivayat 48:95 Ohrmazd will expel the Evil Spirit out of the sky, with the hateful darkness and the evil which he first brought when he invaded, and he will expel all [of it] from the sky through the hole through which he [i.e., the Evil Spirit] invaded. And that hole will make him so stunned and senseless, (that) after that (his) stupefaction will remain.

Pahlavi Rivayat 48:96 There was one who said: 'The eternally-existing ones will make him powerless by killing his form. The Evil Spirit will be no more: no (more) of his creation!

Pahlavi Rivayat 48:97 At that time, when the wicked will have been punished and will have passed through the (molten) metal, there will be the Assembly of Isadwastar and reward and punishment will be to every person [according] to the number of good deeds he has done....

Pahlavi Rivayat 48:99 ...then Ohrmazd and the Amahraspands and all the Yazads and mankind will be in one place, and the star too and the moon and the sun and the Victorious Fire will all be in the form of a man who is strong, and they will all be in the form of a man, and they will come to the earth.

Pahlavi Rivayat 48:100 Then it will be entirely the creation of Ohrmazd.

Pahlavi Rivayat 48:101 And after that it will not be necessary for him to perform any action, and mankind, in the likeness of a body of 40 years of age, will all be immortal and deathless, and ageless, and without feeling or decay.

Pahlavi Rivayat 48:102 And their work will be this, to behold Ohrmazd and to pay homage, and to do for the other lords all (things) which seem to themselves very peaceful. Everyone will love others like himself.'"[69]

With the appearance of the third Apostle, the religion of God is made pure again and an everlasting future existence commences. There is a total annihilation of fiendishness, and the subjugation of disease and decrepitude, of death and persecution, and of the original evils of tyranny, apostasy, and depravity. As to when and where, that is not specified.

❧ CHAPTER 4 ❧

ZARATHUSTRA

THE NATURE OF GOD

God is spirit, not a being, not an entity, but spirit. God is Spirit! This was a drastic new concept for Zarathustra's disciples, followers and times. He could assume any form He might wish, and yet still remain unchanged and undiminished as the "Universal Spirit." God in this aspect is not viewed as an abstraction; instead Zarathustra presents Him as an active "Living Existence" who could be perceived in thought, but whose governance in the universe should be apparent to all. He knew no equal, and was older than anything in the universe. Ahura Mazda was not only the Creator of the material or physical universe, but also the Spiritual universe. He was the creator of water, rock, all that is and all that lives. He was the Almighty Spirit and to be beseeched and worshipped as the "One and Only," the unchanging, through all eternity. He was the Most Beneficent, conferring His blessings upon all things and beings in the physical and spiritual universe.

Early in His ministry, Zarathustra sought to obtain a glimpse of Ahura Mazda:

Shayast la-Shayast XV:1   "It is revealed by a passage of the Avesta that (Zarathustra), seated before Auharmazd [Ahura Mazda], always wanted information [vak] from him; and he spoke to Auharmazd thus: 'Thy head, hands, feet, hair, face, and tongue are in my eyes just like those even which are my own, and you have the clothing men have; give me a hand, so that I may grasp thy hand!'"

Ahura Mazda answered and said,

Shayast la-Shayast XV:2   "" ...I am an intangible spirit, it is not possible to grasp my hand.""[1]

The Avestan name Ahura Mazda translates literally to "the All-Wise Lord" ["Ahura"] meaning "High Being"; "Mazda" meaning "Wisdom", "Wise" or Eternal Light.[2] The Zarathustrian concept of God as Ahura Mazda includes the tenets that God is formless and invisible, uncreated and without duality. It is generally understood that the true nature of God is beyond human understanding.

Yasna XXIX:4 "The Great Creator (is himself) most mindful of the uttered indications which have been fulfilled beforehand hitherto in the deeds of demon-gods and (good or evil) men, and of those which shall be fulfilled by them hereafter. He Ahura is the discerning arbiter; so shall it be to us as He shall will!"[3]

In one chapter of the Dinkard there is a peculiar panegyric of the Creator Ahura Mazda as follows:

"'Sovereign and not subject; father and not progeny; by himself and not descended from; master and not servant; chief and not under a chief; possessor and not indigent; protector and not protected; firm and immaculate; possessing in himself knowledge and not through any medium; disposing and not disposed; distributing but not receiving anything; giving ease to others and not receiving it from them; giving cooperation but not receiving cooperation; esteeming and not in need of estimation from others; directing and not directed'".

"We find also in other writings similar indications of His sublime character, which prove that the honour and dignity of the godhead and Ahura Mazda is fully upheld and maintained in the Zoroastrian sacred writings throughout all ages."

"In the second Gatha (Yasna XLV) we meet with emphatic exhortations of Zoroaster to worship Ahura Mazda and him alone."[4]

Yasna XLV:1   "Yea, I will speak forth; hear ye; now listen, ye who from near, and ye who from afar have come seeking (the knowledge). Now ponder ye clearly all that concerns him."

Yasna XLV:6   ..."Aye, thus will I declare forth Him who is of all the greatest, praising through my Righteousness, I who do aright, those who (dispose of all as well aright). Let Ahura Mazda hear with His bounteous spirit, in whose homage (what I asked) was asked with the Good Mind. Aye, let Him exhort me through His wisdom (which is ever) the best.

Yasna XLV:7   (Yea, I will declare Him) whose blessings the offerers will seek for, those who are living now, as well as those who have lived (aforetime) as will they also who are coming (hereafter. Yea, even) the soul(s) of the righteous (will desire) them in the eternal Immortality. (Those things they will desire which are blessing to the righteous) but woes to the wicked. And these hath Ahura Mazda (established) through His kingdom, He, the creator (of all).

Yasna XLV:8   Him in our hymns of homage and of praise would I faithfully serve, for now with (mine) eye, I see Him clearly, Lord of the good spirit, of word, and action, I knowing through my Righteousness Him who is Ahura Mazda. And to Him (not here alone, but) in His home of song, His praise we shall bear.

Yasna XLV:9   Yea, Him with our better Mind we seek to honour, who desiring (good), shall come to us (to bless) in weal and sorrow. May He, Ahura Mazda, make us vigorous through Khshathra's royal power, our flocks and men in thrift to further, from the good support and bearing of His Good Mind, (itself born in us) by His Righteousness."[5]

The names, titles and descriptions of God throughout the writings of Zarathustra were of use in many ways. They not only offered guidance and a ritual focus, but each name could become the source of a mystical experience in itself. Try meditating upon or slowly speaking the following:

The Sad-o-Yak Nam-i-Khoda

(The Hundred and One Names of the Lord "Ahura Mazda")

Praiseworthy

Almighty

All-Knowing

Lord of All

Without Beginning

Without End

Root of Creation

The End of All

Ancient Cause

More Noble

Most Open (Innocent)

Separate from All

Connected with All

Unreachable by Anyone

Who Can Reach All

Most straightforward; Truest of All

Who Holds Everyone

Without Cause (Does not need a reason for existence)

Reason of All Reasons

Creator of Progress

Creator of Growth

Who Reaches Everyone Equally

Provider

Protector of Creation

Not Different

Without Shape

Most Determined

Most Invisible

Omnipresent

Most Complete

Worthy of Thanksgiving

Completely Good Natured

Completely Good Noble Aura

Remover of Suffering

Mysterious

Immortal

Grantor of Wishes

Creator of Noble Nature

Generous with Justice

Grantor of Generosity

Most Abundant Provider

Who Does Not Get Angry

Independent; Without Worry

Protector from Evil

Who Does Not Deceive

Who Cannot Be Deceived

Without Duality

Lord of Wishes

Wish is His Command

Without Body

Who Does Not Forget

Keeper of Accounts

Worthy of Knowing; All-Knowing

Fearless

Without Suffering

Most High

Always the Same

Creator of the Universe Invisibly

Creator of Much Invisible Creations

Hidden in Invisible Creation

Who Changes Fire into Air

Who Changes Fire into Water

Who Changes Air into Fire

Who Changes Air into Water

Who Changes Air into Dust

Who Changes Air into Wind

Who Changes Fire into Jewels

Who Creates Air in All Places

Creator of Much Water

Who Changes Dust into Fire

Who Changes Dust into Air

Who Changes Dust into Water

Creator of Creators

Fulfiller of Wishes

Creator of Mankind

Creator of All Things

Creator of Four Elements

Creator of Stars

Without Doubt

Timeless

Alert

Always Guarding and Progress Creator

Keeper of Limits

Victorious

Lord of Creation

Wise Lord

Most Capable of Preserving Originality of Creations

Most Capable of Creating New Creations

Who Can Reach All Creations

Who Can Provide Everything

Generous

Lord of Existence

Forgiver

Creator of Justice

Full of Brightness

Full of Aura, Light

Giver of True Justice

Lord of Good Works

Giver of Freedom for Progress

Refresher of the Soul with Progress[6]

Ahura Mazda was not only the creator of all that was, but the creator of all that would be until the end of time. His creation did not cease (as in Genesis) but continues to this day. He was the "Living Active Existence," the Eternal Being who could be perceived only in thought while one was in the material existence, but whose governance of the universe was apparent to all. He sat at the apex among the celestial beings in the highest heaven, and remained immune from the limitations of time and space. He was the Lord of all, the Greatest of all; everything came from Him and through Him. He was brighter than the brightest of creation; He knew no elder and had no equal.[7]

The Mazdayasnian Religion into which Zarathustra was born was a polytheistic, nature-based religion which incorporated the worship of many gods and demi-gods. Zarathustra's revelation of the singleness and intangibility of Ahura Mazda marked a radical departure from not only the Indo-Aryan but all existing world cultures, and created the first monotheistic religion.

The Holy Spirits

1)   The Amesha Spentas

Six attributes of Ahura Mazda, the single Godhead, were represented by Zarathustra in the Gathas as the embodiment of His vision and concept of God.

"...it is obvious that these... names denote the... most sublime characteristics of God. In selecting these from among the other innumerable divine attributes, (Zarathustra) apparently intended to impress the most original and striking of these attributes on the human mind, incapable as it is of comprehending all the infinite attributes of Divinity. Seeing that the one First Cause of all was most wisely ruling everywhere in the invisible or visible worlds—matter, mind, or spirit—always with benevolence, perfect right order and holiness, omnipotence, benevolent love and everlastingness, (Zarathustra) chose these... high and philosophical religious abstractions as the fittest attributes by which to celebrate Him. And accordingly, he composed his sacred poetry of the Gathas in a peculiar style, which is characterized by the reverence of one or more of these... names in nearly every stanza of line of his Gathas, the more readily and forcibly to impress them on the mind."[8]

From an ethical perspective, the Amesha Spentas provided easily understood symbols of divine purity on earth. Zarathustra preached the actualization of these ideals within each man and woman as a means of personal and spiritual growth and as a protection against ungodliness and evil.

The Amesha Spentas were prayed to and beseeched individually, to focus the mind of the beseecher on the subject of his prayer. If the prayer was for better health or a healing, the believer would direct it to that portion of Ahura Mazda referred to as Haurvetat. A prayer for the departed would be directed to Ameretat. In many respects, the Amesha Spentas can be equated with the Archangels of modern Christianity. Their individual qualities are highlighted below:

a. Vohu Manah or Vohuman – represents the quality of the Good Mind. Man increases the qualities of Vohu Manah within himself through good speech and appropriate choices. In the material world, Vohu Manah is the protector of cattle and the animal world. He is also responsible for the preparation of the list of good deeds performed by the individual at the time of the soul's departure from the physical plane.

b. Asha Vahishta – represents the qualities of truth, fairness and justice and in the material world is associated with righteousness, cosmic order and the element of fire.

c. Kshatra Vairya – represents the dynamic, creative power of Ahura Mazda. In the material world, Kshatra Vairya symbolizes physical strength and valor, and is associated with elemental metals.

d. Aramaiti – represents the qualities of service, kindness, faith and devotion. On the physical plane, Aramaiti personifies Mother Earth and fertility.

e. Haurvatat – represents the qualities of beauty, perfection, health and prosperity. She is associated with water and the physical well-being of mankind.

f. Ameretat – represents the quality of immortality and dispels the fear of death. In the material world, she is associated with the plant kingdom and the "tree of life."[9]

2)   The Yazatas

The Yazatas, or "Adorable Ones" were similar to the angels of the Christian tradition, and were hierarchically one level below the Amesha Spentas. While it was said that their number is beyond counting, there were only thirty-three mentioned in the existing writings and the traditions of the Parsi. They were divided into subgroups and associated with specific Amesha Spentas, although their primary purpose was to assist the devout and share the grace of Ahura Mazda with mankind. Their rewards might be physical or spiritual. They may have come in the form of dreams and visions, or literally as "gifts from Heaven." When invoked, the yazatas assisted the Zarathustrian faithful in the performance of their secular and religious duties.[10]

The Avesta mentions approximately forty yazatas by name, of which twenty-four might be considered especially prominent. This number matches the total given by Plutarch in his discussion of Zoroastrianism in "Isis and Osiris."[11]

"...and (Ahura Mazda) created six separate parts of His self, the first of Good Thought, the second of Truth, the third of Order, and, of the rest, one of Wisdom, one of Wealth, and one the Artificer of Pleasure in what is Honourable."[12]

There were two main categories of Yazatas—the celestial and the terrestrial. The celestial, representing Divine Wisdom, included the following:

    a. Sroasha – the guardian of humanity, was the first to worship Ahura Mazda. It was to him Ahura Mazda taught His doctrines so that Sroasha might serve as a missionary to the world. It was his mission to move over the entire earth spreading religious lore so that men would be able to recognize that which was right.

    b. Ashi Vanguhi – the rewarder of good deeds, was the sister of Sroasha. She filled the barns of men with grain and with cattle, their coffers with gold and their fields with foliage. She filled the chests of good and chaste women with jewels, and their wardrobes with fine garments.

c. Asha – the source of all that was right and the protector of the righteous man and woman. Asha transcended both bodily and mental purity; and in that deeper spiritual sense, was equivalent to the Eternal Truth, or the Divine Law. He thus permeated the entire creation and was the essence of that with which God had fashioned the whole Universe.

d. Mithra – the strongest and most active of the Yazatas, was the protector of the lord of the house, the lord of the clan, the lord of the town and the lord of the country, as long as they did not lie to him. He loathed lies and the liars that told them. Mithra was also responsible for seeing that contracts were not violated and that pledges, written or verbal, were upheld.

Mithra was a holdover from the Mazdayasnian religion and as such was also a powerful entity in the Hindu faith of India. It is extremely ironic that it was this very same Mithra, who, in later days, would have his nature changed by other societies into a cult of sensual and insatiable sexual behavior.

The terrestrial yazatas, including those associated with the functions of light, wind, fire, water and earth, mediated the affairs of the material world so that no harm was inflicted on the faithful. They included:

e. Atar – the source of heat and light, was the intermediary through which the faithful might attain to Ahura Mazda. It was he who was sought in the fire temples and upon going out into the sunlight.

f. Ardvi-Sura-Anahita – the undefiled, who presided over all the waters.

g. Zam – personifying the earth, who, with Spenta Armaiti, was responsible for safeguarding the welfare of plants, animals and mankind.[13]

Ahriman and His Cadre of Evil Spirits

The polytheistic religion into which Zarathustra was born was based on the worship of a variety of "daevas" or nature spirits, these spirits were transformed in the new Zarathustrian faith into demons who bore allegiance to the Spirit of Evil, Ahriman.

Ahriman represented all things not of God [Ahura Mazda]. The human vices of laziness, greed, avarice, jealousy, prejudice, gossip, dishonesty, bad sexual behavior, deceitfulness, the causing of doubt in others, the causing of attraction to all things evil, and the urge to cause destruction and annihilation were all a part of the arsenal of Ahriman. Lacks of humility, spirituality, and of "good thoughts, good words and good deeds" were also a part of his "tool chest." In general, these vices were personified by six daevas or archangel counterparts to the Amesha Spentas, and by numerous "druj" or cooperators with evil:

* Akoman – producer of vile thoughts and unrest

* Indra – preventer of the minds of the creatures from practicing righteousness

* Saurva – personifier of evil authority, oppression, unlawfulness and want

* Naonhaithya – producer of discontent

- Taurvi – mingler of poison into the vegetable creations

- Zairi – the venom maker, poisoner of the waters, plants and animals

The druj were many, and were associated with such human and earthly occurrences as scornfulness, revenge, sloth, falsehoods, pollution, drought and earthquake.[14]

The book *The History of the Devil,* cites two of the early Zarathustrian researchers of the nineteenth century:

> "There were two general ideas at the bottom on the Indo-Iranian religion; first, that there is a law in nature, and secondly, that there is a war in nature. There is a law in nature, because everything goes on in a serene and mighty order. Days after days, seasons after seasons, years after years come and come again; there is a marvelous friendship between the sun and the moon, the dawn has never missed its appointed time and place, and the stars that shine in the night know where to go when the dawn is breaking. There is a God who fixed that never-failing law, on whom it rests forever.
>
> There is a war in nature, because it contains powers that work for good and powers that work for evil: there are such beings as benefit man, and such

beings as injure him: there are gods and fiends."[15]

Francois Lenormant described Ahura Mazda and Ahriman thusly:

"The creation came forth from the hands of (Ahura Mazda), pure and perfect like himself. It was Ahriman who perverted it by his infamous influence, and labored continually to destroy and overthrow it, for he is the destroyer as well as the spirit of evil. The struggle between these two principles, of good and of evil, constitutes the world's history. In Ahriman we find again the old wrathful serpent of the Indo-Iranian period, who is the personification of evil and who in Vedism, under the name of Ahi, is regarded as an individual being. The myth of the serpent and the legends of the Avesta are mingled in Ahriman...".[16]

Zarathustra believed that the two primal spirits or essences, Ahura Mazda and Ahriman, "made a deliberate choice (although each it seems, according to his own proper nature) between good and evil, an act which prefigures the identical choice every man must make for himself in this life. The exercise of choice changed the inherent antagonism between the two Spirits into an active one.... Ahura Mazda knew in his wisdom that if he became Creator and fashioned this world, then the Hostile Spirit would attack it, because it was good, and it would become a battleground for their two forces, and in the end he, God, would win the great struggle there and be able to destroy evils, and so achieve a universe that would be wholly good forever."[17]

The Battle between Ahura Mazda and Ahriman

The Zarathustrian account of the battle between good and evil is based on the Indo-Aryan cosmology and understanding of the ancient universe. Traditional accounts divide the eons of time into four spans of 3,000 years each; during the first 3,000 years, Ahura Mazda existed in the endless light of infinite time. At some point during those years, Ahriman became aware of the gloriousness of Ahura Mazda, and became envious. He challenged Ahura Mazda, but the latter, knowing in His omniscience what the outcome of the battle would be, went forth to meet with Ahriman to propose peace, and spoke thus:

Bundahishn 1:13 "Then Ohrmazd, with a knowledge of which way the end of the matter would be, went to meet the evil spirit, and proposed peace to him, and spoke thus: 'Evil Spirit! bring assistance unto my creatures, and offer praise! so that, in reward for it, ye [you and your creatures] may become immortal and undecaying, hungerless and thirstless.

Bundahishn 1:14 And the evil spirit shouted thus: 'I will not depart, I will not provide assistance for thy creatures, I will not offer praise among thy creatures, and I am not of the same opinion with thee as to good things. I will destroy thy creatures for ever and everlasting; moreover, I will force all thy creatures into disaffection to thee and affection for myself.'

Bundahishn 1:15 And the explanation thereof is this, that the evil spirit reflected in this matter, that Ohrmazd was helpless as regarded him, therefore He proffers peace; and he did not agree, but bore on even into conflict with Him.

Bundahishn 1:16 And Ohrmazd spoke thus: 'You are not omniscient and almighty, O evil spirit! so that it is not possible for thee to destroy me, and it is not possible for thee to force my creatures so that they will not return to my possession.'

Bundahishn 1:17 Then Ohrmazd, through omniscience, knew that: 'If I do not offer a period of contest, then it will be possible for him to act so that he may be able to cause the seduction of my creatures to himself. As even now there are many of the intermixture of mankind who practice wrong more than right.'

Bundahishn 1:18 And Ohrmazd spoke to the evil spirit thus: 'Appoint a period! so that the intermingling of the conflict may be for nine thousand years.' For he knew that by appointing this period the evil spirit would be undone.

Bundahishn 1:19 Then the evil spirit, unobservant and through ignorance, was content with that agreement; just like two men quarreling together, who propose a time thus: 'Let us appoint such-and-such a day for a fight.'

Bundahishn 1:20 Ohrmazd also knew this, through omniscience, that within these nine thousand years, for three thousand years everything proceeds by the will of Ahura Mazda, three thousand years there is an intermingling of the wills of Ohrmazd and Ahriman, and the last three thousand years the evil spirit is disabled, and they keep the adversary away from the creatures.

Bundahishn 1:21 Afterwards, Ohrmazd recited the Ahunwar thus: Yatha ahu vairyo ('as a heavenly lord is to be chosen') ...and uttered the twenty-one words; He also exhibited to the evil spirit His own triumph in the end, and the impotence of the evil spirit, the annihilation of the demons, and the resurrection and undisturbed future existence of the creatures for ever and everlasting.

Bundahishn 1:22 And the evil spirit, who perceived his own impotence and the annihilation of the demons, became confounded, and fell back to the gloomy darkness; even so as is declared in revelation, that, when one of its [the Ahunwar's] three parts was uttered, the evil spirit contracted his body through fear, and when two part of it were uttered he fell upon his knees, and when all of it was uttered he became confounded and impotent as to the harm he caused the creatures of Ohrmazd, and he remained three thousand years in confusion.

Bundahishn 1:23 Ohrmazd created his creatures in the confusion of Ahriman; first he produced Vohuman ['good thought'], by whom the progress of the creatures of Ohrmazd was advanced.

Bundahishn 1:24 The evil spirit first created Mitokht ['falsehood'], and then Akoman ['evil thought'].

Bundahishn 1:25 The first of Ohrmazd's creatures of the world was the sky, and his good thought [Vohuman], by the good procedure, produced the light of the world, along with which was the good religion of the Mazdayasnians; this was because the renovation [Frashegird] which happen to the creatures was known to him!

Bundahishn 1:26 Afterwards arose Ardwahisht, and then Shahrewar, and then Spandarmad, and then Hordad, and then Amurdad. From the dark world of Ahriman were Akoman and Andar, and then Sovar, and then Nakahed, and then Tairev and Zairik.

Bundahishn 1:28 Of Ohrmazd's creatures of the world, the first was the sky; the second, water; the third, earth; the fourth, plants; the fifth, animals; the sixth, mankind."[18]

When Ahriman disdained the offer of peace, Ahura Mazda chanted the Ahunwar, or most sacred prayer, and exhibited to the evil spirit what was to come in the final confrontation—the impotence of the evil spirit and the annihilation of the daeva, the Final Judgment and resurrection and the dispensation of immortality to all creatures. Thereupon Ahriman became confounded and fell back into the Abyss where he remained in confusion for 3,000 years.

During the second 3,000 years, Ahura Mazda created the spiritual and material worlds. Ahriman, at the advent of the next 3,000 years, again left the abyss and invaded the material world. He broke through the sky and attacked the earth, its waters, lands and creatures, including man. The creations of Ahura Mazda were now susceptible to pain, hunger, death, disease and decay.

The fourth period of 3,000 years was marked at its beginning by the birth and revelation of Zarathustra. He prophesied the return of His spirit in a "savior" at the end of each of the next two millenia and the appearance of the Saoshyant who would battle the forces of Ahriman and set in motion the Final Judgment.

Punishment and Reward

Zarathustra taught that a man's wickedness and ungodliness would have consequences in this world and/or the next. One would be far better off if the full measure of his punishment could be received in the material world, because afterlife punishments and rewards were greatly diminished by those that you received while on earth.[19] For example, if your wickedness was in the form of stealing and resulted in even more than you stole being stolen from you, you would learn from the experience of cause and effect. Punishment in the afterlife might therefore be greatly reduced. If you became industrious, filled your life with good thoughts, words and deeds and through changing of your life-style found both happiness and wealth, you would need to pray that your full reward had not been given in the material world, and that after death, in the final balancing of good and wicked, you would not be found wanting.[20]

Ahura Mazda intended that all men and women might find the true happiness that came from "Good Thought, Good Words and Good Deeds," and that they would find true joy from teaching the same to their children, friends, neighbors and co-workers. It was through the teaching of ethics and virtue that the druj and daeva could be defeated; it was in the elimination of negativity, gossip and wickedness that the greatest and most lasting joy for man and God would be found.[21]

Uncertainty of Life—A Reason for Living the Good Life

That one should be prepared for the ending of life was an obvious lesson, since death was a certainty and only its timing was unknown. It was for each individual one of the biggest uncertainties of his existence.

Aogemadaeca:41 "...(Now) when a man sets out on a journey, he takes provisions with him;

Aogemadaeca:42 If it be for one day's march, he takes provisions for two days;

Aogemadaeca:43 If it be for two days' march, he takes provisions for three;

Aogemadaeca:44 If it be for ten days' march, he takes provisions for fifteen;

Aogemadaeca:45 And he thinks that he will come back in health to his well-beloved friends, parents, and brethren.

Aogemadaeca:46 How then is it that men take no provisions for the unavoidable journey,

Aogemadaeca:47 On which one must go once for all, for all eternity?"[22]

Heaven and Hell

German Orientalist Martin Haug, describes the Zarathustrian understanding of heaven and hell.

"The idea of a future life, and the immortality of the soul, is expressed very distinctly already in the Gathas, and pervades the whole of the later Avesta literature. The belief in a life to come is one of the chief dogmas of the Zend-Avesta....

"Closely connected with this idea is the belief in Heaven and Hell, which Zarathustra himself clearly pronounced in his Gathas. The name for Heaven is Garotman in Persian, 'house of hymns', because the angels are believed to sing hymns there. Garotman is the residence of Ahura Mazda and the most blessed men....

"Hell is called Drujo demana, 'house of destruction', in the Gathas. The later name is Duzhanha..., which is preserved in the modern Persian Duzakh, 'hell'."[23]

In the Gathas, Zarathustra described heaven and hell not as physical locations, but as timeless states of consciousness where one existed either in oneness [heaven] or separation [hell] from Ahura Mazda. Heaven is referred to as either the "House of Good Thinking" or the "House of Song," a metaphor for the state of perfect Wisdom.

The Soul Immediately Upon Death

There is a kind of detail concerning body and soul, especially at the time of death, which is to be found throughout the writings of the Zarathustrian religion. In his precocious way, Zarathustra wanted to know exactly what occurred, and how difficult was the separation of the soul from the body that it has been attached to and working with for years. In the following description, Zarathustra asked for and was told by Ahura Mazda that four days [actually three nights)]should be allowed after death for the detachment process to be completed.

Yast XXII:1 "Zarathustra asked Ahura Mazda: 'O Ahura Mazda, most beneficent Spirit, Maker of the material world, thou Holy One!

'When one of the faithful departs this life, where does his soul abide on that night?'

Ahura Mazda answered:

Yast XXII:2 'It takes its seat near the head, singing the Ustavaiti Gatha and proclaiming happiness: 'Happy is he, happy the man, whoever he be, to whom Ahura Mazda gives the full accomplishment of his wishes!' On that night, his soul tastes as much of pleasure as the whole of the living world can taste.'

Yast XXII:3 'On the second night where does his soul abide?'

Yast XXII:4 Ahura Mazda answered: 'It takes its seat near the head, singing the Ustavaiti Gatha and proclaiming happiness, 'Happy is he, happy the man, whoever he be, to whom God gives the full accomplishment of his wishes!' On that night his soul tastes as much of pleasure as the whole of the living world can taste.'

Yast XXII:5 'On the third night where does his soul abide?'

Yast XXII:6 Ahura Mazda answered: 'It takes its seat near the head, singing the Ustavaiti Gatha and proclaiming happiness: 'Happy is he, happy the man, whoever he be, to whom Ahura Mazda gives the full accomplishment of his wishes!' On that night his soul tastes as much of pleasure as the whole of the living world can taste.'

Yast XXII:7 At the end of the third night, when the dawn appears, it seems to the soul of the faithful one as if it were brought amidst plants and scents: it seems as if a wind were blowing from the region of the south, from the regions of the south, a sweet-scented wind, sweeter-scented than any other wind in the world.

Yast XXII:8 And it seems to the soul of the faithful one as if he were inhaling that wind with the nostrils, and he thinks: 'Whence does that wind blow, the sweetest-scented wind I ever inhaled with my nostrils.'

Yast XXII:9 And it seems to him as if his own conscience were advancing to him in that wind, in the shape of a maiden fair, bright, white-armed, strong, tall-formed, high standing, thick-breasted, beautiful of body, noble, of a glorious seed, of the size of a maid in her fifteenth year, as fair as the fairest thing in the world.

Yast XXII:10 And the soul of the faithful one addressed her, asking: 'What maid art thou, who art the fairest maid I have ever seen?'

Yast XXII:11 And she, being his own conscience, answers him: 'O thou youth of good thoughts, good words and good deeds, of good religion, I am thine own conscience!'

'Everybody did love thee for the greatness, goodness, fairness, sweet-scentedness, victorious strength and freedom from sorrow, in which thou dost appear to me;

Yast XXII:12 'And so thou, oh youth of good thoughts, good words, and good deeds, of good religion! didst love me for that greatness, goodness, fairness, sweet-scentedness, victorious strength, and freedom from sorrow, in which I appear to thee.'

Yast XXII:13 'When thou wouldst see a man making derision and deeds of idolatry, or rejecting (the poor) and shutting his door, then thou wouldst sit singing the Gathas and worshipping the good waters and Atar, the son of Ahura Mazda, and rejoicing the faithful that would come from near or from afar.

Yast XXII:14 'I was lovely and thou madest me still lovelier; I was fair and thou madest me still fairer; I was desirable, and thou madest me still more desirable; I was sitting in a forward place; and thou madest me sit in the foremost place, through this good thought, through this good speech, through this good deed of thine; and so henceforth men worship me for my having long sacrificed unto and conversed with Ahura Mazda.'

Yast XXII:15   'The first step that the soul of the faithful man made, placed him in the Good-Thought Paradise;

'The second step that the soul of the faithful man made, placed him in the Good-Word Paradise;

'The third step that the soul of the faithful man made, placed him in the Good-Deed Paradise;

'The fourth step that the soul of the faithful man made, placed him in the Endless Lights.'

Yast XXII:16   Then one of the faithful, who had departed before him, asked him, saying, 'How didst thou depart this life, thou holy man? How didst thou come, thou holy man! from the abodes full of cattle, full of the wishes and enjoyments of love? From the material world into the world of spirit? From the decaying world into the undecaying one? How long did thy felicity last?'

Yast XXII:17   And Ahura Mazda answered: 'Ask him not what thou askest him, who has just gone the dreary way, full of fear and distress, where the body and soul part from one another.

Yast XXII:18   '(Let him eat) of the food brought to him, of the oil of Zaremaya: this is the food for the youth of good thoughts, of good words, of good deeds, of good religion, after he has departed this life; this is the food for the holy woman, rich in good thoughts, good words, and good deeds, well-principled and obedient to her husband, after she has departed this life.'

Yast XXII:19   Zarathustra asked Ahura Mazda: 'O Ahura Mazda, most beneficent Spirit, Maker of the material world, thou Holy One!

'When one of the wicked perishes, where does his soul abide on that night?'

Yast XXII:20   Ahura Mazda answered: 'It rushes and sits near the skull, singing the Kima Gatha, O holy Zarathustra!'

'To what land shall I turn, O Ahura Mazda? To whom shall I go with praying?'

'On that night his soul tastes as much of suffering as the whole of the living world can taste.'

Yast XXII:21 'On the second night, where does his soul abide?'

Yast XXII:22 Ahura Mazda answered: 'It rushes and sits near the skull, singing the Kima Gatha, O holy Zarathustra! 'To what land shall I turn, O Ahura Mazda? To whom shall I go with praying?'

'On that night his soul tastes as much of suffering as the whole of the living world can taste.'

Yast XXII:23 'On the third night, where does his soul abide?'

Yast XXII:24 Ahura Mazda answered: 'It rushes and sits near the skull, singing the Kima Gatha, O holy Zarathustra! 'To what land shall I turn, O Ahura Mazda? To whom shall I go with praying?'

'On that night his soul tastes as much of suffering as the whole of the living world can taste.'

Yast XXII:25 At the end of the third night, O holy Zarathustra! when the dawn appears, it seems to the soul of the faithless one as if it were brought amidst snow and stench, and as if a wind were blowing from the region of the north, from the regions of the north, a foul-scented wind, the foulest-scented of all the winds in the world.

Yast XXII:26-32 And it seems to the soul of the wicked man as if he were inhaling that wind with the nostrils, and he thinks: 'Whence does that wind blow, the foulest-scented wind that I ever inhaled with my nostrils?'

Yast XXII:33 The first step that the soul of the wicked man made laid him in the Evil-Thought Hell;

The second step that the soul of the wicked man made laid him in the Evil-Word Hell;

The third step that the soul of the wicked made laid him in the Evil-Deed Hell;

The fourth step that the soul of the wicked man made laid him in the Endless Darkness.

Yast XXII:34   Then one of the wicked who departed before him addressed him, saying: 'How didst thou perish, O wicked man? How didst thou come, O fiend! from the abodes full of cattle and full of the wishes and enjoyments of love? From the material world into the world of the Spirit? From the decaying world into the undecaying one? How long did thy suffering last?'

Yast XXII:35   Angra Mainys, the lying one, said: 'Ask him not what thou askest him, who has just gone the dreary way, full of fear and distress, where the body and the soul part from one another.

Yast XXII:36 'Let him eat of the food brought unto him, of poison and poisonous stench: this is the food, after he has perished, for the youth of evil thoughts, evil words, evil deeds, evil religion; after he has perished; this is the food for the fiendish woman, rich in evil thoughts, evil words, and evil deeds, evil religion, ill-principled, and disobedient to her husband.'"[24]

The soul of the wicked shall realize that he has waited too long to change his destiny and therefore shall lament:

Dadistan-I Dinik 16:4 "... 'Because in my bodily existence and worldly progress there was no atonement for my sin and no accumulation of righteousness'—also in mourning about it thus: 'In the prosperity which this body of mine had, it would have been possible for me to atone for sin and to save the soul; but now I am separated from everyone and from the joy of the world, which is great hope of spiritual life; and I have attained to the perplexing account and more serious danger.'"[25]

According to Zarathustra, all souls have immortality. It is not just the righteous whose souls continue to exist.

Disposal of the Body

This is one of the thorniest subjects to be found in the Zarathustrian Faith, because of the sacredness of both soil and water. Ahura Mazda made Zarathustra aware of the need to dispose of the corpse after death, and the methods of disposal of the body had to protect what was sacred. Soil was a gift from God that should be protected from contamination, and since the bodies of the dead were recognized as a major source of contamination, burial in the ground was not an option.

During the time of Zarathustra, the answer was to take the body to a place far from the village, where it could become a feast for the wild dogs, birds and other animals of prey. In this way, the physical body was being recycled to nature. Today's followers of Zarathustra, the Parsi of India, are known for exposing the bodies of their dead on high platforms to be consumed by vultures.[26] The funeral pyre, or cremation, could not be tolerated because fire was seen as pure in itself and therefore almost divine. It would be wrong to profane such a gift from Ahura Mazda, around which they had built temples for the focus of their worship. There was the fact that cremation would not only defile fire, but also the air.[27] This thinking may seem wrong or barbaric to the western mind, but there was logic in their methodology which made the most obvious use of a beneficent material, the body as food for nature, instead of allowing it to become noxious or the source of illness and disease. Also, this overcame the thoughts of the disintegration of the body and what that brought to mind.

Fargard VII:1 "Zarathustra asked Ahura Mazda: 'O Ahura Mazda, most beneficent Spirit, Maker of the material world, thou Holy One! When a man dies, at what moment does the Druj Nasu rush upon him?'

Fargard VII:2 Ahura Mazda answered: 'Directly after death, as soon as the soul has left the body, O Spitama Zarathustra! the Druj Nasu comes and rushes upon him, from regions of the north, in the shape of a raging fly, with knees and tail sticking out, all stained with stains, and like unto the foulest Khrafstras.'"[28]

Thus the reason that the body should be exposed as food for carrion-eating birds and beasts:

Fargard VI:44 "' O Maker of the material world, thou Holy One! Whither shall we bring, where shall we lay the bodies of the dead, O Ahura Mazda?'

Fargard VI:45 Ahura Mazda answered: 'On the highest summits, where they know there are always corpse-eating dogs and corpse-eating birds, O holy Zarathustra!'

Fargard VI:46 'There shall the worshippers of Mazda, fasten the corpse by the feet and by the hair, with brass, stones or lead, lest the corpse-eating dogs and the corpse-eating birds shall go and carry the bones to the water and to the trees.'"[29]

Fargard VIII:1 "'If a man or dog die under the timber-work of a house or the wattlings of a hut, what shall the worshippers of Mazda do?'

Fargard VIII:2 Ahura Mazda answered: 'They shall look for a Dakhma [Priest], they shall look for a Dakhma all around. If they find it easier, to remove the dead than to remove the house, they shall take out the dead, they shall let the house stand, and shall perfume it with Urvasni [garlic] or Vohu-gaona, or Vohu-kereti [benzoin or aloes], or Hadha-naepata [pomegranate], or any other sweet-smelling plant.'"[30]

In case the death took place in the winter, when the cold would preserve the body and when the corpse-eating creatures might not be available, the following procedure was allowable:

Fargard V:10 "'O Maker of the material world, thou Holy One! If the summer is past and the winter has come, what shall the worshippers of Mazda do?'

Ahura Mazda answered: 'In every house? in every borough, they shall raise three small houses for the dead.'

Fargard V:11 'O Maker of the material world, thou Holy One! How large shall be those houses for the dead?'

Ahura Mazda answered: 'Large enough not to strike the skull, or the feet, or the hands of the man, if he should stand erect, and hold out his feet and stretch out his hands: such shall be, according to the law, the houses for the dead.'

Fargard V:12 'And they shall let the lifeless body lie there, for two nights, or for three nights, or a month long, until the birds begin to fly, the plants to grow, the floods to flow, and the wind dry up the waters from off the earth.'

Fargard V:13 'And as soon as the birds begin to fly, the plants to grow, the floods to flow, and the wind to dry up the waters from off the earth, then the worshippers of Mazda shall lay down the dead (on the Dakhma) his eyes toward the sun.'"[31]

"That the body of the dead be thrown to the birds that wheel in the empty sky for their food. This is the way of things of this earth."[32]

Dadistan-I Dinik 17:1 "The sixteenth question is that which you ask thus: 'What is the purpose of giving up a corpse to the birds?'

Dadistan-I Dinik 17:2 The reply is this, that the construction of the body of those passed away is so wonderful that two co-existences have come together for it....

Dadistan-I Dinik 17:7 "The injury of the destroyer to the body of those passed away is contaminating; the Nasush ['corruption'] rushes on it and, owing to its violence when it becomes triumphant over the life of the righteous man, and frightens it from the place of catastrophe [hankardikih] and puts itself into the place of the body, that body is then, for that reason, called Nasai ['dead matter']."[33]

Ahura Mazda made it clear that the devouring of flesh was well after the soul had departed its host body, and that the soul was totally aware that what was happening to that host body was being done for the health of those remaining in the material world, whom he not only loved, but upon whose goodness he was dependent. Because of his belief, it was a relief to see his host body properly disposed.[34]

There were very detailed instructions as to the carrying of the body to its place for disposal to the birds. It was clearly stated that this should be done, no matter whether the deceased was man, woman or child, in a respectful manner by more than a single individual. The reason was logical, since the natural assumption should be that the single individual carrying the corpse might very likely be a murderer attempting to conceal his crime, or so said the logic of the Avesta.[35]

Heaven, Purgatory and Hell, and the Way Up and Out

Ardwahisht Yast:4 "(Easy is the way to the Garo-nmana [Heaven] of Ahura Mazda): the Garo-nmana is for the holy souls, and no one of the wicked can enter the Garo-nmana and its bright, wide, holy ways; (no one of them can go) to Ahura Mazda."[36]

Shayest Na Shayest 11:3 "Everyone ought to be unhesitating and unanimous about this, that righteousness is the one thing, and heaven [garothman] the one place, which is good, and contentment the one thing more comfortable."[37]

Heaven was the abode of Ahura Mazda and the Amesha Spentas; and from it strains of holy music issued, with the songs of the angels in beautiful harmony, for as it is said in the Gathas:

Yasna L:4 "I will worship you with praise, O Mazda Ahura Mazda, joined with Right and Best Thought and Dominion, that they, desired of pious men, may stand as Judges on the path of the obedient unto the House of Song."[38]

Fragment Westergaard 3:2   "All good thoughts, all good words, all good deeds will reach paradise. All evil thoughts, all evil words, all evil deeds will reach hell. And all good thought, all good words, all good deeds are the badge of the righteous for paradise."[39]

Erpatistan:84   "Woe to the struggler who struggles for the joy of his own soul, O Spitama Zarathustra!

Woe to the deceiver who deceives for the joy of his own soul.

Woe to the Giver who gives for the joy of his own soul.

For the gift that delivers all the bodily world consists in good thoughts, good words, and good deeds."[40]

Should a soul be found wanting of enough good deeds to be accepted in Heaven, but not so evil as to deserve damnation to Hell, then that soul should be sent into a place of non-fulfillment until his sins could be totally expiated either by the purgatorial fires and/or the dedicated "Good Thoughts, Words and Deeds" from the earthly plane.[41] Purgatory was a lonely existence in which a soul had ample time to meditate on his ungodliness, which would generate its own heat of disappointment that would very slowly burn away those individual ungodlinesses.

This excellent explanation of Purgatory, has its place in religion, as well as its reason for existence. It offers a logical reason for funeral and memorial services beyond their value in the closure process for friends and relatives, but also as a focused start to the progression and salvation of the soul of the deceased.

How delightful that in this faith of Zarathustra none of the states of afterlife are totally without the possibility of reprieve, and that the loving God, as described in this religion, allows for the redemption of every soul even after death? Note that the fires of purgatory are not a punishment, but are a part of this expiation. Is it possible that these fires are the realizations of those many wickednesses, not only of deeds and words, that are often not even noticed during lifetime, but the source of hurt and sadness to others? This could even include the mean and hateful thoughts that were never actually put into words or actions. The concept that each sin brings with it its own punishment means that every individual has to take responsibility for their own thoughts, words and deeds or accept the consequences for same on this plane and/or the next.

The Zarathustrian religion states that there must be an accounting or balancing of one's good and bad thoughts, words and deeds as performed by the deceased during his entire lifetime. The only hope for the truly wicked was that there be intercession by Ahura Mazda or one of the "Adored Ones." It must be remembered that it was the individual misdeeds of the deceased which not only caused the soul to go to Hell, but actually created that Hell. Thus this Hell was not a place for the evil to share and compare their evilness, but a state of conscious that could be likened to solitary confinement until the day of Resurrection. For the less wicked, there was the hope of reformation through penance and purgatorial purification, or credit from the righteousnesses of descendants.[42]

The prayers said immediately after death, and for the first three days and nights, by the souls of the deceased and the relatives and friends of the deceased were of tremendous help to the balance sheet of the deceased in that many of the lesser or naïvely-based mistakes in thoughts, words and deeds could be totally forgiven. To a slightly lesser degree, there was a similar erasure by the prayers for the departed said during the period of mourning. To an even or lesser extent were the prayers after the period of mourning had passed. However, there was still reason to think good thoughts for and to say good things about the deceased, not to mention the saying of prayers.[43]

To those who consider themselves Zarathustrian, it should have been of comfort that, as the dead were being memorialized, their station in the afterlife was being affected positively.

In the inexact balancing of good and bad in the life of the deceased, some of the bad which had brought on bad rewards during life would have been counted as having been erased. Likewise, the doctrine of Zarathustra did not say that the all just rewards received during one's life would automatically erase the value of the rewards upon death. Could this mean that there was a potential to "double-reward" for certain good deeds? But if so, would that be unfair?

There were also statements as to how the good works done in the name of the deceased which might be considered to exonerate some of the bad deeds of the deceased, if actively dedicated by the doer, even if said person performing these deeds was not a blood relative. However, in this case, there seemed to be the necessity for the deceased to agree to this, or at least, not to disagree to the application of the good deeds of others. There happily did not appear to be a commensurate transference of the evil thoughts, words and deeds of an offspring; thus again Ahura Mazda offered positive incentives for doing a good job of parenting.[44]

The Sifting Bridge

After the soul had detached from the body, the prayers for forgiveness were fervently sung by the soul, and on behalf of the departed soul, by kin and friends, for three days and three nights. At dawn of the fourth morn, the soul left the body behind and started its journey into the afterlife, still not quite sure of its destination.

Prior to arriving at its final destination, the soul must pass over the Kinvad Bridge. Whether the soul be that of a man or a woman, it is stated that, for the most part, that which had been the right should be allowed to pass over, and that except for the interception of Ahura Mazda, the wicked soul should fall into Hell.[45]

Dadistan-I Dinik 21:6 "And he who is of the righteous passes over the bridge, and a worldly similitude of the pleasantness of his path upon it is when thou shalt eagerly and unweariedly walk in the golden-colored spring, and with the gallant (hu-chir) body and sweet-scented blossom in the pleasant skin of that maiden-spirit, the price of goodness.

Dadistan-I Dinik 21:7 He, who is of the wicked, as he places a footstep on to the bridge, on account of affliction [siparih] and its sharpness, falls from the middle of the bridge, and rolls over head-foremost.

Dadistan-I Dinik 21:8 And the unpleasantness of his path to hell is in similitude such as the worldly one in the midst of that stinking and dying existence (hasten), there where numbers of the sharp-pointed darts [tezo muk dujo] are planted out inverted and points upwards; and they come unwillingly running; they shall not allow them to stay behind, or to make delay.

Dadistan-I Dinik 21:9 So much greater than the worldly similitude is that pleasantness and unpleasantness unto the souls, as such as is fit for the spirit is greater than that fit for the world."[46]

Elsewhere, it was made clear that all things were as willed by God; however, the reward and recompense were basically that as created by oneself, and that God could, in His mercy, only lessen the pain and suffering. It was also clear that the harshness of the reward of the wicked was of one's own making. If the wicked were so foolish as to blame his wickedness, (and thus his just reward) on anyone or anything but himself, this ungodly thought, in itself could make things worse.[47]

Appropriate Periods of Mourning

Zarathustra suggested making the mourning period needed for a wicked man twice as long as that suggested for the righteous man:

Fargard XII:1 "...'They shall stay thirty days for the righteous, sixty days for the sinners.'"[48]

How much of the period of mourning is for the sake of closure for the relatives of the deceased, and how much of it is for the progress of the departed soul? How, and what form, did Zarathustra consider that this mourning should take? Was it merely the wearing of certain clothes, was it work suspension, was it the chanting of prescribed prayers? Should there be acts of contrition? Should the mourning be clearly in the sight of others, or totally hidden from such sight? No matter the substance, it is obvious from the rest of His teachings that the mourning would be for naught if it was not sincere!

There was a definite difference made between the actual act of mourning, and the continuing process of positive remembrance with saying of prayers as well as the dedicating of good thoughts, words and deeds. Once unable to pass over the sifting bridge because of the lives that they had led, were these souls eternally damned? Not by the loving Ahura Mazda, whose mercy was far greater than His justice.

The Resurrection and the Last Judgment

In several places, Zarathustra states that the resurrection will not happen until the time of the "last Judgment," "Adam and Eve" [Mashye and Mashyane], would be raised from the depths of hell first, and made to live again with lasting but blood-free bodies. Then, successive generations would also be allowed to arise likewise, until all the inhabitants of hell and purgatory had been resurrected, and had recognized their parents, their husbands or wives, and most of their nearest relatives. All mankind would stand at this time in that great assembly together, each able to see the good and evil of each other. In that assembly, the wicked man would be as conspicuous as a white sheep amongst those that are black. And therefore, as all things become known, the wicked man should suffer shame, be allowed to apologize and in other ways make penance so that all souls might be freed from all previous attachments and deeds.[49]

There is likewise another resurrection referred to, which was the resurrection of a single soul from either purgatory and, in a very few cases, from Hell itself due to the thoughts, words and deeds of others still living. The reasons for this advancement seem to be that we are tied to our family by far more than heredity.

Ahura Mazda was the fountainhead of the "Good Mind,"[50] and as such is the basis of all good thought, from which originates all right-speaking and all right-doing. On these three pillars; pure thought, pure word and pure deeds, Zarathustra raised the edifice of His ethical code and clearly stated that this was the only source of what could be best termed the "Good Life."[51] He taught that the pivotal problem of life on earth was evil, and that its curtailment was both the destiny and the salvation of mankind. He stated that the physical world of man was full of evil, and that within the heart of man there was a ceaseless conflict between the animal and the spiritual, between the diabolical and the divine natures of man. Therefore, a natural path of this life was steeped in sorrow and pain and yet it was a life worth living.[52]

Zarathustra was constantly offering the inspiring personal example of earnest, ethical endeavor, and calling upon His followers to accept His challenge and to enlist themselves as "comrades in arms" with Him in the actual battle for goodness. This "call to arms" was accompanied by the inspiring message that if man but does his duty, good will prevail at last.[53] Zarathustra stated that the mission of all mankind, despite their religious preference, was to contribute to the containment of that which is evil. This is in line with His religious tolerance and the concept that there is an essential unity in the universe, such that the entire creation should be aimed towards the goal of perfection.[54]

The world was a battle-field, and man was meant to be the ally of Ahura Mazda (God), in combating evil (ungodliness) in all of its manifestations. Zarathustra expected from his followers active and virile cooperation with God in fighting the forces of evil. He taught that mankind should abhor evil, and fight it wholeheartedly. This essentially militant aspect of the "Good Life" was in marked variance to many other religious paths of the world, where evil was to be avoided or ignored. Zarathustra stated that it was through the constant endeavor to conquer evil that one not only built character, but prepared himself for, if not guaranteeing for himself, a special place in the promised after-life.[55] In so stating, Zarathustra had started the education in the concept of the soul as a separate entity from the physical body.[56] It is by facing evil boldly, and fighting it with all of one's might, that man may hope to fulfill his lofty destiny to redeem the world from evil and to establish the "Kingdom of Righteousness" on this earth.[57] He was but animal yesterday, and today he is Man. His destiny is to be Angel, if not all at once, at least as the product of a gradual process of self-perfection.[58]

❄ CHAPTER 5 ❄

The Religion and Ministry of Jesus

Baptism, Temptation, Apostles and the Start of Ministry

We looked at the life of Jesus from shortly after His conception, through the events of the Nativity scene, followed by the exodus with his family to Egypt, the addressing of that one adolescent episode in the Temple in Jerusalem, and then alluded to that eighteen year period known as "the Years of Silence" in Chapter 1. That latter is a time of which there seems to be nothing recorded, at least in the King James Version of the Bible, as presently written. It was said in that way because with new archeological discoveries being made constantly, there may be found proofs of His schooling or of His life during the period of silence. In the meanwhile, let us continue with the life of Jesus after "the Years of Silence." Starting at the age of thirty with the biblical description of what occurred during and after the baptism of Jesus:

Matthew 3:13 "Then cometh Jesus from Galilee to Jordan unto John (the Baptist), to be baptized of him.

Matthew 3:14 But John forbad him, saying, "I have need to be baptized of thee, and comest thou to me?"

Matthew 3:15 And Jesus answering said unto him, "Suffer it to be so now: for thus it becometh us to fulfil all righteousness." Then he suffered (John did baptize Jesus) him.

Matthew 3:16 And Jesus, when he was baptized, went up straight away out of the water: and, lo, the heavens were opened up unto him, and he saw the Spirit of God descending like a dove, and lighting upon him; And lo a voice from heaven , saying "This is my beloved Son, in whom I am well pleased."[1]

Other versions of this event are slightly less clear, but in no way refute the above conclusions:

Mark 1:10 "And straight away coming up out of the water, he saw the heavens opened, and the Spirit like a dove descending upon him:

Mark 1:11 And there came a voice from heaven, saying, "Thou art my beloved Son, in whom I am well pleased.

Mark 1:12 And immediately the spirit driveth him into the wilderness (for his temptation episode)."[2]

Whereas in the Luke rendition:

Luke 3:21 "Now when all the people were baptized, it came to pass, that Jesus also (was) being baptized, and praying, the heaven was opened.

Luke 3:22 And the Holy Ghost descended in a bodily shape like a dove upon him and a voice came from heaven, which said, "Thou art my beloved Son, in thee I am well pleased.[3]

With the exception of several words, each rendition of the baptism of Jesus with the resultant description of the spirit of God onto or into Jesus is very similar. There are definite differences in particular perspectives of that event, which may delight debaters and detractors, such as that the Holy Ghost descended in a bodily shape. However, is it not the end result which is important? Is it not possible that it was at this point in the life of Jesus, not at conception or at birth or upon the return from Egypt or even as he approached John the Baptist, that Jesus had attained his destined station? However, it also seems obvious that John the Baptist had recognized this man for who He was, or was it what He was to become? Was it the potential of Jesus, prior to his baptism, to which John had spoken of earlier in this same chapter when he said:

Matthew 3:11 "I indeed baptize you with water unto repentance, but he that cometh after me is mightier than I, whose shoes I am not worthy to wear: he shall baptize you with the Holy Ghost, and with fire."[4]

As to whether the Holy Spirit was "onto" or "into" Jesus, **Luke 4:1** states, "and Jesus being full of the Holy Ghost returned from out of the Jordan, and was led by the Spirit into the wilderness to be tempted by Satan."[5] There will be a few other places in this chapter that will show an event from more than one Gospel. This will be done so that there will be multiple facets displayed of the life of this gem of a man. This is also being done for those of you who were told not to study the Bible because it would only confuse you. If that is a description of what you were told in Sunday school or Catechism, please enjoy what follows. Such reading should only add to your Faith and understanding.

To assist you in comparing the various Gospel stories, there is a chart of the biblical record of the life and teachings of Jesus as told in the four Gospels included at the end of this chapter.

After the protestation by John concerning the request of baptism, Jesus simply says, "for thus it becometh us to fulfil all righteousness." What was meant by this? Why was it included in the text? Is it possible the choice of words reaches back to a previous time in which the term righteous was so prevalent? What occurs immediately following the beautiful story of the baptism:

Matthew 4:1   "Then was Jesus led up of [BY] the spirit into the wilderness to be tempted of [BY] the devil,

Matthew 4:2   And when he had fasted forty days and forty nights, he was afterwards an hungred (PERSON).

Matthew 4:3   And when the tempter came to him, he said, "If thou be the Son of God, command that these stones be made bread."

Matthew 4:4　　　But he answered and said, "It is written that, Man shall not live by bread alone, but by every word that proceedeth out of the mouth of God."

Matthew 4:5　　　Then the devil taketh him up into the holy city, and setteth him on a pinnacle of the temple,

Matthew 4:6　　　And saieth unto him, "if thou be the Son of God, cast thyself down, for it is written, He shall give his angels charge concerning thee; and in their hands they shall bear thee up, lest at any time thou dash thy foot against a stone.

Matthew 4:7　　　Jesus said unto him, "It is written again, Thou shalt not tempt the Lord thy God.

Matthew 4:8　　　Again, the devil taketh him up into an exceeding high mountain, and sheweth (showed) him all the kingdoms of the world, and the glory of them;

Matthew 4:9　　　And saith unto him, "All these things will I give thee, if thou wilt fall down and worship me.

Matthew 4:10　　　Then saith Jesus unto him, "Get thee hence, Satan: for it is written, Thou shalt worship the Lord thy God, and him only shalt thou serve.

Matthew 4:11　　　Then the devil leaveth him, and, behold, angels came and ministered unto him."[6]

That this story is retold in the Gospel according to Mark 1:12-15, in Luke 3:21-22, in Luke 4:1-13, and lastly in John 1:29-34, attests to its importance to the writers of the Gospels. Why is it that there is not the same emphasis on this temptation event from many in today's clergy? Is that because they feel that this weakens their case as to who Jesus really was at the time of the Nativity story?

Three times Jesus was tempted; twice it was his ego that was tempted. Finally Satan appealed to any greed that Jesus might possess. What is in question here is not whether the claim that Jesus was God incarnate is correct, but as to when in His life does that claim make sense!

Consider if Jesus was God incarnate from conception, or at least at birth, why the biblical story of the baptism with the heavens opening up, and the subsequent descent of the Holy Spirit like a dove and the inclusion of the Spirit of God in Matthew 3:13-16, Mark 1:9-11, Luke 3:21-22, and John 1:29-36? Does the very inclusion of this baptism and the subsequent temptation episode in four separate Gospels shine new light on their importance? Is it just a coincidence that God did not impose the mantle of specialness, but seemingly required the request through an exercise of free will?

What is the significance of the temptation of Jesus by Satan? Does it make sense, other than to test and make firm that infusion of the Spirit of God? There are several ways that this consolidation and purification are presented in the New Testament, but each ends with the same result. (See Matt. 4:1-11, Mark 1:12-15 and Luke 4:1-13.)

Did that infusion of the Spirit of God include an immense gain of new knowledge as well as new powers for Jesus, as was true in the case of Zarathustra? If so, do the temptations take on special meaning? There was an immense amount of both knowledge and wisdom bestowed upon Jesus immediately after the baptism, and it is stated many times and in different ways. For example:

Matthew 12:34 All these things spake [spoke] Jesus unto the multitude in parables [those stories meant to explain his teachings in a way that would be understood by the hearers], and without a parable spake he not unto them.

Matthew 12:35 That it might be fulfilled (that) which was spoken by the prophet, saying, "I will open my mouth in parables; I will utter things which have been kept secret from the foundation of the world."[7]

Miracles

There were many people in those days who thought that because of the healing powers and His new and beguiling sermons, that Jesus was in fact in league with Satan, instead of attempting to save one soul at a time from the insidious temptations of the forces of evil. An excellent example of this from the mouth of Jesus is truly majestic;

Mark 3:22 "And the scribes which came down from Jerusalem said, "He hath Beelzebub [the devil] and by the prince of the devils casteth he out devils."

Mark 3:23 And he [Jesus] called them unto him, and said unto them in parables, "How can Satan cast out Satan?"

Mark 3:24 And if a kingdom be divided against itself, that kingdom cannot stand."

Mark 3:25 And if a house be divided against itself, that house cannot stand."

Mark 3:26 And if Satan rise up against himself, and be divided, he cannot stand, but hath an end."

Mark 3:27 No man can enter into a strong man's house, and spoil his goods, except that he will first bind the strong man; and then he will spoil his house."

Mark 3:28 Verily I say unto you, All the sins shall be forgiven unto the sons of men, and blasphemies wherewith so ever they shall blaspheme:

Mark 3:29 But he that shall blaspheme against the Holy Ghost hath never forgiveness, but is in danger of eternal damnation."[8]

When questioned by the Sadducees, Pharisees or others if the healing of the sick was not some sort of magic or the work of Satan, the answer was that much of the ills of man, especially those of a mental nature, were the result of an imbalance which could best be explained as those individuals had become possessed of evil spirits. Hence, mental illness, leprosy, epilepsy (Mark 1:26 and Luke 9:39), loss of hearing (Mark 9:25), loss of sight (Matt. 12:22) and dumbness (Luke 11:14-16) could all be considered manifestations of demonic influence, and, as such, had a spiritual solution, which was to drive out those evil spirits. Jesus taught the disciples to pray for the deliverance from the "evil one" (Matt. 6:13) and acclaimed Satan as the "prince of this world" (John 12:31, 14; 30 and 16:11) who, with his demoniacal angels, constituted the kingdom which, in the Last Judgment, would be destroyed (Matt. 25:41).

One could argue that the modern practice of psychiatry is assisting patients to identify and destroy the powers of darkness [the evil thoughts and experiences] that they have allowed to enter their minds and bodies.

Among people in the Judaic/Christian faiths, there is ongoing disagreement as to whether Jesus meant to start a new religion, or whether His aim was to refocus the directions of the Jewish Faith of His day, with a return to the laws of Moses but with a new focus. Is it possible that Jesus was attempting to return not only the Judaic faith of the time to its original purity, but also that of Zarathustra and whatever other religion should consider themselves to be from the "One True God"? Upon careful inspection of the teachings of Jesus, there seems to be an outreach far past the people of Jewish ethnicity, a universality which was not restricted to His time, His place or His people. Was he not speaking to all of mankind?

The lack of understanding of Jesus' message by most of the Jews in Israel at the start of His ministry is found and well documented in the Gospels according to Mark and Luke, and yet, that was not the primary reason for His leaving Israel early in His ministry. Yes, it was true that His message had been falling on deaf ears, however, the reason for the travels of Jesus, was the news that His cousin, friend and baptizer, John, had been imprisoned. From the fourth chapter of Matthew:

4:12   "Now when Jesus heard that John was cast into prison, he departed into Galilee;

4:13   And leaving Nazareth, he came and dwelt in Capernaum, which is upon the sea coast, in the borders Zabulon and Nephthalim:

4:14   That it might be fulfilled which was spoken by Esaias, the prophet saying,

4:15   The land of Zabulon and the land of Nephthalim, by the way of the sea, beyond Jordan. Galilee of the Gentiles;

4:16   The people that sat in darkness saw great light; and to them which sat in the region and shadow of death light is sprung up.

4:17   And from that time Jesus began to preach, and to say, "Repent; for the kingdom of heaven is at hand."

4:18   And Jesus, walking by the sea of Galilee, saw two brethren. Simon called Peter, and Andrew his brother, casting a net into the sea: for they were fishers.

4:19   And he saith unto them, "Follow me, and I will make you fishers of men."

4:20   And the straightway left their nets, and followed him.

4:21   And going on from thence he saw other two brethren, James, the son of Zebedee, and John his brother, in a ship with Zebedee their father, mending their nets; and he called them.

4:22   And they immediately left the ship and their father, and followed him.

4:23   And Jesus went about all Galilee, teaching in their synagogues, and preaching the gospel of the kingdom, and healing all manner of sickness and all manner of disease among the people.

4:24   And his fame went throughout all Syria, and they brought unto him all sick people that were taken with divers diseases and torments, and those which were possessed with devils, and those which were lunatic, and those that had palsy; and he healed them.

4:25   And there followed him great multitudes of people from Galilee, and from Decapolis, and from Jerusalem, and from Judaea, and from beyond Jordan.[9]

While the travels of Jesus outside of Israel were brought about by the imprisonment of John the Baptist, and His concern to be of service in releasing John from captivity, this was more from the guidance of God than from a cerebral decision based upon learning, speaking skills, parentage or even the later realization that "a prophet is never appreciated in his own land." This guidance proved to be very important in that He not only found waiting souls, hearing ears, and people capable of becoming believers, but He also found His first Apostles, eleven of whom were Galileans, not Israeli Jews. It should be noted that the term "Galilee" means land of or circle of the Gentiles.[10] Did this choice of Galileans create problems for His later ministry when He returned to Judaea? Especially since he subsequently taught them [His Apostles] his healing powers as well as how to spread the word of his heavenly Father. This conjecture may not hold water, but with the prejudices of the Jews of Judea in that day, it is a question worthy of reflection, thought and another book.

So much of the time of Jesus' ministry was spent healing the sick and even raising those considered to be dead, that it is amazing that He had time to present the message of God that He felt He had been sent to present. And yet, it was because of these healings and other miracles that His fame spread ahead of, and behind, Him. He attempted to minimize these miracles, other than to make use of them to prove the power of God and of prayer. For example, in the ninth chapter of Matthew, verse 23, as Jesus was invited into, and enters, the house of a certain leader and sees that minstrels and others are making noise (for they are commemorating the death of the daughter of their leader):

9:24   "He [Jesus] said unto them [all that were in the house], "give place [make room, step back]: for the maid is not dead, but sleepeth." And they [all of those present] laughed to scorn.

9:25   But when the people were put forth [had been sent out of the room where the maid had been laid], he went in, and took her by the hand, and the maid arose.

9:26   And the fame hereof went abroad into all (of) that land".[11]

Teachings of Jesus (including the Sermon on the Mount)

Jesus preached in synagogues the gospel of the Kingdom of God. It was out of compassion for the sick that He healed them, rather than as some sort of plot to increase the numbers of His followers. Many in the clergy today use as proof of the holiness of Jesus, His miracles and the power of healing with which He had become endowed. To these men, it must be said "please read your bibles more closely," for following the choosing of His twelve apostles it clearly says that:

Mark 3:14 "And he ordained twelve, that they should be with him, and that he might send them forth to preach,

Mark 3:15 And to have power to heal sicknesses, and to cast out devils."[12]

And in **Matthew 10:1**, "And when he had called unto him his twelve disciples, he gave them power against unclean spirits, to cast them out, and to heal all manner of sickness and all manner of disease.

10:2   Now the names of the twelve apostles are these; The first Simon, who is called Peter, and Andrew his brother; James the son of Zebedee and John his brother;

10:3   Philip and Bartholomew; Thomas and Matthew the publican; James the son of Alphaeus, and Lebbaeus, whose surname was Thaddaeus;

10:4 Simon, the Canaanite and Judas Iscariot, who also betrayed him.

10:5 These twelve Jesus sent forth, and commanded them saying, "Go not into the way of the Gentiles, and into an city of the Samaritans enter ye not:

10:6 But go rather to the lost sheep of the house of Israel.

10:7 And as ye go, preach, saying, The kingdom of heaven is at hand.

10:8 Heal the sick, cleanse the lepers, raise the dead, cast out the devils: freely have ye received, freely give.

10:9 Provide neither gold, nor silver, nor brass in your purses,

10:10 Nor scrip for your journey, neither two coats, neither shoes, nor yet staves: for the workman is worthy of his meat.

10:11 And into whatsoever city or town ye shall enter, enquire who in it is worthy; and there abide till ye go thence.

10:12 And when ye come into an house, salute it.

10:13 And if the house be worthy, let your peace come upon it: but if it not be worthy, let your peace return to you.

10:14 And whosoever shall not receive you, nor hear your words, when ye depart out of that house or city shake off the dust of your feet.

10:15 Verily I say unto you, It shall be more tolerable for the land of Sodom and Gomorrha in the day of judgment, than for that city."[13]

In this passage, Jesus emphasizes that He has taught the gifts of healing, even that of the raising of the dead, but that this is a secondary task to spreading the words of His mission.

The Apostles and disciples are given specific tasks by Jesus and are instructed as to how and where those tasks should be carried out. They were to totally trust in God for all things—their food, housing, clothes and their very words. Moreover, there was an acknowledgment that if the energy contained in a house or city that was found to be unworthy of the ministry that Jesus was commissioning, such a house or city was to be left without condemning it, but the Apostles and disciples must be sure to not carry away either its dust nor its bad energy.

10:16 "Behold, I sent you forth as sheep in the midst of wolves: be ye therefore wise as serpents, and harmless as doves.

10:17 But beware of men: for they will deliver you up to the councils, and they will scourge you in their synagogues;

10:18 And ye shall be brought before governors and kings for my sake, for a testimony against them and the Gentiles.

10:19 But when they deliver you up, take no thought how or what ye speak: for it shall be given you in that same hour what ye shall speak.

10:20 For it is not ye that speak, but the Spirit of your Father which speaketh in you."[14]

In a time long before electronic media, Jesus had created His own missionary network. His Apostles were challenged to become far more than devoted followers, they were to become an army of individual extensions of Himself, spreading the Word of God. And the balance of what He had to say was a shocker to those who were hoping that He was the Messiah who had come to bring the promised "peace on earth." Among the shocked were several of the Apostles, who were looking forward to His immediate creation of an earthly kingdom, and very likely to some of the fruits of same for themselves.

Matthew ten continues:

10:34 "Think not that I am come to send peace on earth: I am come not to send peace, but a sword.

10:35 For I am come to set a man at variance against his father, and the daughter against her mother, and the daughter in law against her mother in law.

10:36 And a man's foes shall be of his own household.

10:37 He that loveth father or mother more than me is not worthy of me: and he that loveth son or daughter more than me is not worthy of me.

10:38 And he that taketh not his cross, and followeth after me, is not worthy of me.

10:39 He that findeth his life shall lose it: and he that loseth his life for my sake shall find it.

10:40 He that receiveth you receiveth me, and he that receiveth me receiveth him that sent me.

10:41 He that receiveth a prophet in the name of a prophet shall receive a prophet's reward; and he who receiveth a righteous man in the name of a righteous man shall receive an righteous man's reward.

10:42 And whosoever shall give to drink unto one of these little ones a cup of cold water only in the name of a disciple, verily I say unto you, he shall in no wise lose his reward."[15]

And likewise, in asking the world to change their perspective on their fellow human beings no matter who they are and where they come from; in Mark 3:

3:35 And he looked around him, and said, "Behold my mother and my brethren!

3:36 For whosoever shall do the will of God, the same is my brother, and my sister, and mother."[16]

For those who understood and those who today understand the spiritual importance of this message, Jesus was and is the Messiah, but only on a basis for that individual. What He seems to have stated is that through only the Love of God can mankind hope to see the "Kingdom of God" established on earth. This love, along with confirmed belief in God, must be the determining factor in the decision-making of each and every soul. One must not allow friendships, blood relations or national pride to intervene, in other words, you must first and foremost "truly love the Lord, thy God, with all thy heart, all thy soul and all thy mind."[17]

Wherever Jesus went in Galilee, there were multitudes seeking to be healed. So powerful had His healing powers become that some were healed by merely touching His garments, and yet others by merely seeing Him or hearing His voice.[18]

A part of the ministry of Jesus, which receives little attention, is the difference between being helpful to the poor and the motivation behind the helping. The human sensitivity expressed here is centuries ahead of its time. From the Book of Matthew, chapter six:

6:1   "Take heed that ye do not (give) your alms before men, to be seen of them: otherwise ye have no reward of [by] your Father which is in heaven.

6:2   Therefore when thou doest (give) thine alms, do not sound a trumpet before thee, as the hypocrites do in the synagogues and in the streets, that thou may have glory of men. Verily I say unto you, They have their reward.

6:3   But when thou doest alms, let not thy left hand knoweth what thy right hand doeth:

6:4   That thine alms may be in secret: and thy Father which seeth in secret himself shall reward thee openly."[19]

Two immensely important instances occurred after Jesus received the news of the execution of John the Baptist. They are described in the fourteenth chapter of Matthew. In verse 13, the response of Jesus upon hearing the fate of His friend, relative and baptizer was to board a ship and head to a "desert" place, ostensibly to find seclusion away from the crowds so as to pray and meditate upon what had happened. However, the multitudes which had been so enthralled by the teachings and healings would not be put off and followed their new teacher by foot from the cities to the "desert" place.

What ensued were several of the greatest of the miracles of His ministry, and of which only portions of the story are told at any one time and thus, the telling does not have the beautifully full meaning.

First, however, there needs to be a diversion for that desert place, it is in no way in the desert, but it is very deserted. It is an extremely large grassy pasture on the west side of the Sea of Galilee with a gorgeous view that includes on the opposite side the mountainous area known today as the Golan Heights. Today, the grassy expanse is much as it was 2,000 years ago, with the exception of a gorgeous church built several hundred years ago to commemorate the spot. When friends in the clergy said, "but it says it was a desert place and therefore it is most likely that there have been changes due to different climatic conditions." How beautiful the looks upon their faces when it is pointed out that Jesus, in Matthew 14 verse 19 had commanded that the multitudes sit down upon the grass. Thus, I believe that what was meant by desert was a secluded spot or area, a place of solitude for the purpose of prayer and contemplation. The Sea of Galilee is large, as inland seas go, much larger than just a lake, and yet it is not an immense body of water as might be imagined. The distance to be walked by the multitudes would have been approximately thirty to fifty kilometers and would have taken many hours.[20] Nevertheless, it was a mighty walk and because of this, Jesus was impressed and emotionally moved, as it says:

14:14 "And Jesus went forth, and saw a great multitude, and was moved with compassion toward them, and healed their sick.

14:15 And when it was evening, his disciples came to him, saying, "This is a desert place, and the time is now past; send the multitude away, that they may go into the villages, and buy themselves victuals."

14:16 But Jesus said unto them, "They need not depart; give ye them to eat."

14:17   And they say unto him, "we have but five loaves and two fishes."

14:18   He said, "Bring them hither to me."[21]

It was at this point that Jesus made the statement that showed that this was a secluded place, and not a place of desert land:

14:19   "And he commanded the multitude to sit down on the grass, and took the five loaves, and the two fishes and looking up to heaven, he blessed and brake [broke] and gave the loaves to his disciples and the disciples (then gave) to the multitude.

14:20   And they did all eat, and were filled: and (then) they took up the fragments that remained (and there were) twelve baskets full.

14:21   And they that had eaten were about five thousand men, beside women and children.[22]

(The number that is estimated to have been fed was far in excess of the 5,000 people and very likely in excess of 10,000 individuals.)

The verses of Matthew, starting with the fifth chapter and ending with the seventh, are among the most beautiful and poignant teachings of Jesus. They are seldom read in context for there is so much spiritual truth included that it is hard to complete in one sitting or sermon. Yet this is exactly what we should be able to do, since according to the writer of the Gospel of Matthew this was done at the Sermon on the Mount. Jesus instructed His disciples and at the same time the multitudes assembled to hear Him. This one sermon contains the beatitudes, the admonition to be of the righteous and to let good deeds be the source of glorification of God not of self, the explanation of the juxtaposition between Jesus and the Law, Jesus' thoughts concerning adultery, thoughts concerning an eye for an eye and other judicial and legal matters, love for all mankind including your enemies, the aforementioned discussion of the giving of alms, when, where and how to pray followed by the example of the Lord's Prayer, the how's and why's of forgiveness, the serving of God, the admonition to "Judge not," an exhortation to pray, the simile of the "Strait Gate," the tree which can only bring forth good fruit, the parable of the houses built upon rock or upon sand, and when he was finished with this beautiful but lengthy sermon, the Bible states, "And it came to pass when Jesus had ended these sayings, the people were astonished at his doctrine: for he talked to them as one having authority, and not as the scribes" (Matt. 7:28-29).

The Beatitudes set a new religious tone in the land of Galilee. Matthew 5:1 says, "And seeing the multitudes, he went up into a mountain: and when he was set his disciples came unto him:

5:2   And he opened his mouth, and taught them saying,

5:3   Blessed are the poor in Spirit, for theirs is the kingdom of heaven.

5:4   Blessed are they that mourn, for they shall be comforted.

5:5   Blessed are the meek, for they shall inherit the earth.

5:6   Blessed are they which do hunger and thirst after righteousness, for they shall be filled.

5:7   Blessed are the merciful, for they shall obtain mercy.

5:8   Blessed are the pure in heart, for they shall see God.

5:9   Blessed are the peacemakers; for they shall be called the children of God

5:10   Blessed are they which are persecuted for righteousness sake, for theirs is the kingdom of heaven

5:11   Blessed are ye, when men shall revile you, and persecute you, and shall say all manner of evil against you falsely for my name sake.

5:12   Rejoice, and be exceedingly glad; for great is your reward in heaven: for so persecuted they the prophets which were before you."[23]

Attendees at the Sermon on the Mount included among the multitudes people from Galilee and Israel, but also from Edom, Elam and Ur, and all parts of the former Persian Empire, who had scattered seeking safety during the attacks by Alexander the Great some 300 years before. For them, especially if they were influenced by the same prophesy as the Magi, this sermon would have sounded far more like Zarathustra than what they would have found in the synagogues or in the Old Testament. The entire sermon would have had the ring of truth to those who were Zarathustrian or who were familiar with His teachings. If, like the Magi before them, they were not looking for the actual physical return of their prophet, but for the return of that spirit that had been within Him, they could have become followers of Jesus without but a few questions. The last five verses of the Beatitudes would most definitely have settled the issue. Further confirmation followed with what Jesus said next:

5:17 "Think not that I am come to destroy the law, or the prophets; I am not come to destroy, but to fulfill.

5:18 For verily I say unto you, 'Till heaven and earth pass, one jot or one tittle shall in no wise pass from the law, till all be fulfilled'.

5:19 Whosoever therefore shall break one of these least commandments, and shall teach men so, he shall be called the least in the kingdom of heaven; but whosoever shall do and teach them, the same shall be called great in the kingdom of heaven.

5:20 For I say unto you, 'That except your righteousness shall exceed the righteousness of the scribes and the Pharisees, ye shall in no case enter into the kingdom of heaven'.

5:21 Ye have heard that it was said of them of old time, Thou shalt not kill; and whosoever shall kill shall be in danger of the judgment:

5:22 But I say unto you, That "whosoever is angry with his brother without cause shall be in danger of the judgment, and whosoever shall say to his brother, Raca, shall be in danger of the council: but whosoever shall say, Thou fool, shall be in danger of the hell fire.

5:23   Therefore if thou bring thy gift to the altar and there rememberest that thy brother hath ought against thee;

5:24   Leave there thy gift before the altar; and go thy way. First be reconciled to thy brother, and then come and offer thy gift."[24]

Zarathustrians who had come to hear the ministry of the new prophet of God, would have now come to follow and join with Him, they would have embraced Christianity, but because of their non-Jewish background they would have been extremely important in the establishment of Christianity as a totally separate religion, and not a sect of Judaism.

Also in the Sermon was the beautiful Lord's Prayer, which seems to be a format of how one should pray at all times, with every prayer, and definitely not just a prayer to be recited without neither thought nor feeling. As presented in Matthew 6:9-15 and Luke 11:2-4, the prayer begins with a clear statement as to whom it is addressed:

1) **"Our Father, which art in Heaven"**...

continues with a statement of glorification and recognition of purpose,

2) **"Hallowed be thy Name, Thy Will be done in earth, as it is in heaven"**...

and then, a clear statement as to that which is being requested or beseeched

3) **"Give us this day our daily bread, and forgive us our debts as we forgive our debtors"**...

followed by a request for guidance in this life,

4) **"And lead us not into temptation, but deliver us from evil"**...

and ending with a return to the glorification and station of the One being beseeched

5) **"For thine is the kingdom, and the power and the Glory, for ever."**

It seems as if this is what Jesus felt should be the general format of all prayer, rather than starting a prayer with dear God, give me this and that, or dear God, do that or this, which is heard far too often today. Instead, the bulk of the prayer should be the glorification of God. Only then is it appropriate to list that which is felt to be of greatest importance to the beseecher. It is thus respecting God, as the "All-Knowing."

Jesus taught how individuals should pray in private. The format as suggested by Jesus should create the appropriate juxtaposition between the beseecher and the beseeched. It creates the spiritual atmosphere for the prayer. Two statements prior to the revealing of the Lord's Prayer are the source for the statements concerning the purpose and meaning of prayer:

6:9 "Your Father in heaven knoweth what things ye have need of before ye ask him."

6:10 "After this manner therefore pray ye."[25]

It is suggested that you attempt this format in your personal prayers, be they said in private or public. It is also suggested that you consider prayer to be a two-way communication with that which is greater than yourself, and thus allow time for the conversation to be answered. The results can be phenomenal!

One of the things which many detractors point to as errors or inconsistencies in the teachings of Jesus is exemplified by the various versions of the Gospels. One case is the long and weighty "Sermon on the Mount," which was heard in the open air without microphones or amplifiers by the disciples and the multitudes. It was not recorded, and therefore we are dependent upon what the Apostles heard and remembered not only for accuracy of content, but also for emphasis. There may have been no wind that day, no birds singing or other distractions, but I doubt it. If there were such distractions, it is possible that an Apostle might have missed a word here or there. If Jesus had turned the other way for the sake of the hearing of another section of the crowd, a part or all of a particular parable might have gone missing. To me, the consistencies in Matthew, Mark and Luke are far greater than any differences. Under the conditions and length of this sermon, this is absolutely amazing!

From the desire of Jesus to find a place of solitude to contemplate the death of John the Baptist came only the first of two huge miracles. Was the miracle the fulfilling of the nutritional desires of such a large number of people with such a small amount of physical food, or was it just as importantly the power of prayer, and thereby, of God? To this latter point, let us look at the miracle which followed on that same day:

After the completion of the Sermon on the Mount, in Matthew, the original desire of Jesus to find a place of solitude was realized, and led to the second "miracle" of the day.

14:22 And straightway, Jesus constrained [ordered] his disciples to get into a ship, and to go before [or ahead of] him unto the other side, while he sent the multitudes away.

14:23 And when he had sent the multitudes away, he went up into a mountain apart to pray: and when the evening was come, he was there alone.

14:24 But the ship [on which the disciples had sailed] was now in the midst of the sea, tossed with waves: for the wind was contrary.

14:25 And in the fourth watch of the night Jesus went unto them, walking upon the sea.

14:26 And when the disciples saw him walking on the sea, they were troubled, saying, "It is a Spirit; and they cried out for fear.

14:27 But straightway, Jesus spake unto them, saying: "Be of good cheer, it is I; be not afraid."

14:28 And Peter answered him and said, "lord, if it be thou, bid thee to come unto thee on the water."

14:29 And he [Jesus] said, "Come" And when Peter was come down out of the ship, he walked on the water to Jesus.

14:30 But when he [Peter] saw that the wind was boisterous, he was afraid; and beginning to sink, he cried, saying, "Lord, save me."

14:31 And immediately Jesus stretched forth his hand, and caught him, and said unto him, "O thou of little faith, wherefore didst thou doubt?"

14:32 And when they were come into the ship, the wind ceased.

14:33 Then they that were on the ship came and worshipped him, saying, "of a truth thou art the Son of God."[26]

Would this episode have occurred if it had not been for the death of John the Baptist? And yet, this is a thing of great importance, for the walking on the water fulfilled a prophesy found in the Old Testament, the book of Daniel,[27] and showed the disciples once again about the power of God, and how that power could be passed through to the One whom He had chosen as His special messenger. How could the disciples miss this point, or that Jesus was who He claimed to be? There were things about this man that were totally beyond normal explanation! The events of this particular day should have sufficed, but of course, they did not. In the very next chapter of Matthew, there is need for repetition of the miracle of the loaves and fishes for the unconvinced among the disciples:

Matthew 15:32 says, "Then Jesus called his disciples unto him, and said, "I have compassion on the multitude, because they continue with me now three days and have nothing to eat: and I will not send them away fasting, lest they faint in the way."

15:33 And the disciples say [said] unto him, "Whence should we have so much bread in the wilderness, as to fill so great a multitude?"

15:34 And Jesus saith unto them, "How many loaves have ye?" And they said, "Seven [loaves], and a few little fishes."

15:35 And he [Jesus] commanded the multitude to sit down on the ground.

15:36 And he [Jesus] took the seven loaves and the fishes, and gave thanks and brake them (broke the bread) and gave to his disciples, and the disciples (gave) to the multitude.

15:37 And they did all eat, and were filled: and they (the disciples) took up of the broken meat (the food, both bread and fishes) that was left seven baskets full.

15:38 And they that did eat were four thousand men, beside women and children [again a total of many more than the four thousand]".[28]

How was it that the disciples, those men who were chosen to follow Jesus throughout His ministry, had to be constantly taught the same lessons? However, if you had been one of these individuals, would you not have found it equally difficult to believe what you had witnessed? There should be of no surprise that Jesus asked this exact question in the next Chapter:

16:5 "And when his disciples were [had] come to the other side, they had forgotten to take (bring) bread.

16:6 Then Jesus said unto them, "Take heed and beware of the leaven of the Pharisees and of the Sadducees."

16:7 And they [the disciples] reasoned among themselves, saying, "It is because we have taken no bread."

16:8 Which when Jesus perceived, he said unto them, "O ye of little faith, why reason ye among yourselves, because you have brought no bread?

16:9 Do ye not yet understand, neither remember (the episode of) the five loaves of the five thousand, and how many baskets ye took up?

16:10 Neither (the episode of) the seven loaves of the four thousand, and how many baskets ye took up?

16:11 How is it that ye do not understand that I spake it not to you concerning the bread, that ye should beware of the leaven of the Pharisees and of the Sadducees?"

16:12 Then understood they [the Apostles and the disciples] how that he (had) bade them not beware of the leaven of the bread, but (had instead warned them) of the doctrine of the Pharisees and of the Sadducees".[29]

This started a true transformation in the thinking processes of the Apostles, and their conclusions concerning the meaning of what they had experienced. With the reflection that this demanded on the part of those closest to Jesus, there came some understanding by most and, to an even greater degree, by Peter [Simon Peter], and thus an appreciation of him by Jesus:

16:17 "Blessed art thou, Simon Barjona: for flesh and blood hath not revealed it unto thee, but my Father which is in heaven.

16:18 And I say unto thee, That thou art Peter, and upon this rock I will build my church; and the gates of hell shall not prevail against it"

16:19 And I will give unto thee the keys of the kingdom of heaven: and whatsoever thou shalt bind on earth shall be bound in heaven, and whatsoever thou shalt loose on earth shall be loosed in heaven."[30]

The apostle Peter is the very same man who had been told earlier that he was of so little faith as he began to sink into the sea. What was it that Jesus observed that caused him to make this great change? The change in spiritual mindset of not only Peter, but also the rest of those close to Jesus, laid the foundation for what must be told to them so that they would be prepared, for the Scriptures clearly point out that the future of Jesus and of His teachings were headed for very rough times:

16:21 "From that time forth, began Jesus to shew [show] unto his disciples, that he must go unto Jerusalem, and suffer many things of [from] the elders and chief priests and be killed and be raised again the third day".[31]

It should be also noted that, in the ninth chapter of Mark, only after the temptation and subsequent rejection by Jesus do we find His transfiguration. It is as if this was the acceptance by God of the acceptance by Jesus and his rejection of Satan:

9:1 "And he said unto them [the Apostles], 'Verily I say unto you, That there be some of them that stand here, which shall not taste death till they have seen the kingdom of God come with power.'

9:2 And after six days Jesus taketh with him Peter, and James, and John, and leadeth them up into an high mountain apart by themselves: and he was transfigured before them.

9:3 And his raiment [robe or clothes] became shining, exceeding white as snow; so as no fuller [soap or other cleaning agent] on earth can white them.

9:4 And there appeared unto them Elias with Moses and they were talking with Jesus.

9:5 And Peter answered and said to Jesus, 'Master, it is good for us to be here; and let us make three tabernacles; one for Thee and one for Moses, and one for Elias.'

9:6   For he wist not what to say, for they were sore afraid.

9:7   And (then) there was a cloud that (came and) overshadowed them: and a voice came out of the cloud, saying, 'This is my beloved Son hear him.'

9:8   And suddenly, when they had looked round about, they saw no man anymore, save Jesus only with themselves."[32]

Jesus did not make a big deal of what was seen as miraculous. There has been a separation of the stories of two very famous healings for a most special purpose. The first was the healing from afar of the son of the nobleman from Capernaum early in Jesus' ministry, which set in motion the acceptance of Jesus and His teachings, and therefore deserves special attention.

There was a much different result to be found after His return to Israel with the next miracle, for it started what was to become the end of His ministry and His life.

Besides the acceptance of God through their acceptance of Jesus and His mission, there was in this episode the idea that the disciples needed to realize that this man was far more than a learned teacher, and even more than a prophet of old, and therefore, there was a special need to not only hear His words, but to pay attention and understand what it was that He was saying! But also, by so doing, one was led to and could find, the Kingdom of God; thus for those who were so led by Jesus, He was the Messiah.

Throughout the gospels, we find various miracles performed by Jesus. Several of the miracles seemed to have been solely in the domain of Jesus, and if they had been performed by a practitioner of another faith would have been termed magic, sorcery and very likely the work of the devil. (*Note:* These are terms which have been used by western theologians and philosophers, to describe Zarathustra, the Magi, the Zarathustrian clergy, as well as the priests and shaman of many of the other religious traditions of the world.)

Motivation and reason for a deed were far more important to Jesus than we tend to hear about in today's world. For example, according to Matthew concerning fasting:

6:16 "Moreover when ye fast, be not as the hypocrites, of a sad countenance: for they disfigure their faces, that they may appear unto men to fast. Verily, I say unto you, They have their reward.

6:17 But thou, when thou fastest, anoint thine head, and wash thy face:

6:18 That thou appear not unto men to fast, but unto thy Father which is in secret; and thy Father which seeth in secret, shall reward thee openly."[33]

Likewise, concerning wealth:

6:19 "Lay not up for yourselves treasures upon Earth, where moth and rust doth corrupt, and where thieves break through and steal:

6:20 But lay up for yourselves treasures in heaven, where neither moth or rust doth corrupt, and where thieves do not break through or steal;

6:21 For know that where treasure is so will your heart be also".

6:22 The light of the body is the eye: if therefore thine eye be single, thy whole body shall be full of light.

6:23 But if thine eye be evil, thy whole body shall be full of darkness, how great is that darkness!

6:24 No man can serve two masters: for either he will hate the one, and love the other: or else he will hold to the one, and despise the other. You cannot serve God and mammon."[34]

The Raising of Lazarus from the Dead

The event that heralded the beginning of the end of the ministry of Jesus is the **Raising of Lazarus from the Dead**. This is probably the most famous miracle of Jesus, and definitely told most often from pulpits today, from the Gospel according to John:

11:14 "Then said Jesus unto them plainly, "Lazarus is dead.

11:15 And I am glad for your sakes that I was not there, to the intent ye may believe; nevertheless let us go unto him."

11:16 Then said Thomas, which is called Didymus. Unto his fellow disciples, "let us also go, that we may die with him."

11:17 Then when Jesus came, he found that he had lain in the grave four days already.

11:18 Now Bethany was nigh unto Jerusalem. About fifteen furlongs off:

11:19 And many of the Jews came to Martha and Mary. To comfort them concerning their brother.

11:20 Then Martha, as soon as she heard that Jesus was coming, went and met him: but Mary sat still in the house.

11:21 Then said Martha unto Jesus, "Lord, if thou hadst been here, my brother had not died.

11:22 But I know, that even now, whatsoever thou wilt ask of God, God will give it thee."

11:23 Jesus said unto her, "Thy brother shall rise again."

11:24 Martha saith unto him, "I know that know that he shall rise again in the resurrection at the last day."

11:25 Jesus said unto her, "I am the resurrection, and the life: he that believeth in me, though he were dead, yet shall he live:

11:26 And whomsoever liveth and believeth in me shall never die. Believest thou this?"

11:27 She saith unto him, "Yea, Lord: I believe that thou art the Christ, the Son of God, which should come into the world."

11:28 And when she had so said, she went her way, and called Mary her sister secretly, saying, "The Master is come, and calleth for thee."

11:29 As soon as she heard that, she arose quickly, and came unto him.

11:30 Now Jesus was not yet come into the town, but was in that place where Martha met him.

11:31 The Jews then which were with her in the house, and comforted her, when they saw Mary, that she rose up hastily and went out, followed her, saying, "She goeth unto the grave to weep there."

11:32 Then when Mary was come where Jesus was, and saw him, she fell down at his feet, saying unto him, "Lord, if thou hadst been here, my brother had (would have) not died."

11:33 When Jesus therefore saw her weeping, and the Jews also weeping which came with her, he groaned in the spirit, and was troubled.

11:34 And said, "where have you laid him?" They said unto him, "Lord, come and see."

11:35 Jesus wept.

11:36 Then said the Jews, "Behold how he loved him!"

11:37 And some of them said, "Could not this man, which openeth the eyes of the blind, and caused even this man should have not died?"

11:38 Jesus therefore again groaning in himself cometh to the grave. It was a cave, and a stone lay upon it.

11:39 Jesus said, "Take ye away the stone." Martha, the sister of him that was died, saith unto him, "Lord, by this time he stinketh: for he hath been dead four days.

11:40 Jesus saith unto her, "Said I not unto thee, that, if thou wouldest believe, thou shouldest see the glory of God?"

11:41 Then they took away the stone from the place where the dead was laid. And Jesus lifted up his eyes and said, "Father, I thank thee that thou hast heard me.

11:42 And I knew that thou hearest me always: but because of the people which stand by I said it, that they may believe that thou hast sent me."

11:43 And when he thus had spoken, he cried with a loud voice, "Lazarus, come forth."

11:44 And he that was dead came forth, bound hand and foot with grave clothes: and his face was bound about with a napkin. Jesus saith unto them, "Loose him, and let him go."

11:45 Then many of the Jews which came to Mary, and had seen the things which Jesus did, believed on him.[35]

The telling of this famous miracle normally stops here. However, by continuing on, we get a more complete picture of the fears and mindset of a large part of the Jewish community at that time:

11:46 But some of them [the Jews that had been at the side of and had comforted Mary] went their ways to the Pharisees, and told them what things Jesus had done.

11:47 Then gathered the chief priests and the Pharisees a council, and said, "What do we? For this man doeth many miracles.

11:48 If we let him alone, all men will believe on him: and the Romans shall come and take away both our place and nation."[36]

Note that what is expressed is not the loss of power, prestige or position, but the very existence of the whole nation of the Jews. It was common in those days for armies of Rome to lay waste to a nation which was viewed as a potential threat to the Roman Empire.

11:49 "And one of them, named Caiaphas, being the high priest that same year, said unto them, "Ye know nothing at all.

11:50 Nor consider that it is expedient for us, that one man should die for the people, and that the whole nation perish not."

11:51 And this spake he not of himself: but being high priest that year, he prophesied that Jesus should die for that nation;

11:52 And not for that nation only, but that also he should gather together in one the children of God that were scattered abroad.

11:53 Then from that day forth they took counsel together for to put him to death.

11:54 Jesus therefore walked no more openly among the Jews, but went thence unto a country near to the wilderness, into a city called Ephraim, and there continued with his disciples."[37]

What is seldom made clear today is that there were several important causes for the turning of public opinion on the part of both the priests and of the Jewish people. They saw the rapidly growing numbers of believers of Jesus to be a threat to the Roman Empire and, therefore, to the very continuance of their nation. From this passage, it would seem that the Jewish elite were not feeling hate or jealousy towards Jesus. They felt that just as many a man had throughout history been called upon to sacrifice his life for that of his Nation, so it must be for Jesus. Not only did they see this as being the same thing, but since the followers of Jesus were to be found in many of the small countries surrounding Israel, it was likely that His sacrifice could spare the integrity of those countries as well.

Add to this the incident in the Temple in the last week of Jesus' life as told below. So the religious world of the Jews was in terrible upset as the life of Jesus was drawing to a close. There were among the chief rulers and priests those who believed in Him fully, and those who believed in him not at all, but also a large number who wished to believe but feared for many reasons to confess their belief. This is well stated in John 12:

12:42 Nevertheless among the chief rulers also many believed on him; but because of the Pharisees they did not confess him, lest they should be put out of the synagogue:

12:43 For they loved the praise of men more than the praise of God.

12:44 Jesus cried out and said, "he that believeth on me, believeth not on me, but on him that sent me.

12:45 And he that seeth me seeth him that sent me.

12:46 I am come a light into the world, that whosoever believeth on me should not abide in darkness.

12:47 And if any man hear my words, and believe not, I judge him not: for I am come not to judge the world, but to save the world.

12:48 He that rejecteth me, and receiveth not my words, that one that judgeth him: the word that I have spoken, the same shall judge him in the last day.

12:49 For I have not spoken of myself; but the Father which sent Me, he gave me a commandment, what I should say, and what I should speak.

12:50 And I know that his commandment is life everlasting: whatsoever I speak therefore, even as the Father said unto me, so I Speak."[38]

Jesus makes several points in this gorgeous passage. First is that He clearly says Who and What He is. He is the mirror image of God, and thus if people wish to know God it should be through listening to Him. Thus they would be hearing those things which God wished them to hear, and that through truly observing Him, the spiritual and the physical Him, it will be as if they were observing God. Secondly, He repeats the phrase throughout the quote, "there is One Who sent Him." In verse 46, the phrase; "I am come a light into the world," states so beautifully the station of this individual and how to make use of His words to see that the forces of darkness and evil do not overtake your life choices with temptations.

To those who have the conception that God is a physical being, Jesus tried to make it clear that it was otherwise in John 4:

4:22   "Ye worship ye know not what: we know what we worship: for the salvation is of the Jews.

4:23   But the hour cometh, and now is, when the true worshippers shall worship the Father in spirit, and in truth: for the Father seeketh such to worship him.

4:24   God is a Spirit: and they that worship him must worship him in spirit and in truth."[39]

Throughout the ministry of Jesus there was the lingering problem that many of the people He met, taught and healed had little understanding of the message that was so important to Him. Think if it might be that Jesus was well aware of the fact that His mission was far greater than a simple reorienting of the Judaic religion. Is it not possible that Jesus saw His mission as the reorientation of all faiths, no matter what the source of their belief, nor what they called their God? And thus, His teaching was meant to be timeless and Universal. It would seem that it was meant for generations as yet unborn in the whole world even in lands not yet discovered. If this supposition is correct, is it any wonder that the understanding of most people of the time was too limited in scope?

What is being suggested is that we should consider the recognition of the capacity or the potential of the Man as both the Magi and, much later, as John the Baptist did. That is to say that Jesus was the one whom God had chosen for the special assignment of being His voice at that time. Since the spirit of God was within Him He was able to speak with two tongues, His own and that of His Heavenly Father, God. With His acceptance of that spirit was God diminished or in actuality, greatly enhanced? For once again, there was the voice of God from the physical tongue and lips of an actual man on the physical plane we call Earth. How much better could it be than when the Word of God was enunciated by the most spiritual and greatest orator among men?

Jesus was available in His appointed station to be questioned by common people, Gentile and Jew alike, by the Sadducees, Pharisees and also the priests of other Faiths. When Jesus spoke many of His answers sounded as if they were riddles, but this was a necessity since those answers had to be inclusive of similar questions for generations to come. Therefore, the answers were very likely totally beyond the comprehension of most people of the time.

In like fashion, there was the need to speak in ways that could be understood by a people that had taken the laws of their religion and had found the "do's and don'ts" therein without finding the love and compassion of God, that had originally been revealed in same. Much of what Jesus taught needed to be simplified, and thus He gave examples (parables) in story-form so that the meanings would have both reason and love attached; the God of Love instead of God as the Judge and Avenger.

The message of Jesus was from a God far more inclined to lead His people through guidance and love than through retribution. In the Old Testament it says; "The Lord is my Shepherd, I shall not want. He maketh me to lie down in green pastures: he leadeth me beside the still waters. He restoreth my soul: he leadeth me in the path of righteousness for his name's sake. Yea, though I walk through the valley of the shadow of death, I shall fear no evil for thou art with me; thy rod and thy staff they comfort me."[40]

For you who have yet to take a trip to the Holy Land, there is much desert in that country. With that in mind, you are offered a new perspective on this gorgeous biblical verse. Sheep in the Holy Land quickly learn to trust and follow the shepherd or die. They are taught this lesson by their mothers, who were taught by their mothers before them, that the shepherd is both knowledgeable and loving, but cannot leave the whole herd in the dry expanses of the desert to chase down an inattentive or wayward sheep. Therefore, not only do the sheep follow the way led by their shepherd, instead of being herded by him and his dogs as they would be in much of the Western World, but they also do not drink from a pool unless the shepherd so instructs because, the "still waters" may be foul, contaminated and possibly poisonous. Hence, the sheep would be led beside, and possibly past, the "still waters." The "lying down in green pastures" as opposed to automatically grazing is likewise for the good health of the sheep who, without the guidance of the loving shepherd, might be tempted to overeat, become sick, and thereby easy prey for any of the awaiting predators. The rod and the staff are the methods by which the Old Testament shepherd would instruct the sheep as to when, where and how to go, eat and drink. Therefore, the shepherding tools were a source of reassurance and comfort to the sheep, rather than something with which to be punished or beaten. And, while it is true that the shepherd was doing all of this for his own sake, it was also true that he was doing this out of love for his beloved sheep. The "valley of the shadow of death" could just as easily refer to the illness that could occur from overeating in the green pastures or the result of drinking from bad water, or to the sure death from starvation, lack of water or from becoming food for the many hungry wild animals, including man, roaming the desert.

This Psalm ends with confirmation that God was a loving God at that time for after the comforting of the rod and the staff, it states, "Thou preparest a table before me in the presence of mine enemies, thou anointest my head with oil, my cup runneth over. Surely goodness and mercy shall follow me all the days of my life: and I will dwell in the house of the Lord for ever."[41] This reflects the Jewish feelings about a loving and caring God centuries before the life of Jesus. The clear message in this beautiful Old Testament Psalm is the need for total reliance upon God and His love.

A major part of the message of Jesus was a return to this total reliance upon the loving God, and only after that was secured, and without leaving that reliance, should one go on with one's daily life. This is well illustrated in the verse from Matthew 13:

13:47 "Then one said unto him, Behold, thy mother and thy brethren stand without (outside), desiring to speak with thee.

13:48 But answered and said unto him that told him, "Who is my mother? And who are my brethren?"

13:49 And he stretched forth his hand towards his disciples, and said, "Behold my mother and my brethren!

13:50 For who shall do the will of my Father which is in heaven, the same is my brother, and sister, and mother."[42]

In this passage, Jesus is not denying His Mother, Mary, nor His brother, but attempting to get across a major point of His main message that all, including Himself, must put the love and recognition of God and total reliance upon Him [GOD] ahead of that of the mortal family. And again from Matthew 14:

14:54 "And when he was come into his own country, he taught them in their synagogue, insomuch that they were astonished, and said, "whence hath this man this wisdom and these mighty works?

14:55 Is this not the carpenter's son? Is not his mother called Mary? and his brethren, James, and Joses, and Simon, and Judas?

14:56 and his sisters, are they not all of us? Whence then hath this man all these things?

14:57 And they were offended in him. But Jesus said unto them, "a prophet is not without honour, save in his own country, and in his own house."

14:58 And he did not many mighty works there because of their unbelief."[43]

It should be noted that Jesus was reluctant to preach much in Israel, for the words would only fall on deaf ears. He was of the opinion that healings and the other assorted miracles would be treated as circus stunts and would not lead to new believers, or even to giving hearing to the spiritually deaf.

Jesus had been teaching in the temple according to Luke, but behind the scenes, the negativity from the chief priests and the other powers in Jerusalem was reaching a boiling point. At the same time, it was becoming more obvious that the Apostles and very likely, the seventy disciples had not fully understood what it was that Jesus had said or meant in His teaching. Something definitely needed to change while there was still time; if not, all of the sacrifices and teachings would have been for naught. The healings, the feeding of multitudes with but a few fish and loaves of bread, and the miracles, such as the water-walking would be forgotten within a generation, and the mission He had been sent to accomplish would be unfulfilled. With all of these things in mind, it was necessary that Jesus do something totally out of character. Like a sailor being blown straight towards the cliffs, He had to take a new tack, in such a way that it would cause those close to Him to understand more fully what the mission was, so that they would carry on after His death. There was even the slightest possibility that those in the temple who had begun to believe His message would arise to support His cause. It appears that Jesus felt the need to be outrageous, to "upset the apple cart."

The following is from three different biblical points of view, that outrageous act which Jesus performed. Remember, had He felt the presence of the moneychangers and sellers of doves so onerous, He could have preached against it, either from inside or outside the temple, during the several prior years of His ministry. However, we need to look at not only Matthew 21:12-16, but also in Mark 11:15-19 and Luke 19:4-8:

21:12 "And Jesus went into the temple of God, and cast out all them that sold and bought in the temple, and overthrew the tables of the moneychangers, and the seats of them that sold doves,

21:13 And said unto them, "It is written, My house shall be called the house of prayer; but you have made it a den of thieves."

21:14 And the blind and the lame came to him in the temple; and he healed them."

To compound the problems for the priests and scribes:

21:15 "And when the chief priests and scribes saw the wonderful things that he did, and the children crying in the temple, and saying, Hosana to the son of David; they were sore displeased"

And further adding insult to injury, the story continues:

21:16 "And said [the chief Priests and Scribes] they unto him, "Hearest thou what they say?"[to which Jesus says] "Yea, have ye never read, Out of the mouth of babes and sucklings thou hast perfected praise?"[44]

From Matthew, it would seem that Jesus, by this action, had truly crossed the line that would allow an "out" for the priests and scribes. We need to quote the parallel passages because of what was at stake for Jesus. From Mark 11, after overturning the tables of the moneychangers and the sellers of the doves,

11:17 "And he taught, saying unto them, "Is it not written, My house shall be called of all nations the house of prayer? but ye have made it a den of thieves."

11:18   And the scribes and the chief priests heard it, and sought how they might destroy him: for they feared him, because all the people was astonished at his doctrine.[45]

The differences are neither great nor small, it would behoove you to read that which follows from the rendition of the same episode from the perspective of the Gospel of Luke 19.

19:45   "And he went into the temple, and began to cast out them sold therein and them that bought;

19:46   Saying unto them, "It is written, My house is the house of prayer; but thou has made it a den of thieves."

19:47   And he taught daily in the temple. But the chief priests and the scribes and the chief of the people sought to destroy him,

19:48   And could not find what they might do: for all the people were very attentive to hear him."[46]

The story continues directly into Luke chapter twenty:

20:1   "And it came to pass, that on one of those days, as he taught the people in the temple, and preached the gospel, the chief priests and the scribes came upon him with the elders,

20:2   And spake unto him, saying, "Tell us, by what authority doest thou these things? Or who is he that gave thee this authority?"

20:3   And he answered and said unto them, "I will also ask you one thing; and answer me:

20:4   "The baptism of John, was it from heaven, or of men?"

20:5   And they reasoned with themselves, saying, "If we shall say, From heaven; he will say, Why then believed ye him not?"

20:6   But if we say, Of men; all the people will stone us: for they be [have been] persuaded that John was a prophet."

If these events and quotes were accurately reported, this is probably the best example of being between a "rock and a hard place" that you will find. The priests had to be totally perplexed.

20:7   "And they answered [to Jesus], that they could not tell whence it was.

20:8   And Jesus said unto them, "Neither tell I you by what authority I do these things'"[47]

After this episode, Luke goes on to say that, immediately after, Jesus told the parable of the ungrateful husbandman; it says;

20:19 "And the chief priests and the scribes the same hour sought to lay hands on him; and they feared the people: for they perceived that he had spoken this parable against them.

20:20 And they watched him, and sent forth spies, which should feign themselves just men, that they might take hold of his words, that so they might deliver him unto the power and authority of the governor."

The incident continues with an attempt to trick Jesus by use of compliment:

20:21 "And they asked him saying. "Master, we know that thou sayest and teachest rightly. Neither acceptest thou the person of any, but teachest the way of God truly:

20:22 "Is it lawful for us to give tribute unto Caesar or no?"

20:23 But he perceived their craftiness, and said unto them, "Why tempt ye me?"

20:24 "Shew me a penny. Whose image and superstition hath it?" They answered and said, "Caesar's."

20:25 And he said unto them, "Render therefore unto Caesar the things that are Caesar's and unto God the things which be God's."

20:26 And they could not take hold of his words before the people: and they marveled at his answer, and held their peace."[48]

While the differences are worthy of notice, there is no reason to dispute the fact that Jesus had not only embarrassed the most important leaders in the temple, but challenged their very authority, and by so doing became even more of a "Cult (please pardon the expression) Hero." They had no choice but to seek His arrest and removal from the temple and society; in their minds it was the only answer for the safety of their positions, the temple and the Nation.

Jesus seemed to have knowledge of what was happening behind the scenes in Jerusalem and thus being aware of His impending death, the tone and urgency of His message changed dramatically.

John 12:35 "Then Jesus said unto them, "Yet a little while is the light with you. Walk while ye have the light, lest darkness come upon you: for he that walketh in darkness knoweth not whither he goeth.

John 12:36 While ye have light, believe in the light, that ye may be the children of light."[49]

The die had been cast, there was no turning back; Jesus retired with the disciples to await the inevitable. There was then the withdrawal to Gethsemane, the Last Supper, the betrayal by Judas, the arrest of Jesus, the denial by Peter, the trial before Pilate, the mob psychology of the crowd before Pilate, and the crucifixion, which occurred on a Friday afternoon and ended with the final few words of Jesus, and His death near sunset.

The final week that Jesus spent with the Apostles appears to have been in vain as we read the various accounts of what the Apostles did during, and after, the crucifixion. What seemed to have happened to these once emboldened men with special capacities, who had been capable of speaking the word of God in all arenas and synagogues? Suddenly, they withdrew into hiding and showed less courage than mice.

It was only natural that the Apostles, all of whom had felt that Jesus was either God, the Messiah or, at the very least, from God, were shocked that God had not intervened to save Jesus.

They were aware of the reaction of the crowd before Pilate, and at the crucifixion, and, therefore, were absolutely aware that their lives were also in jeopardy and, therefore, they were fearful. The protection which they had felt in the previous years while in the presence of One whom they had come to call "Master" had been obliterated. What was to become of his beautiful message, and what would they be able to do without Him to guide them?

I submit that this was a time in which the art of praying as taught by Jesus was practiced as they had never before prayed. And that it was from these fervent prayers that what followed did in fact occur.

Is it not humorous that, despite many attempts over the years by the Christian clergy to separate themselves from the Jewish Faith, they continue to refer to the Old Testament for direction and material for their sermons? When you take a close look at the Bible of today, where is the greatest physical weight and the most history? The need of Christianity to make use of the Old Testament is undeniable.

With your refocusing of beliefs held onto for years, please get rid of any lingering prejudices against the Jewish Faith, especially its present day followers. Much of the prejudice against Jews receives its justification from the concept that these people were directly responsible for the crucifixion of Jesus. Surely, we have to admit that none of the present day members of the Judaic Faith were alive at that time, and therefore they should be held totally blameless.

How much time is given today from most Christian pulpits to the fact that the laws, "Love the Lord, Thy God with all Thy Might" and "Liken unto this to Love thy neighbor as thyself," did not originate with Jesus, but were in fact restatements of previously revealed Mosaic Laws (Deut. 6:4 and OT Lev. 19:18, respectively). To emphasize this point:

Mark 12:28   "And one of the scribes came, and having heard them reasoning together, and perceiving that he had answered them well, asked him, "Which is the first commandment of all?"

Mark 12:29   And Jesus answered him, "the first of all the commandments is, Hear O Israel; The Lord our God is one Lord:

Mark 12:30   And thou shalt love the Lord thy God with all thy heart, and with all thy soul, and with all thy mind, and with all thy strength: this is the first commandment.

Mark 12:31   And the second is like, namely this, Thou shalt love thy neighbor as thyself. There is none other commandment greater than these.

Mark 12:32   And the scribe said unto him, "Well, Master, thou hast said the truth: for there is one God; and there is none other but he:

Mark 12:33   And to love him with all the heart, and with all the understanding, and with all the soul. And with all the strength, and to love his neighbour as himself, is more than all whole burnt offerings and sacrifices."

Mark 12:34   And when Jesus saw that he answered discreetly, he said unto him, "Thou art not far from the kingdom of God."[50]

The Execution of Jesus

It is fine if you choose to replace execution with the word crucifixion, but only if, in so doing, you do not forget that, in fact, this was a public and very slow execution. This was not fairly quick like a hanging, although that choice was available, as with the death of Judas after the betrayal of Jesus.[51] This was not a stoning, which is bloody and painful, but with a few well-thrown stones, one is unconscious long before death. This was not the bloody and gruesome but quick beheading inflicted upon John the Baptist. What Jesus was subjected to was one of the most painful deaths devised for the most despised criminals of the Roman Empire.[52] The purpose behind the pain and the long period to death was that it was to serve as a deterrent to those who might think that crime pays. This was the choice of execution chosen for the man, who had been termed before His birth, "The King of Jews."[53]

And it accomplished what it was supposed to for the chief priest in the Temple in Jerusalem, in that the nation of the Jews had stamped out both the emerging Christianity and its source (Jesus), thereby removing the threat to the great and powerful Roman Empire and its domination of the area, as well as the perceived threat of a new religion. In fact, the state of Israel was allowed to continue to exist for some thirty-five years, when an uprising of Jewish people brought forth the wrath of the Roman Empire, in 70 AD. Meanwhile, the Roman Empire not only continued to exist, but to grow and thrive for centuries. So we could say that the crucifixion of Jesus was a win/win situation for not only the Roman Empire, but also for a short while for the religious and civil leaders of the Jewish Nation while the fledgling Christian Faith was sent into hiding and seemingly was in total disarray. In the long run this was not the case. Christianity was the ultimate winner.

The Real Pain of the Cross

To many modern day Christians, the death of Jesus and the pain of the crucifixion has been reduced to describing in great detail the actual physical pain endured by Him. They discuss the actual weight of the cross, the difficulty that Jesus had in carrying it on the road of uneven cobblestones and then how terribly painful the affixing of the body to the cross was in this form of execution, it has been built into something which is surreal. But, in so describing the crucifixion, these members of the clergy are overlooking that this was a form of execution experienced by thousands before Jesus and probably hundreds of thousands after Him.

Consider again the real pain of the cross; for it was much more and far different in that:

1) Jesus knew that His disciples would be driven into hiding, fearful for their very lives.

2) Jesus knew that there was a major lack of understanding of His teachings, and that He had only been allowed to preach to a very small segment of the known world.

3) Jesus seemed to know that the spirit of God within Him would be released and would not return for centuries, and thus probably feared for the billions of people that would be born and die before that next coming.

4) Also, Jesus seemed to know that the message which God had given Him was correct and was for the salvation of mankind, and yet it seemed as if all of that had been for naught.

5) If, as most Christian churches say, Jesus died for the forgiveness of the sins of all of His followers, then would not Jesus find the real weight of all that, rather than the actual weight of the cross?

(*Note*: Jesus did not carry His own cross. A man, Simon of Cyrene, was compelled to carry it for Jesus.)[54]

6) If Jesus saw the future pain and suffering of those who chose to keep His teachings alive in the following centuries, would He not have felt their pain?

8) If Jesus saw further into the future, and saw the killing of young men in many wars in some of which His religion was the main cause of those hostilities, often Christian against Christian, would not the pain have been greatly increased?

There should be little doubt that Jesus suffered in His death in the crucifixion process, but was not the pain of any or all of the above far greater than the physical pain? What do you think?

The Resurrection

For many people and denominations of Christianity, this is the most important event in the story of Jesus of Nazareth. It is what sets Him above all mankind. It is an absolutely wonderful tale, and, again, is told in slightly different words in Matthew, Mark, and Luke. For the sake of simplicity, we will concentrate on the events following the death of Jesus on the cross;

Matthew 27:57 "When the even [evening] was come, there came a rich man of Arimathaea, named Joseph, who also himself was Jesus' disciple:

Matthew 27:58 He went to Pilate, and begged the body of Jesus. Then Pilate commanded the body to be delivered.

Matthew 27:59 And when Joseph had taken the body, he wrapped it in a clean linen cloth,

Matthew 27:60 And laid it in his own new tomb, which he had hewn out in the rock: and rolled a great stone to the door of the sepulchre, and departed.

Matthew 27:61 And there was Mary Magdalene, and the other Mary, sitting over against the sepulchre.

Matthew 27:62 Now on the next day, that followed the day of the preparation, the chief priests and the Pharisees came together unto Pilate,

Matthew 27:63 Saying, Sir, we remember that that deceiver said, while he was yet alive, After three days I will rise again.

Matthew 27:64 Command therefore that the sepulchre be made sure until the third day, lest his disciples come by night, and steal him away, and say unto the people, He is risen from the dead: so that the last error shall be worse than the first.

Matthew 27:65 Pilate said unto them, Ye have a watch: go your way, make it as sure as you can.

Matthew 27:66 So they went, and made the sepulchre sure, sealing the stone and setting the watch."[55]

From Matthew chapter twenty-eight:

28:1 "In the end of the Sabbath, as it began to dawn toward the first day of the week, came Mary Magdalene and the other Mary to see the sepulchre.

28:2 And, behold, there was a great earthquake: for the Angel of the Lord descended from heaven, and came and rolled back the stone from the door, and sat upon it.

28:3 His countenance was like lightning, and his raiment [robe or clothing] was white as snow:

28:4 And for fear of him the keepers did shake, and became as dead men.

28:5 And the angel answered and said unto the women, Fear not ye: for I know that ye seek Jesus, which was crucified.

28:6 He is not here: for he is risen, as he said. Come, see the place where the Lord lay.

28:7   And go quickly, and tell his disciples that he is risen from the dead; and, behold, he goeth before you into Galilee; there shall ye see him: lo, I have told you.

28:8   And they departed quickly from the sepulchre with fear and great joy; and did run to bring his disciples word."[56]

And then, of great interest but seldom read;

28:11 "Now when they were going, behold, some of the watch came into the city, and shewed unto the chief priest all that was done.

28:12 And when they were assembled with the elders, and had taken counsel, they gave large (sums of) money unto the soldiers.

28:13 Saying, Say ye, His disciples came by night and stole him *away* while we slept.

28:14 And if this come to the governor's ears, we will persuade him, and secure you.

28:15 So they took the money, and did as they were taught; and this saying is commonly reported among the Jews until this day.

And then the portion which is read from today's pulpits:

28:16 "Then the eleven disciples went away into Galilee, into a mountain where Jesus had appointed them.

28:17 And when they saw him, they worshipped him: but some doubted.

28:18 And Jesus came and spake unto them, saying, "All power is given unto me in heaven and in earth.

28:19 Go ye therefore, and teach all nations, baptizing them in the name of the Father, and of the Son, and of the Holy Ghost:

28:20 Teaching them to observe all things whatsoever I have commanded you: and, lo, I am with you always, *even* unto the end of the world." A-men."[57]

You will need to decide for yourself which was the greater miracle; that the physical body of Jesus was risen from the dead or that His teachings, which seemed to have become dead with His body, rose from a spark that was itself almost dead to become a flame which eventually circled the entire earth.

We have taken a look at the ministry of Jesus, and several possibly new perspectives on the end of his ministry, as well as reasons for that ministry to create a new religion. It is time to look at a comparison of the religion begun by Jesus and that of the Man who sent the Magi.

A Biblical Record of Jesus According to the Gospels

Event	Matthew	Mark	Luke	John
Birth, Childhood and Ministry				
Genealogy of Jesus	1:2-17		3:32-38	
Birth Announcement to Mary			1:26-38	
Birth Announcement to Joseph	1:18-25		2:1-7	
Birth of Jesus			2:8-20	
Circumcision and Presentation in the Temple			2:21-40	
Visit of the Magi	2:1-12			
Flight to Egypt and Return to Nazareth	2:13-23			
Boy Jesus Visits Jerusalem			2:41-52	

Event	Matthew	Mark	Luke	John
The Period of Silence				
	No Information	No Information	No Information	No Information
Baptism of Jesus and the Temptations				
Baptized by John the Baptist	3:13-17	1:9-11	3:21-22	
The Temptations	4:1-11	1:12-13	4:1-13	
The Early Ministry				
Jesus Calls His First Followers				1:10-51
The First Miracle				2:1-12
Cleansing of the Temple				2:13-25
Nicodemus Visits Jesus				3:1-21
Jesus Baptizes in Judaea				3:22-36
Return to Galilee				4:1-42
Rejection at Nazareth			4:16-31	
Headquarters at Capernaum	4:13-16		4:31	
Call to Discipleship of Peter, Andrew, James and John	4:18-22	1:16-20	5:1-11	
Jesus Teaches in the Synagogue		1:21-22		
Healing of the Sick	8:14-17	1:23-24	4:33-41	

Event	Matthew	Mark	Luke	John
Jesus Tours Galilee and Preaches	4:23-25	1:35-39	4:42-44	
Jesus' Reputation Grows	8:1	1:40-45	5:12-16	
Developing Opposition and The Christian Movement Takes Form				
Healing of a Paralytic	9:1-8	2:1-12	5:17-26	
Jesus Calls Matthew to Discipleship	9:9-13	2:13-17		
Criticized for Attitude Towards Fasting	9:14-17	2:18-22		
Criticized for Desecration of Sabbath	12:1-14	2:23-28, 3:1-6	6:1-11	5:1-18
Jesus' Reputation Continues to Grow	4:24-25	3:7-12	6:17-19	12:15-21
Commissions the Apostles	10:1-4	3:13-19	6:17-19	
Sermon on the Mount	5:1 to 8:1		6:20-49	
Basis for Relationship to Jesus and His Cause				
Jesus Designates His True Relatives	12:46-50	3:31-35	8:19-21	
Parables of the Kingdom	13:1-53	4:1-34	8:4-18	
Necessity of Faith:				
Stilling of the Tempest	8:24-27	4:35-41	8:22-25	

Event	Matthew	Mark	Luke	John
The Gadarene Domoniac	8:28-34	5:1-20	8:26-39	
The Daughter of Jairus	9:18-26	5:21-43	8:40-56	
Two Blind and One Deaf Man	9:27-34			
Second Rejection at Nazareth	13:54-58	6:1-6		
Jesus Instructs the Twelve	9:36 to 11:1	6:7-13	9:1-6	
The Disciples Report to Jesus		6:30	9:10	
Teaches and Feeds the Multitude	14:13-21	6:32-44	9:11-17	6:1-14
Walks on the Sea	14:22-36	6:45-56		6:15-24
Discourse on the Bread of Life				6:25-71
Condemnation of Elders' Traditionalism	15:1-20	7:1-23		
The Various Journeys of Jesus				
Tyre, Heals Daughter of Phoenician	15:21-28	7:21-30		
Decapolis, Heals a Deaf-Mute		7:31-37		
Four Thousand People Fed	15:32-39	8:1-10		

Event	Matthew	Mark	Luke	John
Warns Against Spirit of Pharisees	16:1-12	8:11-21		
Journey into Caesarea	16:13	8:27		
First Mention of Own Death and Resurrection	16:21-28	8:31 to 9:1	9:1-27	
Transfiguration	17:1-13	9:2-13	9:28-36	
Healing of Epileptic Boy	17:14-21	9:14-29	9:37-43	
Second Mention of Own Death and Resurrection	17:22-23	9:30-32	9:44-45	
Return to Capernaum, ½ Scheckel Tax	17:24-27			
Humility, Self-Denial, Forgiveness	18	9:33-50	9:46-50	
Jerusalem, Feast of Tabernacles				7:1-52
Debates in the Temple				8:12-59
Heals Man Born Blind				9:1-41
Discourse on Sheep and Shepherd				10:1-21
Jerusalem, Feast of Dedication				10:22-42

Event	Matthew	Mark	Luke	John
Ministry Beyond the Jordan	19:1-2	10:1	9:51-62	
Mission of the Seventy			10:1-24	
On Marriage and Divorce	19:3-12	10:2-12		
Jesus Blesses the Little Children	19:13-15	10:13-16	18:15-17	
Relationship of Riches to Eternal Life	19:16-30	10:17-31	18:18-30	
Laborers in the Vineyard	20:1-16			
Third Mention of Own Death and Resurrection	20:17-19	10:32-34	18:31-34	
Standards of Greatness	20:20-28	10:35-45	22:24-27	
Blind Beggar of Jericho	20:29-34	10:46-52	18:35-43	
Zacchaeus, Tax Collector of Jericho			19:1-10	
Bethany, Raises Lazarus				11:1-44
The Plots for Jesus' Death				11:45-53
Bethany, Supper in His Honor				12:1-11
End of Jesus' Ministry – The Last Week of His Life				
Entry into Jerusalem	21:1-11	11:1-11	19:29-44	12:12-29

Event	Matthew	Mark	Luke	John
Monday, The Day of Authority				
Curses the Unfruitful Fig Tree	21:18-22	11:12-14, 20-25		
Cleanses the Temple	21:12-17	11:15-19	19:45-48	
Tuesday, The Day of Controversy				
Priests and Scribes Question Jesus' Authority	21:23-27	11:27-33	20:1-8	
Parables of Israel's Unfaithfulness				
Parables of Two Sons	21:28-32			
Parable of Wicked Tenants	21:33-46	12:1-12	20:9-19	
Parable of a Marriage Feast	22:1-14			
Pharisees and Tribute to Caesar	22:15-22	12:13-17	20:20-26	
Sadducees and Resurrection	22:23-33	12:18-27	20:27-38	
A Scribe, the Greatest Commandment	22:34-40	12:28-34	20:39-40	
Questioned About the Messiah	22:41-46	12:35-37	20:41-44	
Pronounces Woe on the Scribes and Pharisees	23:1-39	12:38-40	20:45-47	
A Widow's Mite		12:41-44	21:1-4	

Event	Matthew	Mark	Luke	John
Greeks Seek Jesus				12:30-36
The Jews Reject Jesus				12:37-50
Jesus Talks About What Will Be	24:1-51	13:1-37	21:5-38	
Parable of Ten Maidens	25:1-13			
Parable of Talents	25:14-30			
Describes Judgment to Come	25:31-46			
Judas Conspires Against Jesus	26:1-5, 14-16	14:1-2, 10-11	22:1-6	
Wednesday (No Written Record)				
Thursday, The Day of Fellowship				
Preparation for Passover	26:17-19	14:12-16	22:7-13	
Washes the Disciples' Feet				13:1-20
Passover and the Betrayer	26:20-25	14:17-21		13:21-35
The Last Supper	26:26-29	14:22-25	22:14-23	
Peter and Disciples Forewarned	26:30-35	14:26-31	22:31-38	13:36-38
Friday, The Day of Suffering				
Jesus Prays in Gethsemane	26:36-46	14:32-42	22:40-46	18:1
Betrayal and Arrest	26:47-56	14:43-52	22:47-53	18:2-12
The Trial (Ecclesiastical):				

Event	Matthew	Mark	Luke	John
Before Annas				18:13, 19-23
Before Caiaphas	26:57-67	14:53-65	22:54	18:24
Before the Sanhedrin	27:1	15:1	22:66-71	
Denied by Peter	26:69-75	14:66-72	22:55-62	18:15-18
The Trial (Legal):				
Before Pilate	27:2, 11-14	15:2-5	23:1-5	18:28-38
Before Herod			23:6-12	
Again before Pilate	27:16-26	15:6-15	23:13-25	19:1
Mocked by the Soldiers	27:27-31	15:16-20		19:2
Sentenced to be Crucified				19:16
Road to Golgotha	27:13	15:21	23:26-32	19:17
The Crucifixion	27:33-44	15:22-32	23:33	19:18-24
His Last Spoken Words				
"Father, Forgive Them…"			23:34	
"Today … With Me in Paradise."			23:39-43	
"Woman … Thy Son!"				19:25-27
"My God, My God, Why…"	27:46	15:33-39		
"I Thirst…"				19:28-29
"It Is Finished…"				19:30
"Father, Into Thy Hands…"			23:44-49	

Event	Matthew	Mark	Luke	John
The Burial				
	27:57-61	15:42-47	23:50-56	19:38-42
Saturday, The Day of Silence				
The Guarded Tomb	27:63-66			
Sunday, The Day of Resurrection				
The Empty Tomb, The Risen Christ	28:1-10	16:1-8	24:1-12	20:1-10
Appearance in Emmaus			24:13-35	
Appearance in Jerusalem			24:36-43	20:19-25
Later Appearances of Jesus				
To the Disciples and Thomas				20:26-29
To Seven Disciples by the Sea				21:1-23
To Eleven Disciples on Galilean Mountain	28:16-20			
Ascension into Heaven			24:50-53	

❦ CHAPTER 6 ❦

Parallels and Differences Between Jesus and Zarathustra

The Two Mothers Most Holy

Both Zarathustra and Jesus were born of exceptional mothers, whose holiness and virtue were legendary. Is it possible that God purposely chose these particular mothers to give birth to, and then physically and spiritually nourish their "chosen sons"?

The Avesta tells us that Dughdova, the mother of Zarathustra, was a daughter of the house of Zoish, and possessed a special nature from the time of her birth.

Dinkard 7, 2:1 "About the marvellousness of the manifestations before the birth of that most auspicious of offsprings from his mother....

Dinkard 7, 2:3 Just as revelation mentions it thus: 'Thereupon, when (Ahura Mazda) had produced the material of (Zarathustra), the glory then, in the presence of (Ahura Mazda), fled on towards the material of (Zarathustra), on to that germ; from that germ it fled on, on to the light which is endless; from the light which is endless it fled on, on to that of the sun; from that of the sun it fled on, on to the moon; from that moon it fled on, on to those stars; from those stars it fled on, on to the fire which was in the house of Zoish; and from that fire it fled on, on to the wife of Frahimrvana-zoish, when she brought forth that girl who became the mother of (Zarathustra).'...[1]

Dinkard 7, 2:7 And the father of that girl spoke even these words to those of the district... 'When this girl was brought forth among those of mine, her whole destiny was afterwards set forth by that manifest radiance of fire, where it brought out radiance from all over her in the dark night.

Dinkard 7, 2:8 When this girl sits in the interior of the house, wherein there is no fire, and in the chamber of fire they increase its intensity, it is lighter there, where and when this girl sits, then there where they increase the intensity of the fire; one is dazzled by the radiance from her body, and that of a wizard would not have been so glorious."[2]

Frightened by the obvious blessedness of Dughdova, the local elders pressured her father to have her put out of the district, and she was sent to live with a family in the country of the Spitamas. The Avesta describes her approach to the village which was to be her new home:

Dinkard 7, 2:11 "One marvel is this which is declared, that when that girl, in going to that family, stood on the loftiest place in the country of the Spitamas, and it is surveyed by her, a great wonder is manifested to the girl, just as revelation mentions: 'It is their voice is carried away to her from them; "do thou proceed to that village which is theirs; it is very depressed in height, and very wide in breadth, in which he who is living and the cattle mostly walk together; besides, for thy assistance that village is divinely fashioned and compassionate.'

Dinkard 7, 2:12 Thereupon that damsel stopped, and also fully observed that their recital seems to be for the conveyance of this statement, that my action should be such as was ordered me by my father also.

Dinkard 7, 2:13 Then that damsel thoroughly washed her hands, and proceeded from them to that village which was Padiragtaraspo's, and the glory came to Pourushasp, the son of Padiragtaraspo."[3]

Tradition records both the virginal conception of Zarathustra following the illumination of Dudhdova with a shaft of light,[3] or at least, as the result of a divine intervention. The Dinkard verses report the union of three elements at Zoroaster's conception: the khwarr, or "divine glory" which Dughdova had carried since her own conception, and which had caused her illumination; with the frawahr, or "guardian spirit" which belongs to each individual; and the tan-gohr or "substance" of the physical body. It has been suggested that it was through these three elements that Zarathustra represented all human society, in the metaphors of priest, warrior and herdsman.[4]

Dughdova continued to have miraculous visits and dreams during her pregnancy. It was said that "angels came to her and worshipped and praised the unborn child."[5] Once, she was reported to have dreamt that good and evil spirits were fighting for the child in her womb.[6] At another time, she dreamt that she saw the world being destroyed, and became frightened. An angel came to her in a dream, and calmed her fears with the revelation that she was to bear a great prophet who would be able to avert the impending destruction.[7]

After the birth of Zarathustra, Dughdova was several times required to protect her son from the wrath of the king of the neighboring country of Turan, and from the priests in the region, who feared and attempted to kill the child. The Avesta records attempts to destroy the infant Zarathustra by fire, by stampedes of cattle and horses, by abandonment in a wolf den, and by dagger. In each case, He was protected by Ahura Mazda, and returned to the safety of his mother.[8]

Mary, the mother of Jesus, was born of the Jewish couple Joachim and Anna, who had been previously childless for the many years of their marriage. When the couple was at last blessed with a child, the pregnancy was announced by a divine messenger of God:

James 4:1 "Then, behold, an angel of the Lord appeared and said to her, 'Anna, Anna, the Lord has heard your prayer. You will conceive a child and give birth, and your offspring will be spoken of throughout the entire world.' Anna replied, 'As the Lord God lives, whether my child is a boy or a girl, I will offer it as a gift to the Lord my God, and it will minister to him its entire life'."[9]

At the age of three, Mary was taken by her parents to the Temple in Jerusalem, where she remained for nine years in service to the priests as a consecrated virgin, until her betrothal to the carpenter Joseph.[10]

While Mary resided at home in Galilee with her parents and awaited the formal "home-taking" ceremony of the Jewish marriage rituals, she was visited by the angel Gabriel:

Luke 1:30 "And the angel said unto her, Fear not Mary: for thou hast found favour with God.

Luke 1:31 And, behold, thou shalt conceive in thy womb, and bring forth a son, and shalt call his name JESUS.

Luke 1:32 He shall be great, and shall be called the Son of the Highest: and the Lord God shall give unto Him the throne of his father David:

Luke 1:33 And he shall reign over the house of Jacob for ever; and of his kingdom there shall be no end.

Luke 1:34 Then said Mary unto the angel, How shall this be, seeing I know not a man?

Luke 1:35 And the angel answered and said unto her, The Holy Ghost shall come upon thee, and the power of the Highest shall overshadow thee: therefore also that holy thing which shall be born of thee shall be called the Son of God."[11]

Joseph, too, was visited by an angel in a dream, who informed him of both the virginity of his wife, and the specialness of her son:

Matthew 1:18   "Now the birth of Jesus Christ was on this wise: When as his mother Mary was espoused to Joseph, before they came together, she was found with child of the Holy Ghost.

Matthew 1:19   Then Joseph her husband, being a just man, and not willing to make her a publick example, was minded to put her away privily.

Matthew 1:20   But while he thought on these things, behold, the angel of the Lord appeared unto him in a dream, saying, Joseph, thou son of David, fear not to take unto thee Mary thy wife: for that which is conceived in her is of the Holy Ghost.

Matthew 1:21   And she shall bring forth a son, and thou shalt call his name JESUS: for he shall save his people from their sins.

Matthew 1:22   Now all this was done, that it might be fulfilled which was spoken of the Lord by the prophet, saying,

Matthew 1:23   Behold, a virgin shall be with child, and shall bring forth a son, and they shall call his name Emmanuel, which being interpreted is, God with us.

Matthew 1:24   Then Joseph being raised from sleep did as the angel of the Lord had bidden him, and took until him his wife:

Matthew 1:25   And knew her not till she had brought forth her firstborn son: and he called his name JESUS."[12]

The ancient gospels of Matthew and James record the visit of the Magi to Jesus and His parents shortly after His birth, and describe Herod's wrath when he realized that the priests had not returned to Jerusalem to inform him of the child's location:

James 22:1 "When Herod realized that he had been mocked by the wise men, he grew angry and sent murderers, saying to them, 'Kill every infant, two years and under.'

James 22:2 When Mary heard that the infants were being killed, out of fear she took her child and wrapped him in swaddling clothes and placed him in a cattle manger."[13]

Matthew further records that, following a warning by an angel, Mary and Joseph fled with the infant to Egypt, where they kept the child safe until Herod's death.[14]

Is it not true that it is normally the mothers of mankind who are the first instructors of their children? Mothers must be considered to be, in many ways, the molders of the newborn. Without their nurturing, a child's development with respect to personality, learning ability, self-expression, thought processes, hearing and speech, observation and analysis, is hampered. Was this not even more important in the case of these two women and their special offspring?

Let us also consider the influence of heredity and DNA. Tall parents generally give birth to children who will grow up to be tall. Those with great athletic skills normally have children who grow up with the same. True genius is generally the result of having exceptionally intelligent parents, and so forth. In fact, one might easily question whether optimization over several generations might be required for a person destined to have the infusion of the spirit of God.

What was the relative value of the inherited traits of the mothers of both Zarathustra and Jesus, as compared to their nurturing and their teaching? It is very likely that the answer is not one or the other, but that all of these elements were necessary.

Both mothers were aware, because of the wondrous things that occurred from conception until the births of their special sons, of the uniqueness of their special progeny. Would not each have paid special attention to their nurturing and rearing? It is also good to remember that the rearing and education of both Zarathustra and Jesus were not totally the responsibility of their mothers. They would have interactions with the rest of the family, including the fathers, and with siblings and other relatives. We need to give some credit to their priests, teachers and communities as well. Neither Jesus nor Zarathustra grew up in a vacuum.

As we consider the importance of the genetic makeup in the light of the scientific discoveries of the present day, one might wonder if it was not possible that God predetermined the conception and birth of each of these men? Is it possible that God suspended His rules concerning man's "freedom of choice" and actually predetermined the parentage and DNA of these families for generations?

Both Zarathustra and Jesus were exceptionally bright, even as children. They seemed to have an innate knowledge about things which they could not have been taught, and perspectives and awarenesses beyond those of their peers. Does the fact that both Zarathustra and Jesus had so little recorded about their childhood, adolescence or young adulthood perhaps reflect the circumstance that little out of the ordinary occurred at these times?

First the Spirit of God, Then the Temptation

But these were not common men in any way. It was as if their minds, bodies and souls had been prepared for the occasion when, by their individual free will, they sought and received the specialty for which they were born, the infusion of the spirit of God. The influx of knowledge described by Zarathustra, and that experienced by Jesus, are too extremely similar to be coincidental.

Isn't it fascinating that both, with their acceptance of their spiritual missions, were immediately challenged by the spirits of evil? Both men of God were offered worldly dominance and riches if they would desist from imparting their illumination to mankind.

Jesus was immediately led into the desert by the spirit, where He experienced His temptations.[15] Zarathustra was in the wilderness when He was tempted by Angra Mainyu.[16] In both cases, the "forces of evil" were able to tempt these men without the interruption of other humans.

The temptations were of a kind which the average person would find overwhelming. Consider what might have occurred to these men after the increase in their knowledge and vision, perhaps like the digesting of a modern encyclopedia from several thousands of years into the future. In addition to receiving vast amounts of scientific, physical and intellectual knowledge, they had also obtained the spiritual gifts and understanding that would allow them to preach, teach, heal and attract the multitudes.

Is there a possibility that the records of the temptations attribute an inner conflict to an anthropomorphic "devil," which might better be understood by their followers and other peoples of their time? Or, since a man's thoughts are in fact his reality, might these blessed individuals have needed an actual outside force to properly process their inner temptations. But does it really matter?

In both cases, it would appear that there was less of a true temptation than a process of purification and consolidation of the infusion of the spirit of God. In neither case was there any hint of either individual being interested in the temptation, not even in the slightest.

Other Parallels

Other parallels between the ministries of Jesus and Zarathustra include, but are not limited to:

1. The citizens of their communities and native lands failed to appreciate and understand the teachings of Zarathustra and Jesus at the inception of their ministries. Both prophets were required to travel to neighboring lands where their messages could be shared and appreciated.

2. Neither intended to start a new religion; both openly declared that their mission was to reform the religion of the lands of their birth, which had become corrupted by time and the manmade alterations of the clergy. When the latter occurs in any faith, it is often not for ulterior reasons such as greed and power. It can occur in total innocence, when there is the need to explain a new concept or to further elucidate an old one. The very passage of time seems to demand these manmade redefinitions by the clergy.

3. Both Zarathustra and Jesus were known for their ability to heal the sick and raise the dead, and performed these miracles for much of their ministries.[17] As we have seen in previous chapters, Jesus also taught the art of healing to His Apostles.[18] Zarathustra likewise communicated to His priests the power of healing through the use of the laying on of hands, the arts of surgery and herbology and of the chanting of healing prayers. The Magi, for many centuries, were known to possess this gift, although, outside of their domain, they were sometimes considered to be sorcerers and magicians.[19]

4. Each Man promised a return. Zarathustra made it plain that His return was to be the return of the spirit within Him. The Avesta states:

Greater Bundahishn, XXXIII:36 "As regards these three sons of (Zarathustra), such as Aushedar, Aushedar-mah, and Soshyant, one says, 'Before (Zarathustra) wedded, they had consigned the glory (spirit, khwarrah) of (Zarathustra) for preservation, in the sea Kayansah to the glory of the waters, that is to the Yazad Anahit.'

XXXIII:37 They say, 'Even now they are seeing three lamps glowing at night in the bottom of the sea. And each of them will arrive when it is their own cycle.'

XXXIII:38 It will so happen that a virgin will go to the water of Kayansah in order to wash her head; the glory (khwarrah) will mingle within her body, and she will be pregnant. The will one-by-one be born thus in their own cycle."[20]

Jesus spoke of His return in less detail, but the Bible records the same promise:

Mark 13:26 "And then shall they see the Son of man coming in the clouds with great power and glory.

Mark 13:27 And then shall he send his angels, and shall gather together his elect from the four winds, from the uttermost part of the earth to the uttermost part of heaven."[21]

5. Each religion encouraged its followers to say their prayers through the auspices and person of its founder, such as "this we ask in the name of Jesus Christ our Lord."[22] Likewise, in the Zarathustrian religion:

Farvardin Yasht, XXX:152 "We worship Zarathustra, the lord and master of all the material world, the man of the primitive law; the wisest of all beings, the best-ruling of all beings, the brightest of all beings, the most glorious of all beings, the most worthy of sacrifice amongst all beings, the most worthy of prayer amongst all beings, the most worthy of propitiation amongst all beings, the most worthy of glorification amongst all beings, whom we call well-desired and worthy of sacrifice and prayer as much as any being can be, in the perfection of his holiness."

This particular prayer goes on to say:

XXX:153 "We worship this earth; we worship those heavens;

We worship those good things that stand between (the earth and the heavens) and that are worthy of sacrifice and prayer and are to be worshipped by the faithful man.

XXX:154 We worship the souls of the wild beasts and of the tame. We worship the souls of the holy men and women, born at any time, whose consciences struggle, or will struggle, or have struggled, for the good."[23]

6. Both promised a continuation of life for the soul after the physical death of the body. Both stated that one's place in the afterlife was greatly enhanced by a righteous earthly life, although there were some differences of emphasis within their respective definitions of that righteous life. In both cases, these concepts were in opposition to the teachings of the clergy of their respective times.[24]

7. Another great parallel between the two religions is the positivity of the teachings of both Zarathustra and Jesus. Both came to times and places in which the religions of their people were primarily rules and laws of the "don'ts" of life. They both taught that good things should dominate your life decisions because of your love of God, rather than out of fear of His wrath. Although both espoused a belief in the importance of justice, they encouraged man's spiritual maturation by accentuating the positive aspects and rewards of their religions.

8. The greatest parallel has to be that each spoke in terms of universality of God (or Ahura Mazda) and His Creation. While there were ethnic exclusions that prohibited conversion of non-Aryans to Zarathustrianism, it was very clear that the God of this faith was the God of all faiths. [25] Jesus specifically broke with the Jewish exclusivity of the time by preaching to and about, and accepting one and all into his flock without discrimination.[26]

God

The concept of God, as presented by both Men, was more than parallel. Both believed that God was spirit, should not be represented by an image, or an idol. Further, both men stated that there was pure spirit within every man that differentiated mankind from the rest of the physical creation. Both men taught that we are far more than just physical beings; that we have a spiritual component, our soul. And that therein lies our likeness to God.

> "Man's composition, according to the system of Zoroastrian religion, is of a triple character—material, vital and spiritual—body, life and soul. As his spiritual parts were created before his material and vital parts, they are undying. They combine with his physical parts at birth and separate at his death. Of these spiritual parts the principal are utvan, the soul, and fravashi, the spirit, with their several faculties such as manas, the mind, and bodha, conciousness. The living body [tanu] is to the soul [urvan] and the spirit [fravashi] what an instrument is to the worker, or the horse to the rider, or a house to its master. In this classification are discerned all the elements of the modern tripartite division of man's personality into reason, feeling and will."[27]

To this Zarathustra speaks:

"O Mazda, when I was looking for you with my wisdom and speculation faculties and tried to find you with the eye of my heart, I recognized that you are the starter and the end of everything, you are the source of wisdom and reflection, and you are the creator of truthfulness and purity, and the judge and justice for the behavior of all the human beings."[28]

It was the view of Zarathustra that the God whom He called Ahura Mazda was none other than that which the Jews referred to as Jehovah, and earlier, Yahweh. While He believed that God was one, not many, He had understanding of and compassion for the polytheistic beliefs of such as the Romans and Greeks.

While Zarathustra professed that God was one, not many, He was able to accept and tolerate other faiths. Nowhere does the Avesta record any suggestion that the good and pious can be found only among the believers of the Zarathustrian Faith. This magnanimous attitude displayed excellent public relations and compassion, as well as an astute diplomacy. What better way to work in peace with your fellow man than to find areas of agreement, and to then work out strategies which allowed the dissipation of ideological barriers and the resultant distrust?

The impact of Zarathustra's teachings on the Persian Empire has been made clear through the recently excavated records of the rulers of the Achaemenian Dynasty. Cyrus II, for example, upon his assumption of the role of Emperor following the defeat of the Babylonian Empire, promulgated:

> "Now that I put the crown of kingdom of Iran, Babylon, and the nations of the four directions on the head with the help of (Ahura) Mazda, I announce that I will respect the traditions, customs and religions of the nations of my empire and never let any of my governors and subordinates

look down on or insult them until I
am alive." "...Today, I announce that
everyone is free to choose a religion.
People are free to live in all regions and
take up a job provided that they never
violate other's rights. No one could be
penalized for his or her relatives' faults.
I prevent slavery and my governors and
subordinates are obliged to prohibit
exchanging men and women as slaves
within their own ruling domains. Such
a tradition should be exterminated the
world over. I implore to (Ahura) Mazda
to make me succeed in fulfilling
my obligations to the nations of Iran
[Persia], Babylon, and the ones of the
four directions."[29]

Much of what has been written in this book, up to this point, may
seem to be at variance with the Christian belief in the "God incarnate"
status of Jesus. Here a new perspective is offered which is that, after
the infusion of the spirit of God, both Jesus and Zarathustra were of
a special duality, by which they were able to speak as, and for, God
at the same time that they were capable of speaking as common men
like you and I. In this way, from the time of infusion, they were both
human and "as God." Their very natures were changed. Jesus says:

John 12:44 "Jesus cried and said, 'He that believeth on me,
believeth not on me, but on him that sent me.

John 12:45 And he that seeth me seeth him that sent me.

John 12:46 I am come a light into the world, that whosoever
believeth on me should not abide in darkness.'"

The next verse is usually not included in excerpts of this passage, but probably should be:

12:47 "And if any man hear my words and believe not, I judge him not: for I came not to judge the world but to save the world."[30]

Prophets, Theologians, Manifestations, or Philosophers?

Since Zarathustra did not claim to be starting a new religion, He is sometimes considered by students and academics in the Western World to be a philosopher, or, at most, a prophet, but not a manifestation of God or the founder of a new religion. His mission, as He understood it, was to find and purify the truths of the old Mazdayasnian religion and to add to them what He interpreted as the wishes of Ahura Mazda. He sought to return the belief of His people to the monotheistic tradition which it had observed thousands of years before. These facts, combined with the non-proselytizing aspects of what became the Zarathustrian Faith, seem to make a case for the calling of His belief system a philosophy by the scholars, detractors and theologians of other religions. After all, these people would ask, is not the purpose of all religion to bring new peoples into that faith system? However, there was an ethnic exclusion to this religion for over 2,000 years, and therefore, Zarathustra seemed far more interested in spreading the philosophy that was the basis of His Faith than in bringing an ever increasing membership of new believers, peoples and nations.[31] Add to this the seeming acceptance of the beliefs of other religions and their deity or deities as promoted by Zarathustra, might it not seem logical that He should be considered a philosopher only?

How is this different from Jesus' mission? Jesus was born, and worshipped as, a Jew. If His purpose had been the creation of a new religion, might He not have openly withdrawn from Judaism and become the first member of His Christian Church? The sermons offered in the Gospels of Matthew, Mark and Luke indicate that Jesus was attempting to return the Judaic laws and society of His time to earlier traditions of Moses, David and Isaiah, placing less emphasis on the content of the law and much more on the love and praise of God. The existing beliefs could have easily been given new direction from His teachings. Had the Pharisees been able to hear fairly His words and protestations, might He not have been recognized as a new prophet?

Several Questions Concerning the "What Ifs"?

What if either Man had been heard and understood by the people in His country of birth? How might this have changed His ministry, not to mention the history of the world? Let's consider a few of the possibilities, for mankind as a whole and for ourselves as individuals.

1. **What if** the message of Jesus had been heard by the Jewish Nation alone? Would He have been considered the return of Elijah?[32] With an admission of this would he have had the backing of the Chief Priests? How might this have affected the Jewish people, and would this have reduced the threat to the Roman Empire? Would the Temple in Jerusalem therefore not have been destroyed for a second time, and the Diaspora or scattering of the peoples of Israel been avoided?

2. **What if** the message of Jesus had been heard and believed by the Emperor of Rome in the days of His ministry? In this scenario, the teachings of Jesus might have aroused the curiosity of the Emperor to the extent that He was offered safe passage to Rome. What if the Emperor had been so struck by the message of Jesus that he converted, as did Vishtaspa upon hearing the words of Zarathustra? Might Jesus have been appointed as Imperial Counselor and taken up residency in Rome?

3. **What if** the message of Jesus had been heard and understood by the majority of all peoples? In this scenario, His message could have brought "Peace on Earth," and if this "Peace" had been lasting, there would be little question as to His station as the Messiah.

For that matter, what if either Man's message had been universally heard, understood and believed? The terrible carnage of war might have been reduced, and because many of the world's youngest, healthiest and brightest would not have died, it might have resulted in discoveries in science, medicine, and all of the arts.

Greatest Differences Between the Two Men of God

1. The length of their ministries and hence, the amount of time available to each for revelation.

2. The acceptance of the Zarathustrian Faith by King Vishtaspa, whereby Zarathustra was afforded the protection and encouragement of the monarch during the largest part of His ministry. He had no need to be careful of what was overheard or what miracles were performed. His counsel was sought and made use of in the generation of state decisions and policies. Jesus was under constant threat from both the power of Rome, the house of Herod, and from the Jewish High Priests and secular officials.

3. Zarathustra had the advantage of dictating great amounts of revealed doctrine, knowledge and prayers, and the chance to edit or correct same. There were priests eagerly awaiting whatever was said or revealed by Him. There was no such editorial advantage for Jesus, and the Gospels remained an oral tradition for many years after His death.

4. The confirmation of Zarathustra as a teacher/priest and the founder of His religion by historians of other nationalities was geographically widespread. The historical confirmations of Jesus are almost totally dependent upon Christian sources, with only very minor mentions in Jewish history.[33] There was little mention of Jesus, His teachings, His followers or the effect of His ministry

from any of the great chroniclers of history neither during His time nor immediately after. How different is the historical coverage of the two Men in the religious and history books of today, wherein Zarathustra is all but forgotten.

Most of the above were differences in favor of Zarathustra, in that they were circumstances which were available to Him but not to Jesus. Mindful of this, how great should be our appreciation of the accomplishments of Jesus? Today, Christianity has representation throughout the world, which is absolutely amazing considering the shortness of His ministry.

The INCARNANCY of Jesus and Zarathustra

In the preceding chapters, we have discussed the early lives of Jesus and Zarathustra and their special qualities from conception and birth, through the infusion of the spirit of God. We have had the chance to study their ministries and the many parallels between them. It is the premise of this book that the source of guidance during their ministries was basically the same for each, that is, the infusion of the spirit of God. Differences in revelation and their resultant religions are primarily due to the differences in the length of their ministries, and differences with respect to the societal and religious maturity of mankind at the time of their ministries.

🎔 CHAPTER 7 🎔

INFLUENCES OF TWO MEN AND THEIR RELIGIONS

As similar as the doctrines and teachings of the Christian and Zarathustrian Religions are, their influences, longevity and their histories are as dissimilar as night and day. The reasons for this are many, and much accurate history has been lost with the passage of centuries for both. But it can be said that both Jesus and Zarathustra and their religions have left their mark.

The short ministry of Jesus (one and a half to three years)[1] went basically unnoticed for almost 300 years, during which time his influence was minor because of the small number of followers and because of the harassment and persecution from the Roman Empire.[2] This changed dramatically at the time of the conversion of Roman Emperor Constantine (313 AD). In contrast, Zarathustra's ministry of approximately forty years was well chronicled throughout the civilized world of his day and for the next 1,500 to 2,000 years.[3] His lengthy ministry had the protection of King Vishtaspa and gave rise to what became known as the Persian-Median Empire which influenced many religions and the politics of many nations for centuries. King Vishtaspa of Bactria, who was the first and most important convert to the Faith of Zarathustra, because of his special depth of understanding of his new religion, started the Empire building process.[4] Thanks to the fertility of the land of the Medes and Persians, which included much of what is now called the Fertile Crescent (northern Iraq, northern Iran and the Steppes of Russia), their famous horses, and the forty plus year ministry of Zarathustra, the Empire grew in strength both in geography and manpower.[5] The Medes' army marched down the Tigris River in 614 BC, capturing the city of Assur. In August 612 BC, under the leadership of Cyaxares, the army seized Nineveh, the capital of the Assyrian Empire.[6] The Median Empire now enjoyed its maximum size extending from the

Black Sea to the Persian Gulf and being bordered on the west by the Lydian Empire, on the east by the desert, and on the south by the Babylonian Empire. This extremely valuable territory contained copper, iron and tin mines and included what is today most of Iraq, Iran, Armenia and Anatolian Turkey as well as parts of Saudi Arabia. This was in the era of King Nebuchadnezzar of Babylon, who had invaded Israel, destroyed the Temple in Jerusalem and taken many of the Jewish people back to Babylon as slaves.[7]

Surprisingly, the Medes had become less open to the total teachings of Zarathustra than their ethnic cousins, the Persians, who under Cyrus the Great [Cyrus II] defeated the Medes and took over their Empire in 550 BC. Under the guidance of Cyrus II, who truly followed the teachings of his Faith, the Empire grew to become the largest Empire of its time.[8] Cyrus II treated the Medes as a partner, not as the defeated nation that they were. This kind treatment led to the often used biblical term of linkage, "the Medes and the Persians."[9] Both of these peoples were known for their purity of character and the immutable nature of their laws, which even the king could not alter without the consent of his government or the Chief Priests.

Zarathustrian Influence on Judaism

There was interaction between the Jewish people and those of the Persian Empire in many ways over the years. Sometimes, it was primarily in trade and commerce, and at other times it was in other fields such as education and medicine; these were fields of human endeavor strongly encouraged by both peoples. The best known interaction came in the time of the Jewish Prophet, Isaiah, when under the lead and insistence of the Persian King Cyrus II, the Jewish captives in Babylon were released and allowed to return home.[10] The year was 539 BC, and Cyrus II not only saw that the Jews were released from Babylon, but also signed a decree legally allowing and encouraging the rebuilding of the Temple in Jerusalem which Nebuchadnezzar had destroyed.[11]

For his clemency to subdued nations, and also his deeds on behalf of the returned captives, Cyrus II earned the title of "Yahweh's Shepherd" (Isa. 44:28) and His "Anointed" (Isa. 45:1).[12] He reversed the Babylonian policy of deporting conquered peoples, and actually welcomed them at his court. When they were qualified, he entrusted them with posts of important responsibilities. He allowed and encouraged Babylonian captives to return to their homelands. This was true not only of the Jews, but also the captured Lydians, Armenians, and Greeks.[13] By encouraging the rebuilding of the Jerusalem Temple, Cyrus II set an example of compassion, which was totally within the parameters of his Zarathustrian belief, especially considering that the Jewish people were most like him in their belief in the one Creator, even though by a different name. There is no way of knowing how many of his deeds were the result of being an enlightened wielder of power, and how much were the result of a conscious effort on his part to do that which would bring Joy to Ahura Mazda. Does it really matter?

With the assistance of a healthy donation from Cyrus II, and under the authorization of that edict directly from him (2 Chron. 36:20-22), reconstruction of the Jerusalem Temple commenced. What influence the Jewish Faith had upon the religion of Zarathustra during this period of interaction does not have documentation; however, it has been stated that there was a great influence upon the Judaic religion from Cyrus II and his Zarathustrian Faith concerning[14]:

a)   the introduction of the concept of the Messiah, prior to this the Jewish people looked forward to the emergence of a strong political leader from the House (lineage) of David to defeat their enemies and thus regain their freedom from foreign domination.[15]

b)   the introduction of the concept of Satan.[16]

c)   the Book of Job, origins of which are a total mystery as to its source, author, age and country of origin. The reasons for considering its origin to be from Zarathustrian sources are allusions to the laws and practices mentioned, as well as its location being in Edom, that land at the south end of the Dead Sea, and the land of Moab and on the north of the land of Midian [modern Iraq]. These were both in the Persian Empire at the time. God is not referred to as "Yahweh" in the poem proper, only in the prologue and the epilogue. Where various terms for God are used, the term is often the deity that comes from Teman in Edom. There is a very strong Arabic or Aramaic influence in the language used and the antiquity of the oral form of this story is most likely from between 700 and 400 BC, when the question of divine earthly retribution, both national and individual, was of general concern.[17]

d)   the introduction of the concept of the resurrection of the dead upon the coming of the Messiah.[18]

Whether the whole Book of Job has as its source the religion of Zarathustra will be difficult to prove without proof from further archeological discovery. The timing for its inclusion in the Bible is most likely sometime after the intercession of Cyrus II with the Babylonians on behalf of the captured Jewish people.[19] It should be noted while the concept of Satan is introduced in the Book of Job, this entity appears to have had little significance on Judaism until the time of Jesus.[20]

With the defeat of the Medes in 550 BC, Cyrus II acquired Assyria; he then proceeded to conquer Lydia, which gave him possession of the Greek seaboard cities of Asia Minor. Then finally in 539 BC, proud Babylon, capital of the Chaldean Empire, surrendered without a battle owing to the reputation for compassion and financial gain for those who did not oppose the Persian tide of Cyrus II.[21] It was at this time in 539 BC that Cyrus II by edict established the world's first Declaration of Human Rights, calling for:

1. Total Freedom of Religion, even within families.

2. The abolition of slavery.

3. The establishment of education for all children.

4. The equality of women and men.

5. The right for any nation that wished to leave the Empire to do so, and for any nation that wished to join the Empire the right to do so.[22]

With the fall of Babylon, Cyrus acquired Palestine, and at this point, he turned eastward to extend the borders of the Empire to India. Cyrus II was killed while fighting against eastern nomads in 529 BC, and was buried in a simple tomb in his capital of Pasargadae. The empire building continued unabated in the short seven year reign of his son, Cambyses II, who crossed the Sinai and captured in a quick conflict the nation of Egypt. The reign of Cambyses II lasted for just over a decade, at which point, we have the rise of Cyrus' grandson, Darius I.[23]

Darius I

The next great ruler with Zarathustrian ties to have a major effect upon the Judaic world, Darius I, had to seize the crown of the Persian Empire, which had been usurped by Magian pretenders in late 522 BC. These Magi had started their rebellion during the time of Cyrus II. One of the first campaigns of Darius I was to return the Magi to being a purely religious order and then to retrace the steps of his grandfather, Cyrus II, demanding not only renewed allegiance from the Babylonians, but also to the Jewish people those assets not fully released at the time of their release by Cyrus II. These assets rightfully were the property of the Jewish people and were necessary for the completion of the temple in Jerusalem. With his encouragement the Jerusalem Temple was completed in the sixth year of his reign.[24] This was not accomplished without problems, for there were many complaints lodged against the rebuilding by Tatnai, a governor appointed by Cyrus II, and other complainants.[25] Darius I searched through the well-kept archives of Cyrus II where he found the original decree roll authorizing the work.[26] A new edict forbidding further hindrance to the Temple rebuilding was issued along with a very generous contribution from the Persian treasury towards the completion of the Jewish Temple.[27]

Darius I was a contemporary of the Hebrew prophets Haggai (Hag. 1:1, 2:1-10) and Zechariah (Zech. 1:1, 1:7, and 7:1). He recorded his deeds in a triangular inscription on an almost inaccessible limestone rock above the Iranian village of Behistun. These inscriptions boast of his triumphs, the organization of his far-flung empire, but also are the key to many little known languages of western Asia. They contain carved depictions of Persian power and of his worshipping Ahura Mazda in the presence of royal prisoners. The first English transcription of this detailed account began in 1844 and was completed in 1852 by Henry Rawlinson; it was written in ancient Persian, cuneiform Babylonia and two dead languages: Elamite and Akkadian.[28]

The first two years of the reign of Darius I were occupied with the securing of the borders of his realm militarily; he then turned to securing it economically and governmentally. Under his rule, the Empire flourished. His greatest work was perfecting that system of governance initiated by Cyrus II, by which the empire was divided into twenty provinces [called satrapies], each ruled by a satrap [governor]. He sent officials on regular visits to the satrapies to observe and report back the progress of each. The satrapies paid a fixed annual tax to Darius, and supplied soldiers for the king's armies. Phoenicia, Egypt and the Greek colonies supplied ships and sailors for his burgeoning fleet. From the gold received annually, he minted coins. Commerce was encouraged by the establishment of standardized weights, measures and monies, the founding of a postal system, as well as the building of highways and aqueducts, and the completing of a canal from the Nile River to the Red Sea. All of this won him the goodwill of large portions of the heterogeneous population of the Empire. He was honored not only by the Jews, but also the Egyptians, whose High Priest he was known to have consulted, and by the Greeks whose Oracles gave him support during the revolt by the Greek city states.[29]

Darius II

Years later, a descendant became Emperor Darius II. He was an effective administrator, but not a great king. His understanding of the Zarathustrian Faith was good, although it does not appear to be nearly as extensive nor as decision altering as his predecessors. While he made a grand performance of his religious belief, it appears that this was basically for show. His reign was in the late 400s BC, and because of his lack of passion for the Faith of Zarathustra, there was a decline in its influence and a decay of the moral fabric of the Persian society. As morals decayed, the cohesiveness of the Empire also deteriorated. Now, rebels in the provinces needed to be bought off instead of being sternly but fairly dealt with.

Darius III

Darius III (in the late 300s BC) was a weakling, in religion and leadership, according to most historians. It was he who was on the throne when Alexander the Great of Macedonia led his powerful army into Asia. In 333 BC, Darius III led his troops against Alexander in the battle of Issus, wherein Alexander captured the western half of the Persian Empire. Darius is said to have fled the battlefield during the heat of battle. At Arbela (321 BC), Darius III again led his troops against those of Alexander and again, he fled the battlefield. It should be no surprise that Darius was murdered by a follower and member of his own army, thus bringing to an end the Persian Empire.[30]

The Persian army and all of the massive naval fleet may have been captured or destroyed by the forces of Alexander for both mysteriously disappeared along with a vast majority of the clergy, royalty and Persian Intelligencia. All seemed to have simply vanished into thin air. Is it possible that Darius III created a stalling action that allowed the escape of thousands of people as well as hundreds of military and merchant ships?

Zarathustrian Influence On Christianity

As shown throughout much of this book, the parallels between the teachings of Jesus and Zarathustra are far too great to be simple coincidences. Much more intellectual and spiritual investigation should be conducted into such matters as the introduction of doctrines as confession, atonement, redemption, and contrition; the concept of the "Angelic Hosts," and the inclusion of the immediate afterlife with all its many possible variations. Were these the result of the inspiration and revelation from God, or did a portion come from some sort of training suggested or facilitated by the Magi, and made available to Jesus during his Egyptian stay? Was the direction of teachings in any way influenced by those followers attracted to him from former Zarathustrian lands, many of whom may have been awaiting the start of his ministry? All of the above are possible. But then again, if Zarathustra was correct, then the inclusion into Jesus of the same Spirit with which He had been infused could be explanation enough!

Well Defined Afterlife – Heaven, Purgatory and Hell

Little of what is found in modern Christianity on these subjects was found in the Jewish faith prior to the time of Jesus, although this was a time of tremendous interest in these subjects. The concepts were given great importance in the short ministry of Jesus, and were more fully defined in letters of the apostle Paul.[31] The comparisons of Heaven, Hell and Purgatory as religious realities should become even clearer with the Religion Comparison chart in Chapter 8 of this book.

The Introduction of Angels, and the Other Heavenly Hosts

Biblically speaking, with the exception of the Creation story in Genesis, there is little or no mention of angels, archangels and cherubim, nor any other spiritual assistance to God prior to the New Testament. The fact that the concept of a spiritual realm may owe its very introduction and religious reality to the religion of Zarathustra is given little credit from Christian pulpits, and yet belief in angels was accepted by Jesus, and was a part of His teachings. The first mention of the angels in the New Testament was in the Nativity Story, where the angel of the Lord appeared unto Joseph in his dream (Matt. 1:24-25), and to the shepherds in the field (Luke 2:8-15). Whether this was an accepted concept at the time of the birth of Jesus, or a term used after the beginning of His ministry to explain the story of the dream of Joseph and the vision of the shepherds, there is no way of knowing. Suffice to say that the term "angel" definitely was a part of the religious vernacular from the time of Jesus.[32]

These angels were considered as blameless "sons of God," and were said to have certain spheres of expertise, as well as different ranks, dominions and powers. These "sons of God" or spiritual beings were normally the bearers of heavenly duties, although it was possible for them to fall from grace as Satan did, as well as many who became his assistants.[33] They, too, would have their own specialties and Domains, although much of this detail seems to have come after the direct preaching of Jesus.

Recent Influences of Zarathustra upon Individuals

Friedrich Nietzsche was a well respected German philosopher in the mid-1800s who wrote a book entitled, *Also Sprach Zarathustra: Ein Buch fur Alle und Keinen* (Thus Spoke Zoroaster: A Book for

All and None) [1883 (part 1) through 1885 (part 4)], which was originally published in four parts separately. It was not published as a complete edition until 1892.

Nietzsche had as his focus that segment of society of which he was a highly respected member, the "Intelligencia," the so-called upper class of Europe. This was a period of time which found most of the members of this group, which included professors, doctors, artists, people successful in business and those with inherited wealth, politicians and judges, those who considered themselves to have "class," sneering at religion and those who considered themselves to be religious. Their comments often were super sarcastic. While voicing their opinion that both religion and spirituality were things for the "masses," such as the peasants and "ne'er-do-wells," they believed the only real place or reason for religion was to keep "those people in their place," and from rising up to riot and create great damage. The same intellectuals continued to make use of the churches for their own marriages and funerals, because functions required a physical location of decent size, and they made use of the services of the pastor, priest or Rabbi so that they could make use of the location. The fact is, it was often openly stated in so-called polite society that it seemed very likely that "if God had actually ever existed, he was now DEAD." The "God is dead" attitude was so pervasive among the learned, the wealthy and the powerful throughout Europe and most of the Western World in the 1870s, 1880s and 1890s, that this subject was a laughable conversation piece at their many parlor soirees. It was into that "intellectual atmosphere" that Nietzsche threw his literary bombshell. [34]

Also Sprach Zarathustra contains many quotes which sound as if they could have a Zarathustrian source; however, it has yet to be located. The tone of the writing is often sarcastic and quite negative, definitely not the tone of Zarathustra. Possibly, the sarcasm was something that Nietzsche thought was necessary in order to attract his focus audience. Even so, much of the content could have a Zarathustrian source, either through the many translators who had or were translating the Pahlavi texts of Zarathustra's works such as the Gathos into German, French, English and other languages at that time.[35] Many of the subjects discussed in the book seemed to have roots, or at least parallels, with subjects totally foreign to Christianity, but of a definite Zarathustrian tone. However, at the point of the publication of the entire book, Nietzsche, in a letter to a friend, colleague and professor of philology, Erwin Rohde, stated "Everything in the book is my own, it is without prototype, comparison, predecessor; who has once lived in it will come back to the world with a different face".[36] The interpretation now given to this statement by many students of Nietzsche is that the book is a total fiction.[37]

Because of Nietzsche's enthusiasm and reputation the very people who considered themselves to be the thinkers of the world, reversed their public opinions concerning the death of God and the role of religion. They became enthralled with the subjects so poetically presented, even though the ideas did not in any way flatter their peer group. They grabbed for the concept of there still being a God, and embraced enthusiastically the concept of a God who was not only continuing to create, but making use of man to assist Him in so doing. They publicly found tremendous logic in the concept that man should use his God given talents to actively take part in that continuing creation and that the Will of God would become a reality even if God by Himself needed to create a new race of men. There was a perverse delight in the fact that here was religious thought that was both older than and totally unrelated to Christianity, Judaism or the Bible, and seemingly far more logical than what they found in those sources.[38]

Most intriguing was that the new race of man desired by God would truly be Supermen, the like of which had never been seen on earth. The new race of Supermen were to be created either by the preferred method of the careful and proper breeding of the best humans, male and female, with an eye to an ever advancing species, or strictly by the Hand of God.[39]

It was the concept of careful and proper breeding that found a special reception among these intellectuals, in that, herein, they found a reason to both live and love. It seemed only logical that they should be a very important part of that careful and proper breeding! Nietzsche's chastisement of the clergy was likewise an important attraction for the intellectuals who, in the following statement, found proof that the clergy had been leading the vast masses on a false path:

"You have served the mob and the mob's prejudices, you famous wise men—all of you! You have *not* served the truth, and precisely for that reason you are revered.

"Moreover they endured your lack of Faith because it was a witty detour leading to the mob. Thus a master may let his slaves do as they pleased and be amused by their presumptuousness.

"But there is one that is hated by the mob like a wolf by hounds: the free spirit who is hostile to fetters, who does not adore, who roams in the forests.

"To chase him from his hiding place was always 'a sense for righteousness' to the mob; even now they still sic their dogs with the sharpest teeth on him.

"For truth is manifest: isn't the mob manifest? Woe, woe to him that still searches—so they cried from time immemorial.

"You famous wise men—you wanted to substantiate your mob's claim to revere you; that was your 'WILL TO TRUTH.'"[40]

In the above, Nietzsche was saying that the clergy of the day were catering to the masses so that they could have the adoration of those same masses, as well as to keep them "in line." In addition, the "two theys" in the second paragraph of the quote seemed to refer to the upper class, who endured the lack of faith on the part of the clergy, because it diverted the attention of the masses from their sorry plight of poverty and manipulation, and was a source of humor to them (the upper class individuals).

So dramatic was the paradigm shift in thinking by the Intelligencia that one member, the talented composer Ricard Strauss, an ardent admirer of Nietzsche, wrote one of the truly great symphonic pieces of all time and gave it the same title as Nietzsche's book; it also took on the auxiliary title of *The 2001 Overture*.[41] This was in reference to a prophesy which Nietzsche purportedly made reference to, concerning the date of the fulfillment of the new race of man, the Supermen, that Ahura Mazda would raise up in the latter days. There are many experts who believe that *Also Sprach Zarathustra* had great influence on those in the fields of philosophy, psychology and physiotherapy at that time.[42] In the book, Nietzsche stated emphatically that man was part of an evolutionary process, from the God that never stopped creating, and was still creating, and would continue to create with man as his assistant, if possible:

"Zarathustra looked at the people and wondered. Then he said: 'Man is a rope, stretched between beast and Superman- a rope across an abyss.

"A dangerous cross-over, a dangerous on-the-way, a dangerous looking-back, a dangerous shuddering and stopping.

"What is great in man is that he is a bridge and not a goal; what can be loved in man is that he transcends and descends.

"I love those who do not know how to live except as descenders: for they are the transcenders.

"I love those who have great contempt because they have great reverence. They are arrows of longing toward the other shore."[43]

This quote served as a wake-up call to the Intelligencia, who previously had taken an attitude that they were the absolute end of creation, and most likely evolution; that there was nothing that would ever be better than they themselves, and the feeling and attitude that because of this, there was no need for a God, if there ever had been one. Throughout the book, Nietzsche is putting forth the thought provoking verses that sound very universal.

And likewise:

"Those who sacrifice themselves to the earth so that the earth may someday belong to the Supermen.

"I love him who lives so that he may become aware and who would become aware so that one day the Superman might live."[44]

It was the concept that a truly intelligent God was making use of man's capacity for goodness and intelligence in His process of continuous creation to raise up an ever advancing civilization that would ultimately evolve into His promised race of Supermen.

"And the immaculate perception of all things means to me that I want nothing from them except to lie spread out before them, like a mirror with a hundred eyes.

"Oh you hyper-sensitive hypocrites, you greedy Ones! You are not innocent in your desires and therefore you deny that you have desires!

"Truly, you do not love the earth as the workers do, and creators, who take delight in Becoming!

"Where will you find innocence? Where there is a desire to create? Whoever wants to create something beyond himself, has the pure will.

"Where will you find beauty? Where I must will with all my will; where I am willing to love and descend to the depths, so that an image may become more than just an image.

"Loving and descending they rime (sp) in all eternity. Will to love means will to death (die) That is what I say to you cowards!

"But your castrated ogling wants to be called 'the contemplative life!' And what ever allows itself to be touched by your cowardly eyes is to be baptized 'the beautiful' oh, how you have dirtied noble names!"[45]

Rather than feeling insulted, the intellectuals read, listened and thought because of the respect they had for Nietzsche. He had basically revived the God concept to the upper levels of European society. It was as if he had resurrected God! There were many of his peers who began returning to the Churches, both Christian and Jewish, while a great many more began religious quests, both within themselves by reading, and by traveling in search of the truths of other religions. There was an increase in the funding for the translation of not only the Zarathustrian texts, but also for many of the other known texts of ancient religions, especially those from the Far East, as well as a greatly increased funding for archeological projects.[46]

Where had Nietzsche's inspiration come from? How was he able to have so many Zarathustrian ideas? Whatever his source, the impact of his book throughout Western Europe and parts of the Americas was truly monumental. Many of the translators in the late 1880s were German or Austrian.[47] The influence of Nietzsche's book continued for several decades and was acknowledged by George Bernard Shaw, Jean Paul Sartre, and Max Scheler among others.[48] Many of the talks and studies of Zarathustra quoted in my book were done in the twenty-five years after the publication of *Also Sprach Zarathustra*. What ensued several decades after Nietzsche's death caused the enthusiasm and even the interest to die, or more accurately to be squelched.

After his death, Friedrich Nietzsche's notes and notebooks were taken by his sister, Elizabeth, and given to Nazi political propagandists to be altered and used to further the Nazi goals, with which Elizabeth and her husband were whole hearted sypathizers.

The words and meanings were changed such that it seemed as if the "Supermen and Superwomen" of Nietzsche were not only Germanic but were almost a super race already.[49]

When an individual has great influence on a major or powerful segment of society there will be among the influenced persons those who may misread or misuse the operative portion of the information in such a convoluted way that they not only corrupt the original influence, but sully its entire effect and credibility. The changes and misuse of Nietzsche's notebooks by the Nazi regime may have come close to discrediting both the author and his book, which had caused such a great shift in the philosophical and religious perceptions of both European and American Intelligencia for more than three decades.[50]

The Nazi propagandists' misuse of Nietzsche's book reached its zenith through the actions of our next individual.

Adolph Hitler

Adolph Hitler was so greatly influenced by Nietzsche's book that he stated that *Also Sprach Zarathustra* was a major factor in the writing of his book, *Mein Kampf*, and thus in the establishment of the Third Reich and his overall mindset concerning anti-Zionism. This hate-filled philosophy had become extremely prevalent in the late 1800s, especially in the locality in which Adolph Hitler grew up (Vienna, Austria). The Anti-Jewish feelings were throughout Europe, however, they were extremely intense in Vienna. The concept of racial purity as a necessity for the advancement of humankind had found as its scapegoat, people of Jewish extraction.[51]

Anti-Semitism reached towards an apex in the hands of the composer, Richard Wagner, who articulated his beliefs in both his writings and his operas.[52] To Wagner, the Jewish race was an enemy of the purity of humanity, an enemy to be quarantined and avoided. If it was known that a person had even one quarter Jewish blood, they should not be hired and should be avoided as if they had the plague, according to Wagner.[53] In school Wagner had been a close friend of Friedrich Nietzsche, however, Wagner's growing anti-Semitism caused the end of that friendship.

In Vienna, this anti-Zionism was most visible because the Jewish population, which comprised less than 8 percent of the population, held a much larger percentage (probably over 60 percent) in such professions as journalism, law, and medicine between 1890 and 1910. It was in that political atmosphere that Karl Lueger was democratically elected mayor of Vienna in 1897 and held that office until his death in 1910 on a specifically and exclusively anti-Semitic platform. It was in Vienna that young Adolph Hitler first encountered the anti-Semitic literature that would be a driving force in his ordering the murder of six million of Europe's eleven million Jews. [54]

Had Hitler known what Nietzsche had written or that the Nazi propagandists had altered the book prior to its reprinting or had bothered to understand the real meaning of the actual writings of Zarathustra, how could history have been different? Hitler took what he wished from the rewritten *Also Sprach Zarathustra*, and then considered that he (Hitler) was the promised Messiah, who was to see to the raising up of the promised race of Supermen and Superwomen, who were to be physically perfect as well as mental giants. How could Hitler feel that military victories would provide for the domination of and therefore the salvation of the whole world by his race of Supermen and Superwomen? Would Zarathustra have found it incredulous that there were so many lies built upon lies, and huge misunderstandings of his teachings? Would Zarathustra have said that the Great Deluder, Ahriman had shown the true power that evil can have? In fact, had Ahriman once again influenced the thoughts, the words and the deeds of men, since it was not just one man, but to some degree a whole nation?

If there was any spiritual intercession it was the inverse of what Hitler would have liked. Not only did he lose his war of domination, but his treatment of the Jewish people in the Holocaust so affected the conscience of the world, that the Jewish people were allowed to both return to their homeland Palestine and establish the current state of Israel.

Were the forces of Ahriman still at work in what happened in Nazi Germany? Are they still at work, or are stupidity and narrow-mindedness alive and well? No matter how we answer those questions, the end result of Hitler's attempt to follow what he felt Zarathustra had prophesied, resulted in the fulfillment of biblically prophesied events. The return of Jewish people and the establishment of the State of Israel would most likely not have occurred without the many deaths of the Holocaust. Please do not think that this last statement is in any way an endorsement of the actions of Adolph Hitler, but merely an acknowledgment that the Will of God shall be done one way or another.

Modern Followers of Zarathustra

The number of acknowledged believers in the faith of Zarathustra as of 2010 is thought to be approximately 120,000, with the largest number of these to be found in the area in and around Bombay, India.[55] These Zarathustrians are known as the Parsi, meaning Persians. They continue to follow the tenets of the Zarathustrian faith, with its strong emphasis on the moral and intellectual education of their children, as well as the faithful execution of all of their daily duties in a way that would make Zarathustra proud. In every way, they attempt to lead lives that exemplify the need for prayer, and incorporate those concepts of "Good Thoughts, Good Speech and Good Deeds." Their charity to the poor is exemplary, and this is accomplished in a nation with such a great need of this. The Parsi are also respected for their spirituality, education, honesty and industriousness.[56]

There are many descriptions of the Parsi going to chant their daily prayers on the beach of the Indian Ocean. For example, the description attributed to the industrialist, Andrew Carnegie:

"This evening we were surprised to see, as we strolled along the beach, more Parsee than ever before, and more Parsee ladies, richly dressed, all wending their way towards the sea.... Here on the shore of the ocean, as the sun was sinking in the sea, and the slender silver thread of the crescent moon was faintly shining on the horizon, they congregated to perform their religious rites. Fire was there in its grandest form, the setting sun, and water in the vast expanse of the Indian Ocean outstretched before them. The earth was under their feet, and wafted across the sea, the air came laden with the perfumes of 'Araby the Blest.' Surely, no time or place could be more fitly chosen than this for lifting up the soul to the realms beyond the seas. I could not but participate with these worshippers in what was so grandly beautiful. There was no music save the solemn moan of the waves as they broke into foam on the beach. But where shall we find so mightily an organ, or so grand an anthem? How inexpressibly sublime the scene appeared to me and how insignificant and unworthy of the unknown seemed our cathedrals 'made with human hands' when compared with this looking up through nature unto nature's God! I stood and drank in the supreme happiness which seemed to fill the air. I have seen many modes and forms of worship—some disgusting, others saddening, a few elevating when the organ peeled forth its tones, but all poor in comparison with this. Nor do I ever expect in all my life to witness a religious ceremony which will so powerfully affect me as that of the Parsee on the Beach of Bombay."[57]

Another westerner, Samuel Laing, after observing the same mode of worship, was moved to say:

"Here is the ideal religious ceremony combining all that is most true, most touching and most sublime, in the attitude of man towards the Great Unknown. Compare it with the routine of an ordinary English Sunday, and how poor and prosaic does the latter appear!"[58]

The number of Zarathustrian believers has diminished greatly, but the beauty surrounding their practice of that religion has not. While the majority of the world's Zarathustrians are in India, there are still possibly 10,000 to be found in their native Iran.[59]

Thomas Alva Edison – Inventor Extraordinaire

Thomas Edison was an extremely prolific modern inventor, whose influence can literally be seen day and night around the world. He named his Electric company as well as the light bulbs it manufactured, Mazda Electric. Likewise, the most successful research and development company that the world had known up through 1910 was named the Mazda Development and Service Company by founder and major stockholder, Thomas Edison![60] This company assisted in, and shared, Edison's patent rights on not only electric lights, but, more importantly, the first viable system for centrally generating and distributing electricity, light, heat and power, which soon was built and sold to almost every country in the world. Among Edison's many other inventions were the Dictaphone, motion picture projectors, the talking movie projector, many advances in the telegraph, an electronic vote counting machine, the new and improved stock market ticker, the first phonograph, the first storage battery, the kinescope, the first silent film in 1904, and the ten-minute-long "talky" called "the Great Train Robbery." The Mazda Electric Company was bought by the company known as General Electric at which time, Thomas Edison became a major stockholder of that latter company.[61] Quite a feat for this once hyperactive child, deaf in one ear, and with less than 20 percent of his hearing in the other. He attributed his ability to concentrate on his physical and mental specialness, allowing him to develop and make use of his "out of the box thinking."[62]

The total number of patents attributed to Edison is 1093. The name "Mazda" appeared and was used from 1909 until 1945 by the General Electric Company.[63] Ironic? Yes, but not coincidental. The name was chosen by Edison in part because one of the names of Ahura Mazda, refers to the Eternal Light or "the God of Light." Edison was also impressed by the fact that Zarathustra taught that creation was an on-going process, and that man was to assist Ahura Mazda with that process. Edison was a voracious reader, thanks to not only his home schooling by his mother, but also because his father paid him for every book he read as a youth.[64] Whether he actually read any of the many translations of the writings of the prophet Zarathustra available at the time or read Nietzsche's book is not detailed in his biographies.

You may have noticed that all of the inventions mentioned were of tremendous commercial value. This was not a coincidence. Edison said that he learned his lesson from the failure of his first invention which was not commercially viable (at the time). That first invention was an electronic vote counting machine that he had designed for, but been summarily rejected by, the Massachusetts Legislature because the speed with which the results were given would upset the time-honored tradition of arm-twisting and other forms of influencing changes in votes during the delays due to the votes being counted manually.[65]

The inclusion of Thomas Edison in this chapter and even in the book is not because of his numerous extremely creative inventions, nor, even partially, because of the two companies that bore the name associated with Ahura Mazda, nor even because two of his inventions in just a few years were able to literally light up the whole world, but most importantly because of what he taught by example. This seventh of seven children did not learn to speak until he was almost four years old, and was so very different from most other children. He had a very large head, and extremely broad forehead. His handicaps of looks and behavior convinced his short-tempered schoolteacher that this overly active child's brains were scrambled, and so his formal schooling lasted only slightly more than ten weeks.[66] Modern medicine might well have diagnosed his condition as ADHD (Attention Deficit Hyperactive Disorder), at the very least, and would have slowed him down with prescriptions of Ritalin. This would have been a fate that was still far better than what most parents of his day would have found for him; a stable boy job and to be basically forgotten for the rest of his very existence.[67]

Luckily for Tom and the world, his father and mother were of a different mind.

Nancy Edison, his mother was a very religious woman, who felt that God had sent her a special child, and proceeded to spend an inordinate amount of hours teaching him the Bible and the three R's, while his father was slipping him a dime for every "real" (classic) book that he would read. Because of this, Tom made great use of the public library. By the age of twelve, he had read all of the works of Shakespeare, the World Dictionary of Science, Sear's History of the World, numerous volumes on the science of chemistry, Gibbon's *Rise and Fall of the Roman Empire*, and many more, with the total support of his proud parents, who were stymied by his insightful questions on physics as contained in Isaac Newton's *Principia* and therefore scraped together enough extra money to hire the services of a tutor of the sciences.[68]

In later years, when Edison could well afford an operation that would most likely have returned his hearing, he refused because he was fairly sure that hearing would be an unnecessary distraction to his concentration that had produced an average of one invention every two weeks from the inception of the Mazda Electric and Development Company. Thomas Alva Edison felt that most men's capacities were grossly under-utilized, that they worked with little idea of their self worth, and that people too often allowed those around them to diminish their capacities and potentialities. Many of his pronouncements and encouragements to his fellow workers concerning their latent capacities at Mazda Development sounded like the positive messages of Zarathustra. Despite his "Type A" personality, which kept him busy six days a week, fifteen to twenty hours a day, he found time to keep up with many friends; among the notables were President Herbert Hoover, Marie Curie, Charles Lindbergh and, most especially, Henry Ford.[69]

The life of Thomas Edison was full of events and incidents, many of which were life-altering. He seemed to know how to turn each to his advantage. One example is the day that the very young son of the train stationmaster wandered onto the tracks in front of an oncoming boxcar. At the age of thirteen, Tom jumped onto the tracks, grabbed and saved the child by rolling out of the way barely ahead of the wheels. As a reward, the grateful father taught him the Morse Code and the workings of the telegraph. Before long, this machine was Edison's key to his life full of inventions.[70]

Whether his choice of corporate names was because of his reading or other investigation, or a form of channeling Zarathustra, the beautiful description to his wife of what he saw ahead as he lay on his death bed could have come from Zarathustra himself. On October 18, 1930 at approximately 9 p.m., shortly before his death, Thomas Edison awoke from a coma, and quietly whispered to his wife, Nina: "It is very beautiful over there."[71]

A Giant of the Auto Industry Influenced by Zarathustra

The Toyo Cork Kogyo Company was founded in Hiroshima, Japan in 1920, and called its first three-wheeled truck, which was built in 1931, "Mazda," after the all-knowing God of Zarathustra.[72] The name "Mazda" was also used for their revolutionary car line, which emerged in the early 1960s. Little is known concerning the choice of the name, or the knowledge of those making the choice. No matter, for just as with Edison's ventures, this enterprise was built upon the inventive, totally out of the box thinking in both product and methods of manufacturing.

There have been and very likely will be thousands of people who will claim that their perspective on life or their creative selves were greatly influenced by Zarathustra. But once more there has been a straying from the purpose of this book, that of working with you to refocus your religious conclusions.

Jesus, His Effect and Influences

The influences and effects of the man named Jesus, and the religion based upon His teachings called Christianity, have filled numerous articles and books, many of which are excellent and well worth your consideration. Among the many influences of Christianity must be the billions of good and righteous individuals who have found what they needed to coexist with what they would have viewed as a chaotic, confused world. In addition, we must include the hundreds of thousands who have, because of their beliefs, stepped forward to live lives of service to the underprivileged, the handicapped, orphans and so forth; in other words, those many thousands who have placed the needs of their fellow man above their material desires. However, we will be concentrating on topics generally ignored in both theological and historical studies.

Private Prayer and Lessening the
Importance of Communal Prayer

A new perspective on prayer was introduced by Jesus, in that he taught that one should seek solitude when in prayer, so that the beseecher could focus wholly on the task at hand. His own example was obvious; He would arise early each morning for private prayer, and there were times when He would spend most of, if not the whole night, in private prayer. Just one of those occasions was on that night before he chose the twelve Apostles.[73] He taught that prayer should be a personal thing between man and his God, and that it should not be restricted to what one felt that they needed, but should be a request to know the will of God, and that could best be known by allowing an appropriate time and quietness to allow for an answer to become known. There was definitely still a place for the communal prayers encouraged by the Jewish and most other religions at the time. Jesus did not comment upon the appropriate posturing during prayer. It could be standing, kneeling or sitting, as long as the beseecher assumed fully the attitude of humility, reverence, sincerity, selflessness and faith.

Jesus was totally different than the Jewish prophets of old. While not accepting the mantle of the Messiah per se, and not claiming to be the return of Elijah or any other prophet, He created quite a conundrum for the Jewish leaders of His time. He readily admitted to having the Holy Spirit within Him, and, as such, claimed the right to speak for and as God. Unlike the promised Messiah of the Jewish faith, who was to rid Israel of foreign domination, and rule that nation if not the earth, He clearly stated that His kingdom was not of this world, and further that He had not come to unite the people, but to divide them. By such a claim, can you see how, for those who saw in Him the spirit of God, He was the Spiritual Messiah, and at the same time for those who were seeking an earthly leader, He was only a healer and a claimant of the impossible. For the latter, He was probably a little crazy, and because of the perspective of the Roman Empire, very likely a threat to the nation of the Jews. After all, He had many people believing that He was God Incarnate.

While it is true that Jesus came to refocus the Judaic Faith, it is also true that He offered many seemingly new ideas and spiritual concepts, with the admonition that those who chose to follow Him should seek out and follow the good and Godly path.

The New Definition of the Concept of Sin

Sin took on a new meaning in the Christian teachings in that it is evil, wrong and against the will of God, whereas in the Jewish Faith, then and now, a sin is a missing of the mark, such as when an arrow misses the bulls-eye. And, therefore, the only confession needed in the Jewish tradition is to apologize to the person offended or whom the sin was against. The severity, or at least recognition of such, is far greater in the faith which grew out of the teachings of Jesus, and therefore far closer to the concept of sin or wickedness of Zarathustra, wherein, Sin was an act (thought, word or deed) which was in opposition to the will of God, hence an act of ungodliness or unrighteousness.

The Crusades

After the death of Jesus, there were persecutions of the early Christians for several centuries. After the eventual conversion of the Roman Emperor Constantine in 313 AD, things went far smoother for a while for Christianity (see chapter 5), which is not to totally overlook the split by the Eastern Churches, nor the fact that there was a tendency for there to be a domination by the state into church affairs in such a way that there was a decline in education and general concern for the majority of peoples. In fact, literacy declined to the point that it was only the clergy and the aristocrats that were generally taught to read and write.

When the word came to western Europe of the capture of the Holy Lands and significant parts of Spain by the Moors and other Moslem peoples in 1090 AD, the Church (the Vatican) convinced the kings of Europe that there was a need to expel these invaders (whom they termed infidels) immediately.[74] Initially this was an effort embraced by most European Christian Kingdoms. Great armies were raised, trained and outfitted. It was not enough to count on their professional soldiers, for the size and strength of the armies of Islam were legendary; hence with the encouragement of the Church, recruitment came from the ranks of the lower class. Whether these recruits came from the countryside, where they had been peasant farmers and indentured servants (not much better than slaves), or from the unpaved streets of major cities with slums that had neither running water nor sewage, these masses of illiterate men of poor means marched forth with purpose and resolve to throw back the infidel hordes. Thus occurred what history books refer to as the Great Crusades. This long and bloody conflict was meant to replant the flags of Christendom upon what the church referred to as wrongly captured lands. What these Christian soldiers found when they arrived in such Moslem countries as Spain was its Alhambra, with its marvelous buildings of great beauty and design, beautiful fountains of clear fresh water fed by aqueducts that brought their contents from the mountains far away. They became aware that there were beautifully paved streets that were fully lit at night by gas lanterns. And finally, they became aware that there were sewers to take away excess water and human waste, a system of garbage collection but, most impressively, they found street signs and newspapers on newsstands everywhere that were apparently being read by even the common man. In addition, they discovered that Muslims, Christians and Jews were living and working together in the same city in peace and harmony.[75] Who and what had they come there to save? How did the term "infidel" fit the peoples of these marvelous cities?

Initially ignoring the question above, a fierce war ensued. It was fought on many fronts, and in many lands. There were victories by both sides, but also a tremendous amount of carnage. The vast Christian armies of Europe fought in Spain, across the Straits of Gibraltar, in Northern Africa, throughout the many Islamic countries of the Mediterranean, including Egypt and, finally, in Palestine, the land of Jesus himself.[76] Had there been a single Crusade, it is very possible that the memories of marvelous cities and other things of total wonder might have faded with time, however, the Crusades lasted until almost 1300 AD and thus involved generation after generation of soldiers.[77]

After much death and destruction on both sides in Spain, the lands of the Mediterranean and the Holy Land, the armies of Christendom returned to a Europe that would never again be the same. Education was demanded by the returning solders for themselves, but more importantly for their children. The Crusades were a major motivating factor for the cultural revolution known as the Renaissance, and then for the Industrial Revolution. The returning peasants would not, and did not, return to their lives without seeking both education and opportunity. No longer would they be satisfied with lives of total servitude and poverty. They wanted a better life for their children, if not themselves. To a degree, they began to find support from a clergy, which had become aware of the capacity and potentialities of mankind.

The common man had more than just educational and social desires. He had become armed with an increase in self worth and the ability to be able to read the Holy Words for himself; which then led to a rise in religious dissatisfaction with the Church. This did not generally affect the belief in Jesus, but in those who were His spokesmen, the clergy. It was in part because of this general religious dissatisfaction that Martin Luther was led to post his protests against the Roman Catholic Church that led to the Reformation.

The clergy, which had been subservient to both the Vatican and the royalty of the country in which they resided, became more assertive. Whether it was to promote the conversion of other peoples or to redirect attention away from themselves, they directed their attention as well as the attention of royalty, the landed gentry, the arising middle class, and also the common man to a new challenge to conquer the rest of the world.

Exploration and Colonization of the Earth

The spreading of Christianity after Constantine, from Rome to most of Western Europe, and then to all corners of the world, was due in part to the influence of the Christian clergy. The spread of Christianity was the excuse, or, more correctly, the rationale, given for the expenditure of vast amounts of monetary funds and the utilization of much manpower by many European nations. Vast sums were spent on the building of ships to be sent all over the globe for exploration and colonization. The crusades had ended by 1300 AD, and world travel had begun by the latter half of the 1400s. Would the world have been explored as rapidly if it had not been for the desire of the clergy to find new souls to teach the faith of Christianity? It is very likely that otherwise there would have been diversions of those same funds to wars between those same European nations, or the building of more palaces and cathedrals for the glorification of their rulers. There was a whole world out there, and most of the people were in need of finding Jesus, or so the leaders of France, Spain, Portugal, England and so forth were counseled by the clergy. The kings and rulers were not likely to go against what they became convinced was the Will of God. This very pious argument was not discouraged by the discovery of gold and other items of great value in the newly discovered lands. The riches included not only rare metals and gems, but also new and exotic foods and spices. Initially, it was the desire to do what appeared to be right and the will of God; the riches were merely the proof that the decision makers in the exploring nations had made the correct investment in men and ships.

The most obvious of these exploration discoveries by the various European nations might be in the Americas including the Caribbean Islands, since those were among the first. But these were soon followed by the rest of the world, including Australia, New Zealand, Micronesia, all the islands of every ocean. And there was full contact with Asia by sea, as well as the exploration of the continent of Africa. Wherever the explorers went, they brought priests and clergy to spread the faith of their country. This trend of expansion for the sake of Christian conversion went on from the time of Constantine, and the subsequent exploration, conversion and colonization of the rest of the world through the 1800s. It was through this process that Christianity was able to declare that it was truly well established throughout the globe by the mid-1800s.

Were there other reasons for the exploration and colonization than conversion? Absolutely! However, the driving force was the excuse of the religion of Jesus, which was fairly easily sold to the Nobleman and Commoners alike by their Christian clergy. There is no way of knowing whether the clergy's desire to "spread the Gospel" was a pure motive, or whether there were mixed in personal motives such as creating an advantage with their religious leaders, their kings or their God.

Social Maturity and Reawakening of the Western World

This is a point that can be looked at from many viewpoints; in that the Industrial Revolution, which occurred after the Crusades, was a time in which the Catholic Church had realized that science and discovery could not be stopped by the Inquisition and other fear based attempts at holding mankind's inquisitiveness in check. However, since this is off the point of this book, suffice it to say that the answer for the sake of this book is both yes and no. The "yes" is because with the awakening of the common man the whole structure of society changed. The Church (initially this refers to the Catholic Church, and after Martin Luther it refers to the Protestant Churches also) had been the basis for the creation of many of the laws of Europe, and had given legitimacy to the ruling monarchs, as long as they endorsed the Church. This was a delicate balance which was kept by both the church and the state, each for their protection. The Church, its properties and the clergy were protected by the rulers and their armies in the various Christian countries in which they were located. And the rulers and their countries looked for and received the spiritual endorsement of the clergy, should unrest arise, as long as the rulers showed a reasonable degree of justice and endorsement of the Church in return. There was a large problem with this working relationship, in that it tended to totally overlook the real needs and worries of the workers, peasants and eventually middle classes. This could well have been an added reason for the push by the clergy for the exploration, conversion and colonization of the rest of the World.

Religious Universality

The above was made possible by the non-ethnic approach to Religion, which was a definite part of the teachings of Jesus. This approach was initiated by Jesus with His choice of Apostles, with eleven of the twelve being from Galilee and thus likely to have been of mixed bloodline. Remember, even the term Galilee meant land of the Gentiles, it was the fertile land that the Jewish people had never captured, and had been the land that welcomed people of all ethnicity with very little prejudice. It had been the refuge for Jewish people married to non-Jews when the prophet Ezra had put out the edict that the only marriages that would be recognized were those in which both husband and wife were Jewish (450 BC). In addition, Galilee had been the place of refuge for Phoenicians, Lydians and Persians displaced at the time of Alexander the Great's military campaign. Part of the reputation for lack of virtue of Galileans was due to the fact that this ethnic melting pot did not have the same harsh oversight of virtues that were found in more "pure areas." This was one reason that Mary Magdalene was automatically considered to be a woman of ill-repute, merely because she was from Galilee. This was the land in which Jesus experienced his most successful ministry. Jesus sent His Apostles and the seventy known as His disciples throughout the Middle East, wherever there were ears to hear and eyes that could see that the Kingdom of God was at hand.

After the death and Resurrection of Jesus, this universality was continued by His followers. It was encouraged by Peter, as the head of the new Church, and with great gusto and effectiveness by Paul with his travels and letters to the Romans, Philippians, Thessalonians, Corinthians, Galatians, the Greeks and so on. This evangelical spread of the religion continued uninterrupted despite the tremendous persecution especially by the Roman Empire until 313 AD when the new Emperor of Rome followed the lead of his wife and converted to Christianity. The non-ethnic branches of Christianity have continued this university. Likewise Muhammad and His Islamic followers have done so with equal success.

❄ CHAPTER 8 ❄

THREE RELIGIONS COMPARED

Jesus and Zarathustra would have undoubtedly endorsed the concept that religion should never be the source of distress or conflict between peoples, even if they were from different faiths, nations or races. As such, They would have suggested that there was one thing that would help to mend the perceived differences between various peoples and that was that there be education, which would lead to understanding not only of cultural similarities and differences, but also an appreciation of the various religious beliefs being practiced throughout the world. To include all the major religions presently being practiced would divert the focus of this book, and, therefore, the number has been reduced to only those which we have been discussing—the Faith of Zarathustra, both the Roman Catholic and the Protestant Faiths of Christianity, and an important one which has received too little attention until this chapter, the Jewish Faith. However, it would be helpful to remember that, as Zarathustra so clearly stated, there is but one creation. Therefore, it should not be a surprise that all religions are full of tremendous similarities.

It is generally considered that Christianity has evolved directly out of Judaism, and therefore any differences must be the result of revelation. After all, Jesus was born a Jew, died a Jew and taught the Jewish people. While much of that is true, as you will discover in the balance of this chapter and in the included Religious "Comparison of Beliefs" Chart, there are many reasons to take a separate look at the Jewish Faith as you are refocusing your thinking. For one thing, Judaism maintains its belief in the central revelation, the first five books of the Old Testament, referred to as the Torah. The religious conclusions from the Torah are under constant Rabbinical review as to the real meaning of this basic core. The revisions to the Torah will be a reflection of and find relevance in the time and society in which an individual has been residing. This is in opposition to Christianity, which is setup to resist all change and is heavily dependent solely upon revelation.[1]

With the exception of Moses, the men chosen to have a special place in the Old Testament are called prophets. They saw it was their duty to see into the future for the sake of the Jewish people, and to forewarn them that their violations of the Mosaic Laws would be the cause of serious consequences. Moses is considered the author of the Torah, which includes the story of Creation, the laws of God as revealed by Moses, most of the history of the early Jewish people, as well as the division of the people according to God's Will into the twelve tribes. He had a special closeness to God, even though he did not feel worthy or capable to lead this people. In all, the so-called "books of Moses" take up 365 pages in my King James Version of the Bible, in comparison with 444 pages for the entire New Testament (the entire Old Testament has 1444 pages). Moses was the revealer of 613 laws, thus earning the title of the "Giver of Laws."[2]

Following the death of Moses, the Judaic teachings come from the four major Jewish prophets and are found in the books bearing their names—Joshua, Isaiah, Jeremiah, Ezekiel. Then there are those who are considered the twelve minor prophets—Hosea; Joel; Amos, the Judean fruit grower who first invoked the concept of exile, warning the Jewish people that their devotion to God was meaningless if not accompanied by sincerely just behavior; Obadiah; Jonah, who preached repentance, for, only then would God show the Jewish people mercy, and that was reluctantly after his failed attempt to avoid his calling as a prophet thereby causing his journey in the belly of a whale; Micah, who prophesied the destruction of Jerusalem; Nahum, Habakkuk, Zephaniah, Haggai, who prophesied the building of the second temple in Jerusalem and the end of the Persian empire; Zechariah, who urged the then impoverished Jews to rebuild the temple so as to bring on the Messianic age, and finally Malachi, who was the first prophet to suggest the importance of Elijah as a forerunner of the Messiah.[3]

Judaism tends to emphasize the individual as a part of the whole of society, rather than as an individual in isolation. Therefore, the prayer of a Jew should normally be a communal affair. Public prayer fulfills a universal human need. Jewish prayer rituals are specially designed to reinforce the sense of community. They are meant to lend meaning to a chaotic, arbitrary universe, as well as to offer the comfort of praying with like-minded worshippers.

The Jewish Faith

The Jewish Faith begins with the encounter between Abraham and God that resulted in the covenant of faith. Likewise, it details why this is the Faith of God, and that He is, in fact, the God of Abraham, the God of Isaac and the God of Jacob. The Torah relates the revelation to Moses on Mt. Sinai, when God began to give His Commandments.[4]

Note: Mitzvah is a command of God; mizvot is the plural of mitvah.[5]

The mitzvot guide Jews to fulfill life's purpose and mission to work to end all the ills and evils that beset the world; transform and perfect the world under the Kingdom of God; all of this in anticipation of the day when Jews, and every human being on earth, will welcome the messianic era of harmony, tranquility, peace and perfection. Of the over 613 commandments given by God to Moses, there are 248 which are positive ("thou shalts…") and 365 are negative commandments ("thou shalt nots..."). There are two main categories of mitzvot in the Torah; ritual and ethical.[6]

The ritual mitzvot revolve around ceremonies, rituals and rites of Jewish life, such as the participation in public worship, observing the Sabbath, and the eating of kosher food. The ethical mitvot include the honoring of parents, feeding the hungry, dealing fairly and honestly in business, and not exploiting others. These ethical commands serve to enrich everyday existence by raising ordinary acts to the level of holiness.[7]

In modern times, at least 200 of the mitzvot can no longer be observed, for they are concerned with the duties of priests (who no longer function), animal sacrifice (which is no longer offered), and the living in Israel (which many Jews do not). However, the mitzvot, both of the Torah and the rabbis, form the basis for Jewish ethical and ritual conduct and behavior.[8] The doing of a mitzvah is popularly defined as doing a good deed or the performing of a meritorious act, which implies use of the free choice of the doer. However, the doing of the mitzvah is also the doing of a requirement, an obligation, a commandment, a law, and is therefore not left to whim or chance, but is the sacred responsibility of every Jew.[9]

"The beginning of wisdom is the <u>awe</u> of God."[10] For the individual Jew, and for the Jewish community, the religious quest begins with God in the formation of an individual's personal, and intimate relationship with God, and then with the establishment of an ongoing communal relationship between God and the Jewish People.[11]

Throughout Jewish history, detractors of Judaism have pointed to the concept of "choseness" as an attempt by Jews to flaunt supposed superiority and greatness. In reality, the opposite is true. By the concept of being the chosen people is not meant that Jews were chosen for special privilege, but for sacred responsibility to be a light unto the nations (from Isa. 42:6, and 49:6), a faith community reflecting God's light of love and law.[12]

The Jewish Faith is different from the Faith of Zarathustra and the various forms of Christianity in several important aspects:

1) The Faith considers itself to be a living, organic and evolving entity which sprang from its beginning with Abraham and the concept of monotheism, and has evolved from the Mosaic Laws of the Torah and its history and tradition, but these beliefs are not viewed as being written in stone (yes, the Ten Commandments were written on stone tablets). The Faith is built around the first five books of the Old Testament, the Torah; this is followed by the Mishnah, which is divided into six major chapters in which the various laws were put

into one collection. This is followed by the Talmud, which consists of sixty-three tractates (chapters) commenting on the Mishnah, and that became further updated by liturgical responses and Rabbinical commentary over the ages. Therefore, the basis of Jewish Faith is the Torah, the five books revealed by Moses; however, the outward spiral of belief from Torah to Mishnah and such is what allows the Faith to mature and grow with mankind in a way similar to the stages of maturation of individuals.[13]

2) The Faith recognizes the input from various societies and their religions, and is ever mindful of the fact that this is a people who historically have been militarily defeated, captured and forced for many reasons to disburse, and yet, in the process, have managed to not lose their spiritual identity and, therefore, their uniqueness. The result of these many disbursements has been the introduction of these peoples to many different societies and their religious beliefs. This is not to say that, in the flexibility of their beliefs, they have no belief of their own, but rather to say that it is beautifully organic and constantly growing with the maturity of its individual believers.

3) The individual believer is urged to live a life of righteousness not only for his own sake, but most importantly for his family, fellow believers and mankind as a whole through a lifetime of prayer and study.

4) The Judaic emphasis is on the here and now, and the needs of mankind. Since the overall emphasis is on this plane of existence, there is a subsequent de-emphasis on the afterlife, to the point of questioning if it even exists. Herein lies a marked contrast to Christianity, in which there is emphasis on the individual soul attaining salvation and, thereby, life after life.[14]

5) SIN. Herein, there is another great difference in definition from that found in Christianity or the Faith of Zarathustra, wherein sin is a wickedness (an ungodliness). In Judaism, sin is the mere missing of the mark, such as the archer missing the bulls-eye. It is a misstep which can, and should, be corrected by a simple apology to the offended party. This same definition is true if the error is concerning

God and His laws, and here there is reason to seek repentance, since the laws came directly from God, and are God's will for the Jewish people. There is the need to fervently say, "I'm sorry to the offended," even to God. The conditional nature of God's covenant with the Jewish People was; "If you obey My commandments and observe my *mitzvot,* then, I will reward you. But if you disobey my *mitzvot,* then I will bring punishment upon you" (Lev. 26).[15]

To the people of biblical times, this meant that if they followed God's laws, then the rains would come and the crops would grow. But if they disobeyed those same laws, then they would be thirsty and hungry.[16] The teachings of the prophets take up where the Torah leaves off, foretelling severe punishments for the people and the Jewish nation if God's commands were not fulfilled, linking the transgression of the *mitzvoh* to the eventual conquering of the land of Israel, the destruction of the Holy Temple, and the exile of the Jewish people. Today, for many of the Jews, the above seems a faulty conclusion, since there seems to be little evidence in the relationship between human behavior and whether or not it rains. And yet, there must be an admission that there is a relationship between our actions and what ultimately happens to the world in which we live.[17]

The modern Judaic thought is that God doesn't really have to intervene, because we bring reward or punishment upon ourselves. Every action has consequences, and causes a reaction. Everything that we say or do affects those around us, every word ripples throughout time. Everything that we do or say determines to some degree whether things will turn out good or bad, easy or hard, loving or alienating. And since the whole world is made up of individual human beings, then we can, and ultimately do, have an effect on how our whole world works.

6) While there are differences in the teachings, views and style from one Rabbi to another, this seems to be far more accepted than in the other two faith traditions, and it, in fact, actually seems to be expected.

7) The emphasis in the Jewish faith on communal prayer is multi-faceted, but can be reduced to:

a) History. In the coming together to say the same prayers that have been recited by generations before you, and that generations as yet unborn will recite, you become a part of the continuum of Jewish history.

b) Energy. It is felt that there is deeper joy, richer sharing, and more noble living in the sharing of our most personal moments in the public arena; such as weddings and funerals. It is a richer, fuller, deeper and thus more satisfying experience when in community. When danger lurks, while it could be faced alone, it feels safer, and there is more hope when that danger is shared in community.[18]

The Jewish faith teaches that prayer is the personal journey that brings us to encounter our Creator, the voyage that transcends both time and place, and transforms the very essence of our being. It is the asking of questions, and the hearing of answers, and most of all it is the mutual encounter of love between you and God.[19]

Modern Denominations or Views of Judaism

The Jewish Faith has three main views of their beliefs and outlook on others, which are the Orthodox, the Conservative, and the Reformed, with a fourth presently emerging; the Reconstructionist. The basic differences are:

1) Orthodox Judaism – has been the mainstream Judaism throughout the centuries. The fundamental belief is in the direct revelation, that is to say Divine Law as recorded in the Torah, which the Orthodox Jews believe is eternal and unchangeable, the guide for everyday life and behavior. The most obvious among the Orthodox Jews are the Chasidic Jews, who are recognizable by their distinctive

dress of long black coats, round black hats, long beards and side locks.[20]

2) <u>Reform Judaism</u> – was born in the mid-nineteenth century in Germany in response to the "Age of Enlightenment" in Western Europe. The Reformed Jews rejected the concept of divine revelation, and attributed authorship of the Torah to inspired human beings. Therefore, the Mosaic Law is considered instructional and inspirational, but not binding, with the exception made in the case of the Ethical Laws. In modern times, Reformed Judaism actively affirms its commitment to egalitarianism and the issues of social justice.[21]

3) <u>Conservative Judaism</u> – is a response to Reform Judaism, in that, while accepting the notion that change in the Jewish belief is necessary in an ever-changing world, the Conservative Jews felt that Reformed Judaism had eliminated too many basic Jewish practices, theology and rituals. Hence, there has been a return to a stricter interpretation of the Torah, and the personal adherence thereto.[22]

4) <u>Reconstructionist Judaism</u> – became formalized in the 1950s and rejects the idea of a supernatural God. Instead, the Reconstructionists' understanding is of God as a power in the process that is the sum of all forces that give life meaning and worth. They further assert that Judaism is not merely a religion, but an evolving religious civilization, a culture as well as a faith community.[23]

The four views or denominations mentioned above are only one method of looking at the Jewish Faith. It must be remembered that this is a people that has been in a state of flux since the second Temple in Jerusalem was destroyed in 70 AD and the dispersion of the Jews as ordered by the Roman Emperor Titus. For 1900 years, the Jews have wandered from land to land, lived as guests in some host countries, suffered and died at the hands of persecutors and tyrants in others. It has been said that, during that whole time, most of these people would have crawled on hands and knees, if only they had the opportunity to end their exile and come home to Israel.[24]

The horrific event known as the Holocaust, initiated by Adolph Hitler, and carried out by his Nazi regime from the mid-1930s through the 1945, resulted in the murder, death and extermination of just over six million Jews, nearly one-third of the world's total Jewish population of that day, and emphasized more than ever the need for a safe, free and independent Jewish homeland. Hitler's goal had been the complete world-wide extermination of the Jewish people through inhumane slave and extermination camps. What the Allied Forces discovered upon entering Germany and occupied Poland at such locations as Auschwitz and many other concentration camps so affected the world's conscience that there was a real march forward by the peoples of the world towards the goals of the Zionist movement, resulting in, with the aid of the United Nations, the establishment of the modern State of Israel. Six million Jews had died, but the balance of the Jewish people have risen up, begun new lives, stating that "they are not the victims of Hitler, they are the Victors."[25]

With the establishment of the State of Israel, there was at long last the fulfillment of biblical prophecy, which many felt would lead to "the symbol of the long awaited perfection of the world, the end of days at God's holy mountain, the coming of Masheach [the Messiah], the ultimate redemption."[26]

There are numerous excellent books on the subject of the Judaic religion. One excellent book is *Living Judaism* by Rabbi Wayne Dosick. In a clear, almost conversational, manner he discusses rather fully historical and modern Jewish practices, traditions and beliefs.

Concerning the Comparison Chart (to follow)

Undoubtedly both Zarathustra and Jesus would have suggested that perceived differences could best be overcome through education, and thereby understanding of both cultural and societal similarities and differences as practiced throughout the world. To have included all the various religions presently being practiced worldwide would have diverted the focus of this book, and thus the number was reduced to those we have been discussing, although there is a need to separate Protestant Christianity from the Roman Catholic Church.

(There is a new publication which endorses the concept of universality of religion by his Holiness the Dalai Lama entitled *Toward a True Kinship of Faiths*.)

Despite the differences between the Christian denominations, factions and individual facilities and their clergy, and while those differences may be either significant or insignificant to you and be a reason for your refocus, the chart that follows is an attempt at comparing major teachings, and was compiled with the assistance of many clerical friends from a variety of faith pathways.

Of particular interest, which may require you to flip back and forth from this chapter to the Comparison Chart, may be the following:

  a) The importance of spiritual entities beyond the Creator in all of Christianity and the Faith of Zarathustra, such as Angels, Archangels, Satan and his aides.

  b) Afterlife similarities of same, including Heaven, Hell and Purgatory.

  c) The very definition of Sin.

  d) The revelation basically ceasing with the death of the revealer/prophet.

  e) Confession, renunciation, absolution and penance in the redemptive process.

In all of the above, there is a far greater similarity between the Faith of Zarathustra and Christianity, than there is with Judaism. The biggest similarity between Judaism and Christianity is the end of creation after the sixth day, whereas, according to Zarathustra, the Creator continues to create, at His will, for as long as He wills.

The emphasis in the Judaic belief is on the community of believers and the need in this plane of existence to keep the faith of God alive until the coming of the Messianic Age. This became very obvious when Moses was on Mt. Sinai and, in his absence, feeling abandoned and alone, the people lost faith in their leader and their God. They prevailed upon Aaron, the High Priest, to build an idol, a golden calf, which they could see and worship.[27]

There is a big difference in the treatment of original sin, in that the sins of one's ancestors are said to have little or no effect upon the soul of an individual believer in the Zarathustrian Faith, whereas there is an effect on the souls of innocents in Judaism and Christianity.

At this point, we will not be discussing whether these similarities are the result of a single source of revelation or the result of the socializing needs of various people as designated by human nature, although this would be a fascinating discussion. However, this is neither the time nor the proper venue. Therefore, let us take a look at both the differences and similarities of what we will be calling the four different faith paths. Yet, we must respect the fact that the variances within or on each path are so many that it would be impossible to fully discuss them all within a single book. At the same time, we must continue to be cognizant of how much of what we have believed was filtered through the mind and the imagination of youth, or how much of what has been questioned with that youthful intelligence and curiosity was stifled by the parental or clerical phrase, "Just take it on faith" or "when you are older, you will understand."

Please take enough time on your reflections to become excited by the potentialities and possible ramifications. It is fine to stop and meditate should your thinking become disoriented. But under no circumstance should you allow yourself to become discouraged. Remember that the faiths of God have always contained a certain mystery, or mystical quality. Is this so that there can be individual discovery and thereby astonishment? Is that becoming the case with you?

Concerning the four religious pathways, the most diverse must be that of Protestant Christianity, which has tens of thousands of denominations, each having its own doctrine and dogma, developed from revelation or from intellectual disagreement with a previous belief system at least, or it was so considered by its founder. Many of the differences seem minor to the outside observer, but were of great importance to more than just that denomination's founder at one time. The overriding important difference may have been as simple as the order of the religious service, the method of serving communion, or the vestment to be worn by the clergy; or as major as the status of women in the church or in the eyes of God, including where the women should sit. Also, there have been huge differences of opinion as to whether there should be singing in the place of worship, the language of the scriptural readings or the sermon, the very purpose of the service, not to mention what and who should be included at, or in, the service for marriages and funerals, and so on and so on. In many cases, new churches have been formed, which basically went back to what the old church had taught. Because of the sheer numbers of these denominations, there is a need to take an average in the answering of the questions on the chart. For any single denomination, the answer on one question or another may be incorrect, however, there is so much similarity between the denominations, that it is hoped that you will be able to ignore the minor differences.

Suffice it to say, the Protestant movement was the result of an early sixteenth century Roman Catholic priest, Martin Luther, who felt strongly that the church (Catholic) was drifting away from the real message of Christ, and therefore attempted to set it back on the correct track. The upshot of Luther's action was the establishment of a new church, which is the predecessor of today's Lutheran Church. The flood gates had been opened and the number of new churches grew exponentially.[28]

There seems to be a strong tendency for many of these churches to consider that they have the exclusive spiritual answers and, in many cases, to go to the extent as to deny the validity of the beliefs of anyone else, even those of other Christian Churches. A great amount of this exclusivity may go back to the early days of Christianity and the then legitimate fears of religious competition. It should be pointed out that this negative and seemingly prejudicial attitude has been detrimental to peace and harmony within religious and sectarian spheres.

The thing that almost all Christian Churches seem to agree upon is the concept that Jesus and His teachings grew exclusively out of the Jewish Faith, which they preach was the mission of Jesus to redirect and restore. As you are going from point to point on the Comparison Chart, this conclusion may become more doubtful, in that there are far more similarities between Christianity and the Faith of Zarathustra than there are between Christianity and the Jewish Faith. This is especially true with reference to the Roman Catholic Church. Why this has occurred also must be saved for further research and another discussion, although there will be additional discussion on many of these points later in the balance of the book.

There are some real differences between the Faiths of Jesus and Zarathustra as they have been taught through the years in the treatment and status of women and children who have full and equal status with men according to Zarathustra. Also, what is important is the spiritual journey of the soul not of the individual physical person. The body is but the vessel that is the vehicle for transportation of the soul from conception throughout the physical life. This perception is true for Zarathustrians to the extent that a pregnant woman is counted as two souls with respect to the census.

The issue of the status of women and children was settled by revelation between 2800 and 3700 years ago.

Way To Go – Zarathustra and Ahura Mazda!

Spiritual Healing/Exorcism

Of special interest is the view in the Zarathustrian Faith, the teachings and healings of Jesus and His disciples and following this much of Christianity, for seeing the cause of much illness and disease as sin or evil with the required remedy being some sort of exorcism. This may be viewed as being superstition by many people. However, if you consider as evil, viruses, bacteria, and chemical imbalances, it is not hard to see that a form of cleansing, be it spiritual or pharmaceutical, could offer you a different perspective.

Comparison of Beliefs

Topic	Judaism	Roman Catholicism	Protestantism	Zarathustrianism
Source of Creation	God	God	God	God
God's Name	Yahweh and Jehovah	God	God	Ormazd or Ahura Mazda
God's Form or Nature	Spirit	Spirit	Spirit	Spirit
	Moses stated that he saw God, "I am that I am"	Triune Godhead composed of Father, Son and Holy Ghost	Triune Godhead composed of Father, Son and Holy Ghost	Sevenfold Godhead composed of the Amesha Spentas
Other Spiritual Forces and Beings	Angel of the Lord, Angel of Death, Archangels until the Book of Job, then Satan and his minions. These spiritual forces are de-emphasized.	Archangels, angels, also cherubim and seraphim and fallen angels such as Satan	Archangels, angels, also cherubim and seraphim and fallen angels such as Satan	Archangels, angels, also cherubim and seraphim and fallen angels such as Satan
Human Source of Revelation	Abraham, Jacob and Isaac brought forth the Oneness of God, Moses	Jesus of Nazareth, along with acceptance of the Old Testament	Jesus of Nazareth, along with acceptance of the Old Testament	Zarathustra Spitama
Major Prophets	Isaiah (740 BC), Jeremiah (627 BC), Ezekiel (592 BC), Daniel* (605 BC) *Daniel is an important Biblical figure, but is not considered a prophet in rabbinical Judaism.	Revelation per se ended with the crucifixion; however, with the inclusion of the letters of St. Paul, there is much direction that could be taken as additional revelation.	Similar to Roman Catholic, varies by denomination	None

Minor Prophets	Obadiah (840 BC), Joel (835 BC), Jonah (780 BC), Amos (765 BC), Hosea (755 BC), Micah (740 BC), Nahum (630 BC), Zephaniah (625 BC), Habakkuk (606 BC), Haggai (520 BC), Zechariah (515 BC), Malachi (430 BC) (partial list)	None	None	None, although there were explanations of the revelations by High Priests, which provided additional emphasis.
Creation	Six days + day of rest	Six days + day of rest	Six days + day of rest	Seven stages
Creation Ceased	After six days	After six days	After six days	Continues forever, at God's will
Greatest Creation	Man	Man	Man and Woman	The righteous man, the steward of God's creation
Testing of Divine Calling	By own people	By Satan	By Satan	By Ahriman
Period of Testing	40 years (Moses)	40 days	40 days	40 days
Acceptance by Own People	Slow and uneven	Slow, left Judea for Galilee	Slow, left Judea for Galilee	Very slow, left homeland for Bactria
First Acceptance by Believer	Brother (Moses)	Simon Peter	Simon Peter	Cousin, then King Vishtap of Bactria
Apostles	None found in texts	12	12	None known

Disciples	None known	70	70	None known
Number of Laws Revealed	613	None	None	Many directives, but few laws
Holy Texts	Torah, Mishnah, Talmud, rabbinical commentary on above	Old and New Testaments	Old and New Testaments, varies by denomination	Avesta and its explanation, the Zand
Length of Ministry	40 years	1.5 to 3 years	1.5 to 3 years	Over 40 years
End of Life	Unknown	Crucifixion, at order of Pontius Pilate	Crucifixion, at order of Pontius Pilate	Killed at age 77, defending against an attack in a fire temple
Prophecy of a Savior— What to Look For?	The Messiah, "Wonderful, Counselor, the mighty God, everlasting Father, Prince of Peace, the government shall be upon his shoulders"	The "Son of Man"	The "Son of Man"	Three World Saviors: Aushedar, Aushedarma, Saoshyant
The End of Time	The coming of the Messiah and the resurrection of all souls	Armagedon, then the resurrection of all souls	Armagedon, then the resurrection of all souls	The resurrection of all souls to the Great Assembly
Immortality of the Soul	Not complete until the coming of the Messiah	Only with belief in Jesus	Only with belief in Jesus, varies by denomination	All souls are inherently immortal
Entrance to Heaven	No strong belief in existence of an afterlife; not a strong emphasis on this	Judgment by God or the Archangel Gabriel	Judgment by God or the Archangel Gabriel	Passage over the Sifting Bridge, as a test of righteousness. The truly righteous went straight to heaven.

Progression of Soul in Afterlife?	No	No	Questionable, probably no	Yes
Levels or Stages of Heaven?	No—not a point of emphasis	Possible	No	At least 4
Existence of Purgatory	No	Yes—a state of punishment	No	Yes—a place of holding, without punishment, when one's good and bad deeds during life are equal
Existence of Hell	No	Yes	Yes, varies by denomination	Yes
Description of Hell	Not applicable	Fire and brimstone	Fire and brimstone, absence from God, varies by denomination	A place of discomfort and loneliness
Redemption Available	Not emphasized	Yes, primarily during life	Yes, primarily during life	Yes, in life, heaven, purgatory, and hell
Contact With Physical World after Death?	Not emphasized	Yes, possible through prayer	No, varies by denomination	Yes, through prayer, dreams and the doings of the righteous
Belief in Original Sin?	Yes	Yes	Yes, varies by denomination	Yes, no effect on descendants
After Death— Disposition of Body	Burial preferred, as soon as possible	Burial or cremation	Burial or cremation	Must be non-polluting, burial and cremation forbidden

Purpose of Funeral/ Memorial Service	Closure for community, relatives and friends	Closure for relatives and friends	Closure for relatives and friends	Closure for relatives and friends, plus soul progression of deceased
Separation of Body/Soul	Not specified	Not specified	Not specified	Soul remains with the body for three nights
Proper Time for Grieving	7 to 30 days, not more than a year	30 days is suggested	Varies by denomination	30 days for the righteous, 60 days for others
Remarriage Appropriate?	After 1 year	Not specified	Not specified	After at least one year
Rights of Deceased to Refuse Redemption	Not applicable	Not specified	Not specified	Absolutely no soul need to accept from others
Nature of Sin	A missing of the mark, requires apology to God and the offended; breaking of the Ten Commandments is much more serious	Offenses against God and man, divided into venial and mortal sins, requires confession, renunciation, absolution and penance.	Offenses against God and man; normally requires atonement, not confession, but varies by denomination.	Offenses against man and God, requires confession, renunciation, atonement and contrition as well as the performance of good deeds. A genuine apology, to be followed by an act of charity in the name of the offended.
Value of Good Thoughts	Ideal, but not specified	Ideal, but not specified	Ideal, but not specified	Of value, necessary for good words and deeds

Value of Good Words	Ideal, but not specified	Ideal, but not specified	Ideal, but not specified	Of value, good words are a source of soul progression for ancestors
Value of Good Deeds	Ideal, but not specified	Necessary, with baptism and confession, for entry into heaven	Not specified, but an important part in qualifying for heaven	Of value, good deeds are a source of progression for ancestors
Preceding Manifestation of God	Abraham	Moses	Moses	Yima (Jamshid)
Founder of Denomination	Moses	Jesus Christ	Jesus Christ, then varies by denomination	Zarathustra Spitama
Doctrines Intrinsic to the Faith	Not specified	Salvation through belief in Jesus, baptism, confession of sins at point of death (Last Rites)	Salvation through belief in Jesus and living a righteous life, baptism, varies by denomination	Existence of afterlife for all souls
Views Upon:				
Contraception	Permitted	Not permitted, agitation for loosening	Permitted, varies by denomination	Not specified
Abortion	Not specified	Not permitted, agitation for loosening	Permitted, varies by denomination	Only if the mother's life is in danger
Physical/ Mental Handicaps	Probably due to sins of parents	Probably due to sins of parents	Due to physical malfunctions	Not specified
Premarital Sexual Relations	Not condoned	Not condoned	Not recommended	Not condoned
Adulterous Behavior	Forbidden by law	Not condoned	Not condoned	Forbidden

Remarriage After Divorce	Permitted, after reasonable waiting period	Not permitted, unless annulment is granted	Permitted, varies by denomination	Permitted
Remarriage After Widowhood	Permitted, after reasonable waiting period	Permitted, after a respectable time	Permitted, after a respectable time	Permitted
Divorce	Not preferable, but permitted	Not permitted, unless annulment is granted	Permitted, varies by denomination	Not condoned
Priesthood— Available to Men and Women?	Yes (only recently)	No, to men only	Yes, but varies by denomination	Yes
Priesthood— Marriage Allowed?	Yes	No	Yes	Yes
Priesthood— Celibacy Required?	No	Yes	No, varies by denomination	No
Status of Women Within the Faith	Worship separately from men	A diminished role, with no female priests	Varies by denomination	Spiritually and socially equal
Status of the Soul of Young Children	Depends on age and spiritual education	Depends on baptism and spiritual education	Varies by denomination	Soul is intrinsic, and eternal
Spiritual Training	Yes, to Bar Mitzvah or Bat Mitzvah	Yes, Catechism Classes to Confirmation	Yes, Sunday School, to Confirmation	Youth training on spiritual life to supplement parental training. Begin by age 3, complete by age 6 to 10, dependent on intelligence of the child

Perspective Towards Non-Members	Gentiles	Not permitted in Heaven, intermarriage is discouraged	Varies by denomination from acceptance to not permitted	Respected for their beliefs
Prayer:				
To Whom	To God	To Jesus or God	To God, in the name of Jesus, varies denominationally	To Ahura Mazda (God)
Intercession Through	immediate family ancestors	Saints, angels and archangels	Not applicable	Amesha Spentas, angels and archangels
Preferred Posture	Standing	Kneeling	Sitting or standing	Not specified
Value of Private Prayer	De-emphasized; prayer has more significance in community	Extremely important	Extremely important	Extremely important
Preferred Location	Synagogue, or with a minion of 13 Bar Mitzvahed men	Church	Church	Temple
Method of Prayer	Verbalized or chanted	Verbalized or silent	Verbalized or silent	Chanted or verbalized
Reading of Scripture, Personal	Greatly encouraged; Torah, Talmud, Mishnah	Greatly encouraged; Old and New Testaments	Recommended; Old and New Testaments	Strongly encouraged; Zend Avesta. Prayers are required 5 times daily.
Reading of Scripture, Congregational	Major portion of Sabbath liturgy, as well as part of devotionals	Important at Mass, worship services	Important at worship services	Important at worship and community services

				At the end of time, all souls which have been in hell or purgatory shall be brought forth to face the righteous and be made whole in the eyes of God in the highest spiritual realm, starting with the oldest— Adam and Eve, and progressing to the most recent.
The Last Judgment and Final Resurrection	With the coming of the Messiah, there will be a resurrection of the dead, and all souls shall be made physical and whole	Armagedon With the Second Coming, all souls shall become alive	Armagedon With the Second Coming, all souls shall become alive	

Are you as surprised at the similarities on the chart between the Faiths of Zarathustra and Christianity, especially with the Roman Catholic Faith, and to a lesser degree, the Protestant churches? Also, what about the many differences in view, definition and doctrine between Christianity and Judaism? What it all means, you must decide for yourself, for there is no way of knowing; however, it goes a long way in showing the validity of the teachings of Zarathustra, while in no way does it diminish either the validity nor the beauty of the Jewish Faith. And as to the possible influence of the Faith of Zarathustra upon the Jewish Faith, one need only look to the entire book of Job, or even more to the book of Isaiah wherein God says:

Isaiah 44:28 "That saieth of Cyrus, He is my shepherd, and shall perform all my pleasure: even saying to Jerusalem, Thou shalt be built; and to the temple, thy foundation shall be laid."[29]

Isaiah 45:1 "Thus saieth the Lord [GOD] to his anointed, to Cyrus, whose right hand I have holden, to subdue the nations before him; And I will loose the loins of kings, to open before him the two leaved gates and the gates shall not be shut;

Isaiah 45:2 I will go before thee, and make the crooked places straight: I will break in pieces the gates of brass, and cut in sunder the bars of iron:

Isaiah 45:3 And I will give thee the treasures of darkness, and the riches of the secret places, that thou mayest know that I, the Lord, which calleth thee by name, am the God of Israel.

Isaiah 45:4 For Jacob, my servant's sake, and Israel mine elect, I have called thee by thy name; though thou hast not known me.

Isaiah 45:5 I *am* the Lord, and there is none else, there is no God beside me: I girded thee, though thou hast not known me:"[30]

One needs to know that this was recorded according to the Prophet Isaiah, even though it sounds as if it was addressed to the Persian King Cyrus II, who herein is referred to as God's "Anointed One." Just as important can be the repeated phrase, "thou hast not known me" which seems to be less for Cyrus II, than for the Jewish people, so that they would know that what Cyrus had done, and that he had so done for the sake of, and at the behest of God! Cyrus was fully aware that God, the one Creator, was the same by whatever name any people or faith might call Him. To this point, again in Isaiah, verse 12:

45:12 "I have made the earth, and created man upon it: I, *even* with my hands, have stretched out the heavens, and all their host have I commanded.

45:13 I have raised him up in righteousness, and I will direct his ways", saieth the Lord of Hosts. He shall build my city and he shall let go my captives, not for price nor reward"[31]

Can you find another explanation for this glorious commendation from the God of Israel to His servant, Cyrus II, the King of Persia, who had performed His will with no other reason or excuse than the wish to do His will without thought of reward other than doing the will of God, the Creator by whatever name the various peoples should choose for Him?

❧ CHAPTER 9 ❧

A Few Thoughts and Final Focusing

Pragmatism in Your Conclusion Can Lead to AWE

It is time to concentrate on the process of refocusing and updating your spiritual beliefs so that those can become comfortably compatible with your intellectual maturity. It is suggested that no matter what these new conclusions are, that they be more pragmatic than they may have been in the past so that there can be adjustments made more easily with the input of new data. Things of a spiritual nature are so difficult to make firm because by their very nature they are ethereal. Just as it is impossible to catch a cold winter's breeze in a jar for use the following summer, so it is just as impossible to make permanent that which is spiritual. Has your journey through the reading of this book endorsed that last statement? By taking a truly pragmatic stance you will become somewhat prepared for the unexpected and thus be able to manage if not enjoy what will happen to you in the rest of your physical life.

To achieve this balance your attention is directed to the appropriateness of several points made by the Jewish scholar and philosopher, Abraham Joshua Heschel, in his statement partially entitled "Between God and Man"… "What is unknown and concealed from us is open and known to God"… "Ultimate meaning and ultimate wisdom are not (and cannot be) found within the world, but in God. That relationship is *awe*"… "Awe, in this sense, is more than an emotion; it is a way of understanding… an act of insight into a meaning greater than ourselves…. Awe is a way of being in rapport with the mystery of all reality…. Awe is an intuition for the creaturely dignity of all things and their preciousness to God... for the reference everywhere to Him who is beyond all things."

"The meaning of awe is to realize that life takes place under wide horizons, horizons that range beyond the span of individual life, or even the life of a nation, generation or an era. Awe enables us to perceive in the world intimations of the divine, to sense the ultimate in the common and the simple, to feel in the rush of the passing the stillness of the eternal.... Awe, unlike fear, does not make us shrink from the awe-inspiring object, but, on the contrary, draws us near to it. This is why awe is compatible with both love and joy." [1]

This statement by Herschel is appropriate for your spiritual refocus in that not being God, you can never be all-knowing. It is hoped that you have had some "Ah-ha" moments, as well as some that truly fit the description of "awe." Consider that there is no way that any person, other than one infused with the Spirit of God, can definitely say a fact means this or that. It is suggested as you are pragmatically concluding exactly what it is that you believe, that you allow new data to be a source of joy and to create added love for that which is greater than you. If you have identified yourself and your beliefs with a religion or with that man who either founded that religion or revitalized another, it is suggested that new religious thinking may be in order. The two religious Men you have been reading about both tried to make it clear that they were offering the Word of God, and that what was important was neither themselves nor their religion, but GOD [aka Ahura Mazda] and thus the "RELIGION OF GOD."

Remember that greatest law, "To love the Lord your God with all your heart, with all your soul and with all your Strength." With this in mind, do you think it is possible that God finds Joy in the arguments, let alone the wars, between peoples of different faiths? As you consider this, please allow Zarathustra to be your Spiritual Rosetta stone in that His teachings, His example and that of His followers spoke to and exemplified not only tolerance but an understanding that as other peoples found ethics and truths in their beliefs they were in their own way loving and obeying God, even if they used different names or called them gods.

In this book, there has been much more about Zarathustra and His religion than there has been about Jesus and the beautiful religion that has come from His teaching. This was because Zarathustra's ministry was ten to twenty times longer than that allowed to Jesus, because much of Zarathustra's ministry can no longer be found in history books, and even more because of the precocious nature of this man with His constant questioning of God (Ahura Mazda) for more answers, and then asking for more details to the answers which had just been given. That great detail is another reason for considering Zarathustra as a Religious Rosetta Stone, a means by which there can be understanding of multiple religious mysteries and concepts. For example, Ahura Mazda informed Zarathustra, as the Creator, He would continue to Create, and that he wished mankind to assist in that deed. Further, He informed Zarathustra that from time to time the faith of God would become corrupted by the well-meant meddling hands of man [both Clergy and Laymen] and thus need redirection and renewal through the return of His spirit in similar fashion as it had occurred to Zarathustra. It is the contention of this book that it was the first of these returns that was marked by the journey of the Magi to the birthplace of and to honor the birth of Jesus. Zarathustra was also informed that there would be a need for at least two further Saviors [Messiahs] in centuries to come.

During the reading of this book there should have been a part of you that has been touched, a part other than your body, which is changing and aging by the day, other than your mind, which has a way of distorting, forgetting and denying truths, a part of you which has been the real you for as long as you can remember! That touched part is the real you, it is your soul. This book has been a success if your soul recognized or felt what it is that you truly believe. Along with this, there should have been a recognition that you came into this life and are still alive because of more than random chance or coincidence. If this is what you feel at this moment, then what is it that you should be taking from your reading?

It is sincerely hoped that while thinking about and adjusting your long held beliefs, you now find yourself closer and more in awe of your Creator and His very special spokesmen. It is further hoped that you will take the opportunity to try the prescription for living offered by Zarathustra which is to think only "the good thoughts"; further, to speak only "the good words", and to concentrate on alleviating all activities other than "the good deeds", even if it is for but a single day. Remember, just one day, and you get to pick the day! At the point that you have accomplished this, as you get into bed after that one full day, ask, "Do I not feel better about myself and the world around me?" Can you honestly say that you gave it your best attempt and you feel you can follow that prescription for another day? For the sake of both your body, soul and for the sake of those around you, please try to do so!

Have you succeeded in truly living the "Good Life", for more than one day? Now, you have a new challenge which is to go for a full week without verbalizing a single untruth, not even the smallest white lie! Of course, some of your friends may become upset. They may tell you that they did not need to hear the truth! When you explain to them what you are attempting, chances are they will think that is great, even though it may be that they will stop seeking your opinion, except when they want a truthful one! Of course, you will need to use wisdom with this new you so that you deliver this truthfulness empathetically with tact and love. You will need to find a way to keep from being hurtful while remaining fully honest. You should find that this new attitude towards life is not at all bad! Remember that people can find plenty of acquaintances who will tell them whatever it is that they want to hear. In addition, you may just have found a way to stop wasting a lot of unproductive time. Shortly you should feel less stressed! No longer will you need to remember or worry about exactly what it was that you said. The absolute truth is so much easier to remember than non-truth even if you have told the smallest of white lies. You should soon feel the grip of Ahriman slowly losing hold! Remember that in chapter 2, when we looked at the Creation story as told by Zarathustra, that in this rendition;

1. God [Ahura Mazda] first conceived of Creation.

2. Ahura Mazda then created the Spiritual Universe.

3. It was only then that Ahura Mazda created the Physical Universe, which He based upon the model of the Spiritual Universe. Thus, in this rendition, there is a clear description that Creation was the result of premeditation followed by action, not the mere result of chance. It should also be noted that up to this point Satan (Ahriman) was not allowed to take part in the Creation process, which tends to disprove the often stated "dualistic aspect of the Zarathustrian faith," a complaint often heard from detractors of Zarathustra's Religion.

4. Ahriman [Satan, by any name] is released only after the creation of everything except Man, and thus is a part of the plan of God, and thus the reason of many Zarathustrians that the very existence of Ahriman was allowed so that mankind would have Freedom of Choice in that rendition. For without the existence of temptation and alternatives while doing the Will of God there is no freedom of choice. Therefore, Ahriman and his minions of ungodliness operate with the acquiescence of God. If the thoughts, words and deeds of mankind are with a real choice, men and women can no longer use the excuse that "the Devil made me do it." For those who choose to do what is RIGHT Ahriman is but a DELUSION. The fact the Ahriman is a delusion can be arrived at from (A) Scripture, and from (B) logic.

Satan [Ahriman] is a Delusion of Man?

A. "Concerning Ahriman it is related that he hath no real existence." [2] This is not to say that there are people who do evil and thus can be called the beloved of the Daeva, for in

Yasna XXXII, 4: "for ye have brought to pass that men who do the worst things shall be called the beloved of the Daevas, but excluded from the Good Mind, departing from the will of God [Ahura Mazda] and from the Right."[3]

"God [Ahura Mazda] and the place, the religion and the time of God were and are and shall be, world without end; While Ahriman, in darkness, with backward understanding and desire to destroy, exists only in the abyss and it is he who shall not be."

B. In the Zarathustrian rendition of the Creation story, ultimately Ahriman is to lose all power over humankind, at which time according to the proponents of Absolute Dualism Ahriman will be cast in to the Abyss by the good thoughts, words and deeds of the transformed humankind so as to no longer be a source of discord and ungodliness. Whereas the Relative Dualism proponents would declare that Ahriman was allowed to exist so that humankind would have true Freedom of choice, and that with eventual spiritual maturity all of humankind would determine that the distractions of ungodliness were totally undesirable and with a mature Free Choice dispense with the unnecessary delusion. Logically, anything spiritual that can be dispensed with permanently through the actions and prayers of humankind cannot be real.

It would seem that what truly brings Joy to GOD [Ahura Mazda] is when a person makes the Right decision because it is Right and not out of Fear nor because of the promise of a reward, but strictly because it is the RIGHT THOUGHT, RIGHT WORDS, and THE RIGHT DEEDS.

The other side of this theological discussion is that if God [Ahura Mazda] is all good, how is it possible that there could be Earthquakes,

Tsunamis, Epidemics and such, and thus it was necessary that Ahriman, the destroyer of good, be a part of Creation from the start. Since mankind has been made a partner by God, albeit a limited and minor partner, in the process of continuing creation, is it possible that it is up to mankind to find answers to the above mentioned negatives through science, or by education to avoid those disasters?

It is hoped that in your spiritual refocusing, this book has been of help. How are you feeling about whatever changes you have made concerning your spiritual and religious training? The results of this process should help you to sleep like a baby. Whether it will be that sleep, or the smile that you will be unable to take off your face, you will soon discover a new you emerging, and after the first three people you see comment on what they consider to be a new and happier you, there will be no turning back. Which is not to say that people and circumstances can't cause you to revert to old habits for a short while, but now, with your awareness of the value of living the Good Life, you should be able to return to it with a simple apology to the individual who caused you to lose that new character, even if the cause was God.

Zarathustra taught that a main purpose of this life was the gaining of religious skills and knowledge as a preparation for the next life of the soul. If this man of God is correct in His description of the afterlife as a continuing spiritual journey, the process of questioning and refocusing should go far past the reading of this book. That journey should continue for the rest of your physical life and beyond. What has been started can be exciting, fulfilling and at the same time make you into a more delightful person for those around you on this plane of existence. You will be a part of the never ending Creation, and the afterlife should be anything but boring.

Upon finishing this book, and attempting to adopt the "good thought, word and deed" process, you should find new joy in your life. It is suggested that when you are asked what is new, that you mention what has caused the emergence of the new you, instead of just saying "Oh nothing." The purpose of this is to start a wave of positivity within your sphere of influence, which will make the maintaining of the new you far easier to keep going.

Think of how else you can effectively make a difference by eliminating the negative, and accentuating the positive. When your boss or your best friend asks you to do anything that in the past you would have done, but felt bad about it for hours and even days, explain to this person that you are working on a new you, and, as such, you really cannot do what is being asked, that it hurts to even think about it. There may be a bristling or a saying that you have to do this or that. Politely refuse by saying that the new you is attempting to do those things that are right, fair and just, which is to say, that in your mind, "the end no longer justifies the means." When the asking party's forehead shows upset, point out that as the new you is successful, you will become totally trustworthy. If this conversation is with your boss, and he is still not convinced, then insist that the balance of this discussion be held in the presence of his boss, or even that boss's boss. By this process, you will be a real part of bringing back honesty in the work place. Not only will you sleep better at night, you will lower both your blood pressure and your stress level, while helping the world at the same time.

Do not allow yourself to be the fall guy for the dishonesty of others. Be assured that the person who asks you to do what you know is wrong, will be the first to deny same. They will say that you must have totally misunderstood them, and that they never would have asked such a thing. In other words, take the full responsibility for all of your actions before, during and after you take said actions.

One thing which became obvious in the writing of this book is that the ethical truths of Zarathustra are as important today as they were thousands of years ago. All that has changed is today's technology, not the people making use of it. Yes, we have electricity and the appliances which make use of it, telephones, trains, satellites, airplanes above and submarines under the sea, computers with Internet functions which allow instantaneous written communication to anywhere in the world, and before long we will be traveling to, and then colonizing, first, the moon and the planets of our solar system and then what has been science fiction will become reality. We will be traveling way beyond what can be seen from the earthbound telescopes by the end of this or at least the next century. With the rapidity of inventions and technology, there is little doubt that we will conquer space, and mankind will commence an era of colonization in the actual foreseeable future.

Looking at the writings of Zarathustra and realizing that human nature has yet to change, we should see that the teachings of Jesus, Zarathustra and the other men of God warn that "what we sow, we shall reap." Does it not hold true for all of mankind? We must learn to solve the problems of this planet, rather than running away from them. We must learn to make use of, without using up, our natural resources, eliminate the extremes of poverty and wealth among both individuals and nations. We must find that which will end War as the solution to International disputes, and will bring about universal education for all children on Earth. We must solve such problems as starvation, global warming and pollution. Then, and only then, will it be the correct time to conquer space and inhabit other worlds.

For all of this to occur, it seems that there is an absolute necessity for a rebirth of ethics for all of mankind. This is something which can start with you, and then grow. This rebirth requires certain realizations, which probably include the acquiring of new spirituality on the part of most of society. However, this cannot happen through the dictates of any one person, not even the most benevolent of dictators. Nor can it occur as the result of the best intentioned legislation. It cannot even be brought about by the order from the return of God or one of His representatives, for this would be no different than the most benevolent of dictators. There can be no lasting change unless it is brought about by the free-will choice of all who accept the Zarathustrian prescription, or that of God's special Prophets, to happiness and well-being. This would not require such acceptance by all of mankind since most people are not trendsetters, but as followers they will follow what they see the thinkers and the balance of society doing. They will do so to keep friends, in which case in their faking the "good life," these followers will discover the hidden beauties, and really join in with the rest.

YOU have the opportunity of being a trendsetter for what will bring joy to you and to God. While you are perfecting the new you, find ways of suggesting the same to those in your sphere of influence, and further start voting with your wallet, and your emails. Refuse to give financial support to those who sponsor TV, radio, newspapers and internet programming which includes voyeurism, violence and ungodly behavior by not only stopping the buying of products, but by writing the sponsors and letting them know the reasons for your boycott. It is time that a large enough portion of society insists on healthy programming to effect a true change. This in no way suggests that this should be accomplished through either censorship or legislation, but only by not watching such programming and by economic boycott. This should happen because we begin to believe there are many reasons to look past ourselves to our children and grandchildren. Mankind must speak out with intelligent proofs emanating from his "good thoughts."

If Ahriman [Satan] is in fact a delusion of mankind that draws His power from the ungodliness [or less than godliness] of man, then it is time that we start putting this unwanted and unnecessary essence back in the "bottle" by purifying our thoughts, speaking only what is right and good, and being examples of righteousness, and not giving comfort or money to the purveyors of that which is less than godly.

YOU are but a single individual; however, there is a lot that each person can accomplish if they will make use of their particular God-given capacities. It can start with a friendly and genuine smile wishing a good morning or "have a great day" to your neighbor, or to the people standing like statues as you enter the elevator. (Is there some law that says upon entering an elevator that you should find the greatest open space, do a complete 180 degree turn like a robot, face the elevator door, and without acknowledging any other occupants, silently tilt your head back so that you can help the numbers on the floor indicator to move?)

The focus of your speaking should be what will encourage good thoughts in others and thus emphasize first the points of agreement and only then the points of disagreement. Winning in the thought and speech arena should no longer be the goal. Encouraging intelligent, positive thinking should be the focus, with the final goal being the follow-through with "good deeds." Just as in the days of Zarathustra, we must be willing to act on our own good thoughts, words and deeds so that every action produces a positive and pleasurable result for one and all, not just our self. As others are viewing this, they should find such positivity that they wish to know the secret of your joy. By working on following the "Good Life" formula, we will distance ourselves from a few that we have considered to be friends; however, the attraction of joyful new friends will more than make up for the loss.

The good words and deeds will be rewards in themselves as they change the attitudes of your children, friends and co-workers in positive ways. YOU should soon see the emergence of good thoughts, words or deeds on the part of others. As this occurs, please positively acknowledge same, while remembering that even this will be unexpected at first. YOU must absolutely learn to listen to the words of others carefully, not just so that your new words will be listened to, but because from others the seeds of good thoughts can be nourished and evolve into true positivity. "You shall be known by the company that you keep,"[4] …. And that this will soon be become very nice company.

The transformation of society can be lasting only if parents will wake up to the true needs of their children, which must include seeing that the education they receive has a basis in not only the sciences, but also ethics and virtues. Too many parents today seem to feel that this is the job of the schools, along with sex and drug education. This is a total cop-out, especially since the teachers and school administrators have been rendered emasculated by the prohibition of almost every form of punishment including verbal chastisement.[5] Virtues training must begin in the home with the parents and siblings, to be endorsed and enhanced with training from their churches, and organizations such as Scouts. It is not enough that the parents be actively involved in the training, they must actually become "role models." Parents must find quality time to spend with their kids and like minded people for two reasons:

1)   Childhood passes so very quickly, and you will never get it back.

2)   Trying to replace time by spending money means that you have to earn that much more money.

Parents must be guided away from the concept of "ownership of their children" and begin to reflect the attitude in their thoughts and actions, that "this is a blessing which has been lent to me, to assist in the maturation process to a happy, and fulfilling adulthood."

As you look back upon the teachings of Zarathustra, logically it makes sense that you should worry about the quality of the lives of your offspring, if only because your progress in the afterlife may be greatly enhanced by the good thoughts, good words and good deeds, as well as the prayers, from these same offspring. There is so much to be gained by intelligent parenting. The pattern which you set up for your children should include that the same be passed on to your grandchildren, and on. But then, do you really need that incentive? Isn't the genuine joy and happiness of your children reward enough for you?

Good Thoughts? Good Words? Good Deeds?

Let us now look at the potential losses of incorporating these attributes into your everyday life. How will you explain this new you? How will it feel to remain silent, or to even politely move away from the conversation that has turned to gossip or smut? Do you really enjoy the downgrading of another's reputation? Do you honestly think that you won't be the target of similar talk, when your back is turned? Stop feeding the fires of Ahriman! Be an adult! Stand up for the new positivity! Do not do it meekly, be proud to do what is right because it is right!

If you lose a friend or two at first, that, of course, is a shame. However, the chances are if they are truly friends, they will not only return, but thank you for your change. If not, there are many very nice people who will be attracted to the new you. Do you think that a man should pick his friends to have similar ethical behavior? If the less than godly man with a fair and rational warning, followed by a lessening of your time of association, he would seek to change in order not to be isolated. Thus, he can begin to feel that true happiness that comes from being a part of the whole, especially a positive whole. He, too, can learn to make use of "good thoughts, good words and good deeds." Should this individual decide not to change his ways, he will soon find his circle degenerating as he drifts further from the will of his Creator.

Do not be one who simply gives lip-service to ethical behavior. Engage in positive conversations, accentuating the positive and spending time with those who do the same. Likely there will be changes on the part of those who in the past have been able to get our attention only if they had a problem, some gossip or by bewailing in a "poor-me-voice" the happenings of the day. Many people in our society have been able to get the attention they need only through negative behavior. Rather than ostracizing these individuals, start by praising some of this person's positive virtues. If you are questioned as to what you are doing, explain the new you and offer to assist them to find a brand new them! What a gift, if they only can accept it.

The Power of Positive Thinking

The Reverend Norman Vicente Peale created a sensation in the middle of the twentieth century with his doctrine of the "power of positive thinking."[6] For many, it was a brand new concept, the application of which was literally transforming for them, having survived a world war and a worldwide depression. Like many things in this modern day, Peale's admonition was soon forgotten by most people such that it proved to be little more than a "fad." Was this because it was not embraced by enough segments of society, such as the schools and churches, or because there was a war going on? However, an excellent concept disappeared from the social scene all too quickly.

It is hoped that the Christian and Jewish clergy will assist in the rewriting of future history by acknowledging Zarathustra and His teachings for His positive contributions to their faiths, dropping some of their religious exclusiveness, fears and prejudices so as to honestly look for the voice and true meanings of God in other religions. In so doing, they will be giving new recognition to the fact there definitely is but one Creator, who is the source of true religion. With that positive starting point, it is more than possible that shortly the seats in their "religious sanctuaries" will be finding new occupants. It might also help if the clergy could get out of the business of politics and get back into the business of teaching and promoting the words of God. When Jesus said, "leave unto Caesar that which belongs to Caesar," could he have been referring to the noninvolvement in politics?

We started by looking at the story of the Magi in great detail. In the process, we discovered many items seldom openly analyzed. We were then led to look at the man whose centuries old prophesy sent the Magi. We learned about the way Zarathustra received the spirit of God, and that He prophesied that the same spirit would be received by special men in the future as needed, and that these people would most likely receive the spirit in a similar way when appropriate. By looking at the evidence in the Bible, it would seem that the spirit was received by Jesus as a thirty-year-old adult as prophesied. If so then the dreams and visions around the time of the Nativity, plus the arrival of the Magi pointed to the future of this exceptional child. We have learned many things about the religion which Zarathustra introduced to the world, as well as a few of His prophecies yet unfulfilled, such as future Saviors and the future of Medicine, and that in the future mankind would become so mature that evil will cease to exist. Then we returned to the life of Jesus, after the "years of silence" to that episode in which He was baptized by John the Baptist, and how, upon leaving the baptismal water, the spirit of God descended upon Him like a dove, and then He was led by that spirit into the desert to be tempted by Satan. And finally Jesus was allowed to begin His short but valuable ministry.

We have looked at the parallels and differences of Jesus and Zarathustra, Their lives and Their teachings of what They called the word of God. We have looked at many of the long range influences of both men to date, and very possibly, into the future. While there may be some differences in your conclusions from those that have been suggested, that is more than okay, since you have available that all important freedom of choice. The fact is that a person's thoughts are their reality, and therefore it is your conclusions that are important, and that YOU are comfortable with those conclusions.

We have looked at how following the simple prescription for the "Good Life" can improve the quality of our lives, and of those people around us. Also, the idea was put forward that as individuals we could actually make a difference in the world by becoming activists.

There has been ample discussion about how you can make use of the tools to be found in the Zarathustrian doctrines for yourself, and how those tools can be offered to and made use of in the lives of those in your immediate sphere of influence. Is that enough or do you wish to make a difference on a larger scale? What are your special capacities? We each have them, often latent and unused! Is it in the Arts, such as painting, drama, music or writing? How about in motivating others? You can be of assistance to adults, teenagers, or children! You can assist by helping immigrants with their language skills. What is being suggested is that you personally do not need to be the one that changes the World, but can be like Thomas Edison's mother, the facilitator for the doer that does change the world. You can be the peacemaker who upon observing that well attended meeting on an evening positively changes the collective negative energies of the occasion by pointing out how wonderful it is in a society that is normally so noninvolved to have such magnificent and dynamic attendance. After a very short pause, you could add, "what a shame it would be to waste time with a gathering of so much talent." Then suggest that everyone realize that if it is possible to offer ideas without names or egos attached, and to offer them, not as the solution, but as one brick in the foundation upon which other ideas could be added and again without egos or even a person's name attached until there could be a consensus which would be the property of all in attendance. Then point out that this is exactly what this energetic and intelligent assemblage is capable of and what the problem at hand requires. YOU have just supplied the positive process by which the creation of solutions can appear and supplied the manpower to effect the positive results. One of the rules should be that only comments of merit should be made or how the last point offered might be made better. It sounds utopian, but it works! It is a change in approach that can cause people who could never see eye to eye before, to see real value in each other. It is not necessary that your idea is supported, because that idea ceased to be yours as soon as it was verbalized. YOU gave it to the entire group. This format works, because participants start listening to the ideas not to who is offering them.

What a blessing it would be if this format could become the norm for all conversations whether at a small tea party, the school board meeting, or Congress. The value of far too many beautiful ideas are never given a chance, because of who put the idea forth, the manner in which it was transmitted, or because while awaiting their turn to speak others were too busy thinking what it was they were going to say and how best to say it, to actually hear the ideas of the person before them. If there is a spokesman who has difficulty articulating an excellent idea, before others can attack this individual; if only someone could find a way to lovingly offer clarification through restatement of what will otherwise become lost. We do not learn from our own ideas and speaking, only from that of others. Does all of that make sense?

Other Comings or Returns of Saviors

There are a few loose ends that probably should be addressed which you will find in the New Testament of the Holy Bible. Remember that Ahura Mazda (God) informed Zarathustra that there would most likely be a necessity for more than one Savior. Is it possible that this can be combined with what Jesus had to say about his return? Try to forget what you thought you heard in your church concerning this matter long enough to see what it is that Jesus had to say. Remember that the early church was not aware of these teachings of Zarathustra. Remember also what we have said about the first coming of the spirit of Ahura Mazda [God] named Hushedar. This was Jesus as shown by the journey of the Magi. Will the coming of Hushedarmah as named by Zarathustra also be the return or second coming of Jesus? What should be looked for in this coming? Unfortunately, the writings which were detailed enough for the Magi concerning the birth of a child with the capacity to become the recipient of the spirit of God, have been lost, as have those detailing the specific times and locations of that next coming. However, if the next coming is the same as what Jesus was speaking about when He was describing His return, we should be able to look for clues in what Jesus said about that return:

1)   In several places Jesus says that, in the second coming, "He shall come in the clouds".

a) **Mark 13:25-26:** "and the stars will be falling from heaven, and the powers in the heavens will be shaken. And then they shall see the Son of Man coming in the clouds with great power and glory."

b) **Matthew 24:30:** "then will appear the sign of the Son of man in heaven, and then all the tribes of the earth will mourn, and they will see the Son of man coming on the clouds of heaven with power and great glory."

c) **Revelation 1:7:** "Behold, he is coming with the clouds."

d) **Mark 14:61-62:** "Again the high priest asked him, 'are you the Christ, the Son of the Blessed?' And Jesus said, 'I am; and you will see the Son of man seated at the right hand of Power, and coming in the Clouds of heaven'."

What does it mean when it is stated that "He shall come from the clouds"? That could mean that Jesus will arrive in an airplane or space ship! But that would seem to refer to the clouds of earth, whereas the above Scriptures refer to the coming of the "Son of Man" appearing from the clouds of heaven. There have been sermons preached that this event could not have occurred any earlier than the present with our satellite communications and the Internet. This could be true if the "clouds" referred to physical clouds, that is, the clouds of earth. However, two of the above verses mention specifically that the "clouds" will be the "clouds of Heaven." What if what is returning is again the spirit of God, and since God is spirit, the returning is far more spiritual than physical. In other Scriptures Jesus says that His coming shall be as a thief in the night;

a) **2 Peter 3:10:** "But the day of the Lord will come like a thief...."

b) **Revelation 16:15:** "Lo, I am coming like a thief! Blessed is he who is awake, keeping his garments that he may not go naked and be seen exposed"

c) **1 Thessalonians 5:2-3:** "For you yourselves know well that the day of the Lord will come like a thief in the night. When people say, 'there is peace and security,' then sudden destruction shall come upon them as travail comes upon a woman with child, and there will be no escape."

d) **Matthew 24:42-44:** "watch therefore, for you not know on what day your Lord is coming. But know this, that if the householder had known in what part of the night the thief was coming, he would have watched and would not let his house be broken into. Therefore you also must be ready; for the Son of man is coming at an hour you do not expect."

e) **Mark 13:33-37:** "Take heed, watch: for you do not know when the time will come. It is like a man going on a journey, when he leaves home and puts his servants in charge, each with his work, and commands the doorkeeper to be on the watch. Watch therefore—for you do not know when the master of the house will come, in the evening, or at midnight, or at cockcrow, or in the morning—lest he come suddenly and find you asleep. And what I say to you I say to all: Watch!"

The coming as a "thief in the night" is not the kind of second coming that will be accompanied by the sounding of trumpets nor will it be likely viewed by the entire world on CNN, the Internet, or even on the greatest religious reality show on earth. Could the Scriptures be hinting at an arrival similar to that of Jesus, such that there could be the physical birth of a child with little notice by the world at large, and that the spiritual coming would be after that child had grown to adulthood and maturity? At that point, with full freedom of choice, he or she could accept the appointment to be the messenger of God by allowing the infusion of the Spirit of God, and most likely in a way that very few would notice. How can these descriptions be made to be in agreement with the ones that say that he shall come from the clouds of Heaven?

There is a third grouping of quotations concerning the coming of the Son of Man in which it clearly states that in His coming "he shall have a new Name":

a) **Matthew 24:4-5:** "And Jesus answered them, "Take heed that no one leads you astray. For many will come in my name, saying, "I am the Christ," and they will lead many astray."

b) **Revelation 2:17:** "He who has an ear, let him hear what the Spirit says to the churches. To him who conquers will I give him a white stone, with a new name written on the stone which no one knows except him who receives it."

c) **Revelation 3:11-12:** "I am coming soon; hold fast what you have, so that no one may seize your crown. He who conquers, I will make him a pillar in the temple of God; never shall he go out of it, and I will write on him the name of my God, the new Jerusalem which comes down from my God out of heaven, and my own new name."

d) **Revelation 21:22-24:** "And I saw no temple in the city, for its temple is the Lord God and the Lamb. And the city has no need of sun or moon to shine upon it, for the glory of God is its light, and its lamp is the Lamb. By its light shall the nations walk; and the kings of the earth shall bring their glory into it."

He Shall Appear as a Thief in the Night
He Shall Descend From the Clouds of Heaven
He Shall Have a New Name

These quotations from the King James Version of the Bible seem to throw the whole second coming issue into confusion for many Christians. Let us try to give new meaning to the return of Christ. If the second coming is not the physical person of Jesus, but, instead, the spirit that was within Him into the form of yet another person, as it was with Zarathustra, this would seem to give new meaning to the quotations above. The time, place and manner of the coming would be cloaked in mystery and thus it would be as a "thief in the night." Likewise, the descending from the clouds could simply mean that the spirit of God would descend from heaven similar to the spirit descending like a dove as was described when Jesus was baptized by John, the Baptist, or as it is written happened with Zarathustra. The appearing with a new name could simply be that this is the same spirit but in a different body.

The purpose of this book has been to inform, to offer spiritual insights that will help you think and refocus your spiritual conclusions with the hope that in so doing, your life will become even happier than it was before. It is hoped that your refocusing will help you establish an improved appreciation of and love for God, that source, that essence, that force of creation, which can go by any name you choose to become an even greater source of wonderment and awe, and further that this awe and happiness shall be infectious to your immediate world.

Further, it is hoped that you have become aware that you have far more capacity than you may have realized and that you can make a difference in the world. With that knowledge, you will!

At most times, the concepts and quotes used in this book have come from of the Avesta or from the Holy Bible. There is a quote which I have been unable to locate, the source of which may have been a personal dream. It is offered to you because it has the ring of truth and may assist you in your quest as to the nature of God [Ahura Mazda]. This quote states that His love is for all of His Creation, even when if what is included has the appearance of ungodliness. All was necessary for the sake of the education of mankind:

"Zarathustra wished to know specifically what was least pleasing and what was most pleasing in the eyes of Ahura Mazda:

"Least pleasing in my eyes, O Zarathustra is that man with no belief;

More pleasing is that man who worshipeth Idols

Still more pleasing is he who worshipeth daeva [the spirits of Nature]

More pleasing than this is the man who worshipeth many gods

But most pleasing in mine eyes, Oh Zarathustra, is that man who worshipeth Me, the one God, and for you of the Aryan [Iranian] race, my name shall be Ahura Mazda".

In this wonderful litany, even if it be from a dream, Ahura Mazda states that He loves all mankind and how He views the spirituality of mankind. He has love for the non-believer, merely finding his lack of belief to be the "least pleasing." In this answer, Ahura Mazda speaks not just as the God of Zarathustra and the Persians, but as the God of all Creation, thus all of mankind. The quote would explain the very tolerant interactions of Zarathustra and His followers with individuals and nations of varied beliefs. This tolerance offers a historical explanation for the release of the Jews from their Babylonian captivity via Cyrus the Great. For by freeing the monotheistic Jewish nation from the hands of the idol-worshippers, Cyrus would surely bring joy to his God, Ahura Mazda.

Although I may not have met you, however, the fact that you have read this far in this book, I now consider you a friend and as such, have spiritual love for you.

MAY THE BLESSINGS AND JOY OF AHURA MAZDA
[OR WHATEVER YOU CHOOSE TO CALL THE SOURCE OF ALL CREATION]
BE WITH YOU NOW, AND FOREVER MORE!

STUDY GUIDE

INTRODUCTION

1. Do you enjoy and feel comfortable questioning and analyzing your spiritual and religious knowledge?

2. Are you totally satisfied with that knowledge or are you willing to add to your thoughts and conclusions concerning the what's, whys and how's of religion?

3. Can you discuss and converse on religious thoughts without feeling threatened and becoming defensive? To this end, try and remember that only the source of creation is all knowing, and therefore you do not need to agree with those in your study group, they also are not God!!

4. Did your basic religious education end with Catechism or Sunday school? In which case, is it possible that what you learned has faded with time or was simplified to be made age appropriate?

5. Has your spiritual training become less than satisfying now that you are an adult?

CHAPTER 1: THE BIRTH AND EARLY LIFE OF JESUS - THE IMPORTANCE OF THE STORY OF THE MAGI

1. List the ten most important thoughts as to the importance of the journey and visit of the Magi as presented in the Gospel of Matthew. Why it was recorded in such detail?

2. Why had the Magi come so far to acknowledge the birth of one whom they described as "The King of the Jews"?

3. They traveled into what, for them, was enemy territory, to bring Him expensive gifts. Did they explain the reason for their bowing down to worship the baby, not the parents?

4. What happened to those gifts? Might they have been sold to enable the flight of the family to Egypt?

5. Discuss with your study group what your own reaction would have been to have had important world leaders visit the birth place of a child of yours. What questions or advice might have you asked of these individuals? Would your life or that of your child possibly have been the same after this incident?

6. As we look at the possibilities not detailed in the biblical account of the Magi story, it becomes obvious that the story is less than complete. What would help to fill in the gaps?

CHAPTER 2 - ZARATHUSTRA

1. What are the similarities in the birth of Jesus and Zarathustra? What are the differences?

2. How and why was he disturbed at an early age by the condition of the religious faith of his parents as it was generally being practiced?

3. When Zarathustra retired into the wilderness on His religious quest, what was it that He was seeking? He prayed to God, who He was to call Ahura Mazda, for enlightenment, what was it that He received and how?

4. He ultimately became the founder of a new religion, replacing that which the priests and the people had damaged beyond repair. Finding that His teachings were ignored by His own people, Zarathustra was forced to travel to the neighboring kingdom of Bactria. Why is it difficult for a True religious leader to be recognized by His own people?

CHAPTER 3 - ZARATHUSTRA -
THE RELIGION, TEACHINGS AND PROPHESIES

1. Zarathustra's revelation and ministry lasted for over forty years, during which time He revealed many laws, doctrines, prayers and prophecies. He provided detailed descriptions of angels and other assistants of the Creator God, whom He called Ahura Mazda. He introduced the concept of Satan, whom He called Ahriman. He introduced the concepts of the rites of confession, renunciation, penance and absolution through the priests, a continuation of the life of the Soul after the death of the physical body, an explanation of and an introduction of Heaven, Hell and Purgatory, a detailed explanation of the process needed for the proper detachment of the soul from its host body after physical death, the values of prayers during life and after death, and new rules for the disposal of the body of the dead. What of these teachings and doctrines did you find of particular interest?

2. Is this religion in any way a copy of either Christianity or Judaism? If so, discuss how this could have occurred.

3. Zarathustra taught that it was not enough to avoid Evil, but that it was necessary to actively combat it within oneself and without. Is this only an old fashioned idea? Why does it make sense to you in this day and age?

CHAPTER 4 - ZARATHUSTRA -
THE NATURE OF GOD AND HIS CREATION

1. This Chapter relates that God is a Spirit which is responsible
    for all that is and as such, is vitally interested in all of
    Creation. He is a God who continues to create and which
    looks to His finest creation, Humans, to assist him in that
    continuing creation. How does this compare with your
    conception of God? What aspects of this conception of God
    are disturbing and what are comforting and why?

CHAPTER 5 - THE RELIGION AND MINISTRY OF JESUS

1. What occurs to Jesus with His Baptism by His cousin John, the Baptist? Discuss the meanings and the possible ramifications.

2. The temptation of Jesus occurs after the incident at the time of the Baptism, what are your thoughts concerning this temptation? How important was this? Was it actually a temptation or merely a way of Jesus finding a method of explaining the otherwise unexplainable? Are your thoughts of the temptation different than they were prior to the reading of this book?

3. Did the similar happening (both infusion of the spirit of God and the Satanic temptation) take on new meaning for you after the similar description of what happened in the case of Zarathustra?

4. Discuss with your group why Jesus chose most of His Apostles to be from Galilee. Was this merely a coincidence? Is it possible that this choice of Apostles could have influenced the reception of His message in Jerusalem?

5. This chapter discusses the teachings of Jesus and their impact on the Jews of Jerusalem and more particularly of both the Jews and Gentiles of Galilee and surrounding lands. Were you aware that Galilee was considered the "land of the Gentiles"? Were you aware that many Galileans with Jewish blood were in Galilee because of the ethnic decrees of the Jewish Prophet Ezra some three hundred years before the time of Jesus?

6. Were you aware that many of the Gentiles of Galilee were there because of the disruption of their ancestor's lives 300 years before with the military conquests of Alexander, the Great? And that these "Gentiles" included Zarathustrians, Babylonians, Sumerians and other ethnic peoples displaced and dispersed at the time of the invasion by Alexander, the Great?

7. Why is the fact that Jesus taught the Healing "Arts" to apostles and disciples not given much importance in many Christian churches today?

8. Can you list at least five reasons that Jesus stated that He had come to divide, not to unite people?

Chapter 6 - Parallels and Differences between Jesus and Zarathustra

1. As we look at the amazing similarities only of these two special men of God, and the messages that They brought to humankind, and also the awesome circumstances concerning Their conception, birth, and childhood, is it possible that all of this is merely coincidence? Consult with the members of your group. Again it is Okay if there are differences of opinions, hopefully you are still among friends.

2. In Their childhood, WHY the "years of silence" wherein almost nothing was recorded for either man until adulthood? We question why both Men then experienced similar heavenly intervention, establishing them as sources of revelation, healing powers and miracles. Is it possible that these parallels can all be coincidence?

CHAPTER 7 - INFLUENCES OF THE TWO RELIGIONS

1. Many assertions are made in this chapter concerning the influences of the religion of Zarathustra upon both Judaism and Christianity, discuss this in your study group and learn from the thoughts of the other members. This is a place where there can be many opinions, and the only ones that will count for you are those that after reflection make sense to you!

2. Discuss how and why the edict on Human Rights made by Cyrus was ahead of its time and whether this same edict would not have a new reality if adopted by the United Nations today! Check the United Nations Charter to see how many of the items from Cyrus' edict are included partially or in full.

3. Research the history of Cyrus and Darius further and discuss the biblical meanings of the declarations of Isaiah concerning each, with such terms as that Cyrus should be known as "the Lord's Shepherd" and God's "Anointed One."

4. Discuss with the members of the study group what seems to have occurred to Christianity before the conversion of Roman Emperor Constantine and in the centuries after. NOTE: There are positives and negatives in both periods.

5. The discussion of the Crusades and their impact on the western world is far too simplistic and deserves further study and discussion as does the effect that Islam had upon the maintenance of scholarship and the sciences while the western world was in what has been termed the Dark Ages.

6. Discuss in your study group the positive and negative influence that religion can have upon the society in which it is practiced.

7. Discuss various aspects of the exploration and colonization of the world by the Christian nations of the western world. What lessons are there to be learned by this history?

8. "GOD IS DEAD!" was the attitude of a great number of the Intelligencia of the United States and of Western Europe in the 1800s. Is this attitude emerging in "polite society" again? Can a revival of the teachings of Zarathustra make a difference again?

9. Nietzsche's book was misused by a Hate-filled group, and because of that his reputation and philosophy have been rendered totally superfluous, discuss the fairness and lack of justice and what can or should be done!

10. Discuss in your study group the stories of Thomas A. Edison and the founder of Mazda Motors. What lessons should be learned from these individuals?

Chapter 8 - Three Religions Compared

1. Traditionally Christianity has been considered an outgrowth, or successor religion, of Judaism. Review this chart and comparison of the Jewish Faith and the Talmud, and a study investigating some of the ways in which it differs from Christianity and the faith of Zarathustra. In the process, remember that the differences are just differences and do not make any one of the religions better than the other and definitely not wrong. These differences include the Jewish perspectives on the individual, on prayer, the afterlife, community, the purpose of religion and even the definition of sin. How is it that, in contrast, the Christian and Zarathustrian religions appear so similar in these same areas? There is an honest attempt by the author to express that each faith is a valid and true gift of God, and that none is superior to the other, just not completely the same. Is any religion which makes you a better or happier person worthy of your consideration?

Chapter 9 - A Few Thoughts and Final Closing

1. This chapter brings to an end the reader's spiritual journey of refocusing. If the book has had anywhere near the effect upon the reader that the writing of it has had upon the author, this will have been a journey well worth having, and, hopefully, it will have whetted the reader's appetite for further spiritual travel, as well as a journey of new optimism. The Reader and also the group of individuals with whom you have been studying is reminded that according to the teachings of Zarathustra each of us has a long line of ancestors with hopes and expectations to be fulfilled. Further, as the previous eight chapters have been telling us; as individuals we can assist in the continuing creation such that every person can do what will truly change the world in which we live now, and in which mankind will hope to live for generations to come. Discuss separately the items mentioned bove with your group.

2. Is there more hope for the world than you thought before you started this book?

3. Can you think of and share with your group at least three ways that you can make a real difference in the World?

4. GO GET 'UM TIGERS—WITH GOOD THOUGHTS, GOOD WORDS, AND GOOD DEEDS!

BIBLIOGRAPHY

Barclay, William. *Herod, The Great*. Philadelphia: Westminster Press, 1958.

Bharucha, Ervad. *A Brief Sketch of the Zoroastrian Religion and Customs*. Duffer Ashkari O.Y. Engine Printing Press, 1893, reprint General Books, 2009.

Boyce, Mary. *A History of Zoroastrianism: The Early Period*, 2nd ed. Chicago: University of Chicago Press, 1984.
    -----*Textual Sources for the Study of Zoroastrianism*. Chicago: University of Chicago Press, 1990.
    -----*Zoroastrians, Their Beliefs and Practices*. London: Library of Religious Beliefs and Practices, 1979.

Brown, E.G., *A Year Amongst the Persians*. 1893, reprint Elibron Classics, Adamant Media, 2005.

Champion, Selwyn, and Dorothy Short. *Great Religions of the World*. Los Angeles: National Geographic Society, 1978.

Clark, Peter. *An Introduction to Zoroastrianism*. Portland, OR: Sussex Academic Press, 2001.

Darmesteter, James (trans.) *Avesta Fragments*. See Mullen, F. Max (ed.), *Sacred Books of the East*.
    -----*Fargard*. See Muller, F. Max (ed.), *Sacred Books of the East*.
    -----*Khorda Avesta*. See Muller, F. Max (ed.), *Sacred Books of the East*.
    -----*The Zend Avesta*, Part II. See Muller, F. Max (ed.), *Sacred Books of the East*.
    -----*Zend Avesta Vendidad*. See Muller, F. Max (ed.), *Sacred Books of the East*.

Dawson, Miles. *The Ethical Religion of Zoroaster.* New York: AMS Press, 1931.

Dhalla, M. *Zoroastrian Theology.* Reprint in History of Zoroastrianism. New York: Oxford Press, 1938.

Dosick, Wayne. *Living Judaism.* New York: Harper-Collins, 1998.

Duchesne-Guillemin, Jacques. *Zoroastrianism, Symbols and Values.* U.S.A. : National Geographic Society, 1971.

Figueira, Dorothy. *Aryans, Jews, Brahmins: Theorizing Authority Through Myths of Identity.* Albany State University of New York Press, 2002.

Fuller, Reginald C., Johnston, Leonard, and Kearns, Conleth (eds.). *A New Catholic Commentary on Holy Scripture.* London: Thomas Nelson and Sons Ltd, 1969.

Hanna, Nabil. *Bible Proofs.* Los Angeles: Kalimat Press, 1988.

Haug, Martin. *Essays on the Sacred Language, Writings, and Religion of the Parsis.* Bombay Gazette, 1862.

Heschel, Abraham Joshua. "Between God and Man." *Zarathustrian Assembly Spenda Periodical*, vol. 2, nos. 5-6, vol. 3, nos. 1-2, 1993.

His Holiness the Dalai Lama. *Toward a True Kinship of Faiths.* New York: Doubleday Religion, Random House, 2010.

Hoffmeier, James. *Ancient Israel in Sinai: The Evidence for the Authenticity of the Wilderness Tradition.* New York: Oxford University Press, Inc., 2005.

The Holy Bible, King James Version. Chicago: Windsor Publishing.

Jackson, A.V. W.. *The Prophet of Ancient Iran*. New York: Columbia University Press, 1899.
-----*Persia, Past and Present*. New York: MacMillan, 1910.

Laing, S. *A Modern Zoroastrian*. London: Chapman and Hall Ltd, 1890.

Masani, Rustam. *Zoroastrianism: The Religion of the Good Life*. New York: The MacMillan Co., 1968.

Miller, Madeline and J. Lane, *Harper's Bible Dictionary*, 8th ed. New York: Harper and Rowe, 1973.

Mills, L. H. (trans.) *Avesta Fragments*. See Mullen, F. Max (ed.), *Sacred Books of the East*.
-----*Avesta-Yasna*. See Muller, F. Max (ed.), *Sacred Books of the East*.
-----*Avesta*, Part III. See Muller, F. Max (ed.), *Sacred Books of the East*.
-----*Gathas*. See Muller, F. Max (ed.) *Sacred Books of the East*.
-----*Miscellaneous Fragments*. See Muller, F. Max (ed.), *Sacred Books of the East*.
-----*The Zend Avesta*, Part III. See Muller, F. Max (ed.), *Sacred Books of the East*.

Moulton, J.H. *The Treasure of the Magi*. London: Oxford Press, 1917.
----Early Zoroastrianism. Hibbert Journal, 1913, ed. Jack, L.P. and Hicks, G. Dawes

Muller, F. Max (ed.); Darmesteter, James (trans.), Mills, L.H. (trans.), West, E.W. (trans.). *Sacred Books of the East*, vols. 1, 4, 5, 7, 18, 23, 31, 39. Celho, India: Motilal Banarsidass, 1897.

Nietzsche, Friedrich. *Thus Spoke Zarathustra*. Gateway ed. Translated by M. Cowan. Chicago: Henry Regnery Co., 1957.

Pagels, Elaine. *The Gnostic Gospels*. New York: Random House, Inc., 1979.

Sharma, Suresh K. and Usha Sharma, (eds.). *Cultural and Religious Heritage of India: Zoroastrianism*. New Delhi: Mittal Publications, 2004.

Tilak, Bal Gangadhar. *The Orion—Researches into the Antiquity of Vedas*. Poona City, India: Tilak Bros. Publishers, 1893.
-----*The Artic Home in the Vedas*. Poona City, India: Tilak Bros. Publishers, 1903.

Webster's Collegiate Dictionary. New York: Random House, 2000.

Webster's New World Dictionary. Cleveland/New York: The World Publishing Co., 1964.

West, E.W. (trans.). *The Bundahishn*. See Mullen, F. Max, *Sacred Books of the East*.
-----*Dadistan-I-Dinik*.   See Muller, F. Max, *Sacred Books of the East*.
----- *Pahlavi Texts,* Parts I-V. See Muller, F. Max, *Sacred Books of the East*.
----- *Shayest-Na-Shayest*.   See Muller, F. Max, *Sacred Books of the East*.
----- *Vohuman Yasht Dadistan-I-Dinik*.   See Muller, F. Max, *Sacred Books of the East*.

Woolson, Gayle. *Divine Symphony*. New Delhi: Baha'i Publishing Trust, 1971.

Internet Sources

http://ancienthistory.about.com
http://avesta.org
http:// classics.mit.edu
http://dictionary.reference.com
http://lifestyle.iloveindia.com
http://normanvincentpeale.wwwhubs.com
http://stanford.edu
http://zoroastriankids.com
http://www.archive.org
http://www.avesta.org
http://www.bellaonline.net
http://www.bradshaw foundation.com
http://www.bringyou.to
http://www.caissoas.com
http://www.dlshq.org
http://www.farsinet.com
http://gnosis.org
http://www.heritageinstitute.com
http://www.hinduwebsite.com
http://www.historylearningsite.co.uk
http://www.historyworld.net
http://www.iranchamber.com
http://www.livius.org
http://www.nytimes.com
http://www.persiandna.com
http://www.presstv.ir
http://www.sacred-texts.com
http://www.themystica.com
http://www.usccb.org
http://www.zoroastrian.org

Endnotes

Chapter 1

1   Miller, Madeline S. and Miller, J. Lane (eds.). *Harper's Bible Dictionary*, p. 254.

2   Barclay, William. *The Gospel of Matthew*. pp. 14-25.

3   *Harper's Bible Dictionary*, p. 254.
    The *Harper's Bible Dictionary* makes note that there were many individual rulers in the Herod family. At the time of the birth of Jesus, the man that called himself Herod the Great, was the second in family line of eleven rulers of Judaea. He died in the year 4 BC. His son, Herod Antipas, ruled from 4 BC until he was deposed in 39 AD. Under the "Herod Family" reign of power, there was a tremendous amount of construction, road and aqueduct building, the creation of new and the rebuilding of cities including the port city of Stratos Tower, which as a sign of his political astuteness he renamed Caesarea in honor of his patron, Augustus Caesar. In Jerusalem and other cities, Herod had stadia erected, along with public baths, theaters and amphitheaters. His major building included the reconstruction of Sepphoris (just four miles north of Nazareth) and was a likely work site for Jesus and His carpenter father, Joseph.

4   Boyce, Mary. *A History of Zoroastrianism: The Early Period* (Brill, 1989, 2nd ed.), vol. 1, pp. 10–11.

5   West, E.W. (trans.). *Yasna* 48:11-12; *Yasna* 43:30. *Sacred Books of the East*.

6   Williams, A.V. (trans.) *"Pahlavi Rivayat"*, 48:1-6. 1990. http://www.avesta.org/zcomet.html.
    Gathas defined hymns with spiritual value or instruction, very similar to the Psalms of the Old Testament. Since so much of religion depended on verbal transmission, accuracy was very often assisted by the singing of the holy verses

7   Boyce, Mary. *Textual Sources for the Study of Zoroastrianism, Zand of Yahman Vasht* 9:1, p. 53.

8   Ibid. *Greater Bundahishn* 35:56-60, pp. 52-53.

9   Ibid. *Gathas, Yasna* 48:11-12; *Yasna* 43:30; pp. 39-40.

10 *The Holy Bible, King James Version*, Matt. 2:1-12.

11   Ibid. Matt. 1:18-23.

12   Ibid. Luke 1:26-33.

13   Ibid. Isa. 60:1-6.

14   Fuller, Reginald C., Johnston, Leonard, and Kearns, Conleth (eds.). *A New Catholic Commentary on Holy Scripture*. 713:e-k, p. 908.

15   *The Holy Bible, King James Version,* Matt. 2:12.

16   Ibid. Matt. 2:16.

17   Ibid. Matt. 2:1-9

18   Hoffmeier, James. *Ancient Israel in Sinai: the Evidence for the Authenticity of the Wilderness Tradition.* pp.119-

19   *The Holy Bible, King James Version,* Matt. 2:12

20   Egypt was not yet a part of the Roman Empire at the birth of Jesus and was no longer a part of the Macedonian Empire which had disintegrated after the death of Alexander. It seems to have reverted to being a Persian protectorate. According to the Map of Nations at the time of Christ's Birth. Map no. 11. *Harper's Bible Dictionary.*

21   *The Holy Bible, King James Version,* Matt. 2:7-8.

22   *Harper's Bible Dictionary,* p. 49.

23   Pamphlet printed in 1976.

24   *Harper's Bible Dictionary,* p. 814.

25   Interaction of the Persian and Judaic cultures was between equals in perceived or historical power, at least in the eyes of the Magi. *Harper's Bible Dictionary,* p. 123.

26   *The Holy Bible, King James Version,* Matt. 2:2.

27   Ibid. Hos. 11:1.

28   Ibid. Luke 2:21-40.

29   Ibid. Matt. 2:19-20.

30   Ibid. Matt. 2:13-15.

31   Ibid. Matt. 2:19-23.

32   Ibid. Luke 2:41-7.

33   The chronological life of Jesus is in the back of most King James Bibles. A
      copy may be found at the back of Chapter 5.

34   *Harper's Bible Dictionary.* pp. 254-57.

35   Masani, Rustam. *Zoroastrianism: The Religion of the Good Life.* p. 7.

36   Ibid. p. 10.

Chapter 2

1.   Oppenheimer, Stephen. *Journey of Mankind Interactive Trail.* http://www.
      bradshawfoundation.com/journey/timeline.swf.
      Author's Note: The term "nuclear winter" is an apt description of the result of
      the eruption of Mt. Topa approximately 74,000 years ago. There is geological
      evidence that the skies were so filled with volcanic debris that the sun did not
      shine on land for approximately six years.

2   Masani, Rustam. *Zoroastrianism: The Religion of the Good Life.* p. 30.
      Author's Note: There are two beautiful books substantiating this fascinating
      subject by Bal Gungahdar Tilak, "The Arctic Home in the Vedas" (1903)
      and "The Orion" (1893). The astronomy, mathematics and history are very
      convincing.

3   Eduljee, K.E. *Location of the Aryan Homeland, Airyana Vaeja.* http://www.
      heritageinstitute.com/zoroastrianism/aryans/location.htm.
      Author's Note: With the return of an Ice Age there was reason the Aryan
      peoples to resettle many miles southward. That this move could have come
      rather suddenly would have necessitated taking with them only the barest
      essentials; their animals, their seeds, enough food for hard times, plus the
      knowledge learned in the twenty to forty thousand years of long winter's
      night. Their myths say that they had not only domesticated cattle, sheep,
      horses and especially dogs, which were bred for hunting, herding, and
      protection. They had developed rudimentary weapons including spears
      swords, and two and four wheeled chariots. They had developed the some
      skills of construction and of boat building. They credited Mazda for the
      revelation which had allowed these creations. That proof of all of this cannot
      be found is probably owing to the fact that much of the Arctic Home has been
      and continues to be under an ice sheet. Wild speculation, of course it is. But
      it does make sense the tower of Babel may not be just a myth and that the
      skill to build the pyramids, cities and the Arc of Noah may have been skills
      learned in ancient times, over the one hundred and fifty thousand years prior

to the known history of mankind! While thinking about these things, that prior to the Aryan's move southward that in the approximately 30,000 years stay above the Arctic Circle, during the six month long days of winter, the hunter/gatherers would have had ample time for contemplation, prayers, and creativity. Remember we are talking about modern man.

4   Figueira, Dorothy M. *Aryans, Jews, Brahmins: Theorizing Authority Through Myths of Identity.* p. 130.

5   Boyce, Mary. *Textual Sources for the Study of Zoroastrianism.* p. 8.

6   *Zoroastrianism: The Religion of the Good Life.* p. 30.

7   *Textual Sources for the Study of Zoroastrianism.* p. 9.

8   *Webster's New World Dictionary.* p. 84.
    Author's Note: Refers to the language and those peoples of Caucasian background whose ancestors spoke the Indo-European language that preceded the languages of Hindi and Pahlavi (later Farsi), and were the ancestors of the greater populations of India, Iran and Afghanistan.

9   *Textual Sources for the Study of Zoroastrianism.* p. 9.

10 Mobin, Abolhassan. *History of Iran: The Aryan Movement.* http://www.iranchamber.com/history/articles/aryan_movement.php

11 *Zoroastrianism: The Religion of the Good Life.* p. 33.

12 Ibid, p. 32.

13 *Textual Sources for the Study of Zoroastrianism.* p. 9.

14 *Zoroastrianism: The Religion of the Good Life.* pp. 32-33.

15 Eduljee, K.E. *Aryan Religions*, in *Zoroastrianism.* http://www.heritageinstitute.com/zoroastrianism/aryans/religion.htm.

16 *Zoroastrianism: The Religion of the Good Life.* pp. 33-34.
    Dawson, Miles M. *The Ethical Religion of Zoroaster.* p. xiv.
    Zarathustra and His Religion. 1996. http://www.iranologie.com/history/zarathustra.html
    Boyce, Mary. *Textual Sources for the Study of Zoroastrianism.* pp. 11, 15.
    The date of 300 BC makes absolutely no sense in that this would place the birth of Zarathustra after the invasion and destruction of the Persian Empire by Alexander, the Great. Zarathustra must have lived long before Cyrus I, the first Persian Emperor, who not only freed the captive Jews from Babylon in the year 530 BC, which had to be after he defeated the Medes whose Empire

had come about by the political and religious advice of Zarathustra. The dates of 8000 BC and 10,000 BC come from Babylonian and Assyrian Historians, who do not feel that the amount of his teachings could have been produced by only one man. They seem not to take into account the concept of Revelation nor the length of Zarathustra's ministry, and instead theorize in the concept of multiple Zarathustras'. The varying dates of the Birth of Zarathustra include the following also 1000 to 6000 BC from classical writers as Xanthus, Plato, Pliny the elder, and Plutarch. Mary Boyce makes an excellent case for a date of 1600 to 1700 BC based on language in the Gathas, which agrees closely with the Persian Year 3748 as of 2010 AD.

17 *Zoroastrianism: The Religion of the Good Life.* p. 33.

18 Darmesteter, James (trans.). *The Zend Avesta: Part 1, Sacred Books of the East,* vol. 4. http://www.heritageinstitute.com/zoroastrianism/reference/darmesteter3.htm.

19 *Zoroastrianism: The Religion of the Good Life.* pp. 36-38.

20 Cann, Rebecca. *The First Prophet: The Story of Zarathustra.* http://zoroastriankids.com/story2.html.

21 Pliny, *Naturalis Historia*, in *Zoroastrianism: The Religion of the Good Life.* p. 33.

22 *Zoroastrianism: The Religion of the Good Life.* p. 36

23 Author's Note: The stories of His childhood vary greatly, but all seem to have been written many hundreds of years after the fact and seem mythical in nature.

24 Woolson, Gayle. *Divine Symphony.* p. 32.

25 Ibid. p. 32.
    Sivananda, Sri Swami. *Zoroaster,* in *Lives of Saints.* http://www.dlshq.org/saints/zoroaster.htm.

26 *Yasna* 44:3-5. http://avesta.org/yasna/yasna.htm#y43.

27 *Zoroastrianism: The Religion of the Good Life.* p. 40.

28 *Yasna* 33: 7. http://avesta.org/yasna/yasna.htm#y28.

29 *Yasna* 43: 5. http://avesta.org/yasna/yasna.htm#y43.

30 *Yasna* 31: 8. http://avesta.org/yasna/yasna.htm#y28.

31 *Zoroastrianism: The Religion of the Good Life.* p. 53.

32 Ibid. pp. 40-41.

33 Ibid. p. 53.

34 Ibid. pp. 59-60.

35 Ibid. p. 24.

36 Ibid. p. 51.

37 Ibid. p. 60.

38 Ibid. p. 41

39 Darmesteter, James (trans.). *The Zend Avesta*. pp. 211-12: *Fargard* 19:6-9. *Sacred Books of the East*.

40 *Zoroastrianism: The Religion of the Good Life*. pp. 41-43.

41 Muller, F. Max (ed.) *Sacred Books of the East*, vol. 31. pp.134-5: Yasna 46:1-2

42 "Zoroaster". *Lives of Saints*. http://www.dlshq.org/saints/zoroaster.htm

43 Darmesteter, James (trans.). *The Zend Avesta: Part II*. pp. 325-27: *Yast* 23:1-8. *Sacred Books of the East*.

44 Taraporevala, IJS.. *The Divine Songs of Zarathustra*. Bartholomae, C. (trans.) http://www.avesta.org.

45 Ferdowsi. *The Shahnameh*. Zimmern, Helen (trans.). www.classics.mit.edu/ferdowsi/kings.mb.txt.

46 *The Divine Songs of Zarathustra*. Bartholomae, C. (trans.). http://www.avesta.org.

47 Kapadia, S.A. *The Teachings of Zoroaster & the Philosophy of the Parsi Religion*. p. 15. http://www.archive.org/details/teachingzoroast00kapauoft.

48 Mills, L.H. (trans.) *Yasna* 30:2. *Sacred Books of the East*, vol. 31. p. 29.

49 *The Divine Songs of Zarathustra*. Bartholomae, C. (trans.) http://www.avesta.org.

50 Ibid.

51 Ibid.

52 *Frequently Asked Questions On Zorastrianism and the Avesta*. http://www.avesta.org/zfaq.html

53   Taraporevala, Sooni. "Parsis – Zarathustrians of India." http://www.the-south-asian.com/April2001/ Who%20was%20Zarathustra.htm

54   *Textual Sources for the Study of Zoroastrianism.* p. 1

55   *The American Heritage Dictionary of the English Language*, 4th ed. http://dictionary.reference.com/browse/Zend-avesta.

56   *Textual Sources for the Study of Zoroastrianism.* p. 1

57   *The Holy Bible, King James Version*, Matt. 2:2.

58   *Textual Sources for the Study of Zoroastrianism.* p. 154.

59   *Zoroastrianism: The Religion of the Good Life.* p. 12

60   Darmesteter, James (trans.) *Avesta: Khorda Avesta. Frawardin Yasht: II:* 20-21. http://www.avesta.org/ka/yt13sbe.htm.

61   Dawson, Miles M. *The Ethical Religion of Zoroaster.* p. xiii.

62   Ibid. p. xiii.

Chapter 3

1   West, E.W. (trans.). *The Bundahishn. Sacred Books of the East,* vol. 5. http://avesta.org/mp/bundahis.html.

2   Mills, L.H. (trans.). *Avesta: Yasna.* http://www.avesta.org/yasna/yasna.htm.

3   Ibid.

4   Boyce, Mary. *Textual Sources for the Study of Zorastrianism.* pp. 48-49.

5   *The Bundahishn. Sacred Books of the East,* vol. 5. http://avesta.org/mp/bundahis.html.

6   Bharucha, Ervad Sheriarhi Dadabhai. *A Brief Sketch of the Zoroastrian Religion & Customs.* pp. 20-21.

7   Ibid. p. 21.

8   *Avesta: Yasna.* http://www.avesta.org/yasna/yasna.htm.

9   *The Bundahishn. Sacred Books of the East,* vol. 5. http://avesta.org/mp/bundahis.html.

10   *Avesta: Yasna.* http://www.avesta.org/yasna/yasna.htm.

11   Darmesteter, James (trans.). *Avesta: Vendidad.* http://www.avesta.org/vendidad/vd2sbe.htm

12   *Textual Sources for the Study of Zorastrianism.* p. 100.

13   Ibid. p. 100.

14   *Avesta: Vendidad.* http://www.avesta.org/vendidad/vd3sbe.htm

15   Masani, Rustam. *Zoroastrianism: The Religion of the Good Life.* p. 105.

16   *Avesta: Vendidad.* http://www.avesta.org/vendidad/vd3sbe.htm

17   *Zoroastrianism: The Religion of the Good Life.* pp. 124-26.

18   *Avesta: Vendidad.* http://www.avesta.org/vendidad/vd3sbe.htm.

19   *Zoroastrianism: The Religion of the Good Life.* p. 126.

20   Ibid. p. 126. Quoting E.W. West.

21   Ibid. p. 127.

22   *Avesta: Vendidad.* http://www.avesta.org/vendidad/vd3sbe.htm.

23   Darmesteter, James (trans.). "Tahmuras' Fragments". *The Zend-Avesta. Sacred Books of the East*, vol. 1-2. pp. 295-97.

24   *Avesta: Yasna.* http://www.avesta.org/yasna/yasna.htm.

25   Ibid.

26   *Avesta: Vendidad.* http://www.avesta.org/vendidad/vd5sbe.htm.

27   *Avesta: Yasna.* http://www.avesta.org/yasna/yasna.htm.

28   Jafari, Ali A. *Woman in the Gathas and the Later Avesta.* http://www.caissoas.com/CAIS/Religions/iranian/Zarathustrian/woman_in_the_gathas.htm.

29   *Avesta: Yasna.* http://www.avesta.org/yasna/yasna.htm.

30   Mills, L.H. (trans.). *Avesta:Visperad. Sacred Books of the East, American Edition.* http://www.avesta.org/visperad/vr_tc.htm.

31   Darmesteter, James (trans.). *Avesta: Erpatistan and Nirangistan. Sacred Books of the East,* vol. 5.

32 Jahanian, Darius. *Women in the Avestan Era.* http://www.iranchamber.com/society/articles/women_avesta_era.php.

33 *Herodotus: On the Customs of the Persians, c. 430 BCE*, p. 3. http://www.heritageinstitute.com/zoroastrianism./reference/herodotus.htm

34 Xenophon. *Cyropaedia of Xenophon: The Life of Cyrus the **Great**.* http://www.iranchamber.com/history/xenophon/ cyropaedia_xenophon_book1.php.

35 *Avesta: Yasna.* http://www.avesta.org/yasna/yasna.htm.

36 *Avesta: Vendidad.* http://www.avesta.org/vendidad/vd19sbe.htm.

37 Noori, Ahmad. "The Medical Sciences in the Avesta." http://www.iranchamber.com/culture/articles/medical_sciences_avesta.php.

38 Price, Massoume. "Pre-Zoroastrian Religions of Iran." http://www.iranchamber.com/religions/articles/pre_zoroastrian_religions.php.

39 *Avesta: Vendidad.* http://www.avesta.org/vendidad/vd7sbe.htm.

40 "Ancient Healing: Baresman (Barsom)." http://www.heritageinstitute.com/zoroastrianism/barsom/index.htm
"Ancient Healing: Haoma." http://www.heritageinstitute.com/zoroastrianism/haoma/index.htm.
"Cleanliness and Purification." http://www.heritageinstitute.com/zoroastrianism/purification/index.htm.
"The History of Medicine in Ancient Persia."
http://www.presstv.ir/detail.aspx?id=40689&sectionid=3510304.

41 Darmesteter, James (trans.). *Avesta: Vendidad.* http://www.avesta.org/vendidad/vd7sbe.htm.

42 Ibid.

43 West, E.W. (trans.). *Avesta: Dadistan-I Denik. Sacred Books of the East*, vol. 18. Also http://www.avesta.org/mp/dd94.htm.

44 Ibid. Also http://www.avesta.org/mp/dd38.htm.

45 Karkaria, R.P. (trans.). *Avesta: Denkard. Sacred Books of the East,* vol. 7. Also http://www.avesta.org/denkard/dk3s275.html.

46 *Avesta: Yasna.* http://www.avesta.org/yasna/yasna.htm.

47 Kohiyar, Ratanshah E. (trans.) *Avesta: Denkard.* http://www.avesta.org/denkard/dk3s.html.

48 Bowker, John. *The Oxford Dictionary of World Religions.* pp. 763-64 as cited in http://www.themystica.com/mysticval/articals/p/prayer_zoroastrian.html.

49 *Zoroastrianism: The Religion of the Good Life.* pp. 56-57.

50 *Khorda Avesta* (Book of Common Prayer). http://www.avesta.org/ka/ka/_part1.htm.

51 *Khorda Avesta* (Book of Common Prayer). http://www.avesta.org/ka/yt1_bi.htm.

52 *Zoroastrianism: The Religion of the Good Life.* p. 135.

53 *Khorda Avesta* (Book of Common Prayer). http://www.avesta.org/ka/ka/_part1.htm.

54 *Avesta: Denkard.* http://www.avesta.org/denkard/dk3s.html.

55 *Avesta: Yasna.* http://www.avesta.org/yasna/yasna.htm.

56 Jafari, Ali A. "The Zoroastrian Priest in the Avesta." p. 7.

57 Dawson, Miles M. *The Ethical Religion of Zoroaster.* p. 200.

58 "Zoroastrian Priesthood." pp. 1-2. http://www.heritageinstitute.com/Zoroastrianism/priests/index.htm.

59 West, E.W. (trans.). *Avesta: Dadistan-I Denik. Sacred Books of the East*, vol 18. Also http://www.avesta.org/mp/dd94.htm.

60 *Avesta: Vendidad.* http://www.avesta.org/vendidad/vd3sbe.htm.

61 *Avesta: Yasna.* http://www.avesta.org/yasna/yasna.htm.

62 *Textual Sources for the Study of Zoroastrianism.* p. 91.

63 West, E.W. (trans.) *Avesta:Zand-I Vohuman Yasht. Sacred Books of the East,* vol. 5. http://www.avesta.org/mp/vohuman.html.

64 Ibid.

65 Williams, A.V. (trans.) *"Pahlavi Rivayat".* http://www.avesta.org/zcomet.html.

66 Ibid.

67 *Avesta: Zand-I Vohuman Yasht. Sacred Books of the East,* vol. 5. http://www.avesta.org/mp/vohuman.html.

68 *The Bundahishn. Sacred Books of the East,* vol. 5. http://www.avesta.org/mp/bundahis.html.

69 *"Pahlavi Rivayat".* http://www.avesta.org/zcomet.html.

Chapter 4

1 Dawson, Miles M. *The Ethical Religion of Zoroaster.* pp. 20-21.

2 Ibid. p. 18.

3 Mills, L.H. (trans.). *The Zend Avesta, Part III.* p. 8. http://www.sacred-texts.com/zor/sbe31/sbe31006.htm.

4 Sharma, Suresh K. and Usha Sharma. *Cultural and Religious Heritage of India: Zoroastrianism.* p. 209-10.

5 Mills, L.H. (trans.). *Yasna. Sacred Books of the East,* vol. 31. p. 122-23.

6 "101 Names of the Lord 'Ahura Mazda'". http://www.persiandna.com/101Names.htm.

7 Masani, Rustam. *Zoroastrianism: The Religion of the Good Life.* p. 53.

8 Bharucha, Ervad Sheriarhi Dadabhai. *A Brief Sketch of the Zoroastrian Religion & Customs.* pp. 12-13.

9 *Zoroastrianism: The Religion of the Good Life.* pp. 12-13.

10 Ibid. p. 72.

11 Ibid. p. 47.

12 Ibid. p. 72.

13 Ibid. pp. 73-79.

14 V, Jayaram. "Zoroastrian Cosmogony or Theories of Creation." http://www.hinduwebsite.com/zoroastrianism/cosmogony.asp.

15 Darmesteter, James. *Sacred Books of the East, vol. 4.* p. vii.

16 Carus, Paul. *History of the Devil: Persian Dualism.* p. 56. http://www.sacred-texts.com/evil/hod/hod07.htm.

17 Boyce, Mary. *Zoroastrians: Their Religious Beliefs and Practices. p. 27.*

18   West, E.W. (trans.). *Bundahishn. Sacred Books of the East,* vol. 5. pp. 6-7.

19   West, E.W. (trans.). *Dadistan-I Dinik. Sacred Books of the East,* vol. 18. pp. 26-28.

20   Ibid. pp. 28-32.
     The Ethical Religion of Zoroaster. pp. 239-40.

21   Boyce, Mary. *Textual Sources for the Study of Zoroastrianism.* p. 100.

22   *The Ethical Religion of Zoroaster.* p. 210.

23   Haug, Martin. *Essays on the Sacred Language, Writings and Religion of the Parsis.* p. 311.

24   Darmesteter, James (trans.). *The Zend Avesta, Part II. Sacred Books of the East, vol.23.*pp. 314-321.

25   *Dadistan-I Dinik. Sacred Books of the East,* vol. 18. p. 36

26   *The Ethical Religion of Zoroaster.* pp.213-220.

27   Ibid. p. 213.

28   Darmesteter, James (trans.) *Avesta: Venidad. Sacred Books of the East, American Edition.* http://www.avesta.org/vendidad/vd7sbe.htm.

29   Ibid. http://www.avesta.org/vendidad/vd6sbe.htm.

30   Ibid. http://www.avesta.org/vendidad/vd8sbe.htm.

31   Ibid. http://www.avesta.org/vendidad/vd5sbe.htm.

32   *The Ethical Religion of Zoroaster.* p. 33.

33   *Dadistan-I Dinik. Sacred Books of the East,* vol. 18. pp. 38-39.

34   *The Ethical Religion of Zoroaster.* pp. 212-226.

35   Ibid. p. 218. *Fargard III: 14.*

36   Darmesteter, James (trans.). *Avesta: Khorda Avesta* (Book of Common Prayer). *Sacred Books of the East, American Edition.* http://avesta.org/ka/yt3_bi.htm.

37   West, E.W. (trans.). *Shayest Na-Shayest. Sacred Books of the East,* vol. 5. p. 335. http://avesta.org/mp/shayest.html#chap11.

38 Mills, L.H. (trans.) *Yasna. Sacred Books of the East, American Edition.* http:// avesta.org/yasna/yasna.htm#y47.

39 Champion, Selwyn and Dorothy Short. *Great Religions of the World.* p. 87.

40 Darmesteter, James (trans.). *The Zend-Avesta. Sacred Books of the East.* pp. 355-56.

41 *The Ethical Religion of Zoroaster.* p. 248.

42 Ibid. pp. 237-240.

43 Darmesteter, James (trans.). *Avesta: Venidad. Sacred Books of the East, American Edition.* http://www.avesta.org/vendidad/vd12sbe.htm

44 *The Ethical Religion of Zoroaster.* pp. 247-249.

45 Masani, Rustam. *Zoroastrianism: The Religion of the Good Life.* p. 1.

46 Dawson, Miles M. *The Ethical Religion of Zoroaster.* p. 193.

47 *Zoroastrianism: The Religion of the Good Life.* p. 11.

48 Darmesteter, James (trans.) *The Zend Avesta, Part 1. Sacred Books of the East,* vol. 4. *http://www.sacred-texts.com/ zor/sbe04/sbe0418.htm.*

49 *The Ethical Religion of Zoroaster.* pp. 253-256.

50 *Zoroastrianism: The Religion of the Good Life.* p. 10.

51 Ibid. p. 10.

52 *The Ethical Religion of Zoroaster.* p. 193.

53 *Zoroastrianism: The Religion of the Good Life.* p. 11.

54 Ibid. p. 103.

55 *The Ethical Religion of Zoroaster.* p. 193.

56 Clark, Peter. *Zoroastrianism : An Introduction to an Ancient Faith.* pp. 69-75.

57 Ibid. p. 29.

58 *Zoroastrianism: The Religion of the Good Life.* p. 11.

Chapter 5

1   *The Holy Bible, King James Version.*

2   Ibid.

3   Ibid.

4   Ibid.

5   Ibid.

6   Ibid.

7   Ibid.

8   Ibid.

9   Ibid.

10   Miller, Madeline S. and Miller, J. Lane (eds.) *Harper's Bible Dictionary.* pp. 212-13.

11   *The Holy Bible, King James Version*, Matt. 9:24-26.

12   Ibid.

13   Ibid.

14   Ibid. Matt. 10:16-20.

15   Ibid.

16   Ibid.

17   Ibid. Deut. 6:5.

18   Ibid. Luke 8:43-47.

19   Ibid. Matt. 6:1-4.

20   Crawford, Deborah. "Average Walking Pace or Speed." http://www.bellaonline.net/articles/art20257.asp.

21   *The Holy Bible, King James Version,* Matt. 14:14-18.

22   Ibid. Matt. 14:19-21.

23   Ibid.

24   Ibid. Matt. 5:17-24.

25   Ibid. Matt. 6:9-10.

26   Ibid. Matt. 14:22-33.

27   Ibid. Dan. 12:5-7.

28   Ibid. Matt. 15:32-38.

29   Ibid. Matt. 16:5-12.

30   Ibid. Matt. 16:17-19.

31   Ibid. Matt. 16:21.

32   Ibid. Mark 9:1-8.

33   Ibid. Matt. 6:16-18.

34   Ibid. Matt. 6:19-24.

35   Ibid. John 11:14-45.

36   Ibid. John 11:46-48.

37   Ibid. John 49-54.

38   Ibid. John 13.

39   Ibid. John 4.

40   Ibid. Ps. 23:1-4.

41   Ibid. Ps. 23:5-6.

42   Ibid. Matt. 13:47-50.

43   Ibid.

44   Ibid. Matt. 21:12-16.

45   Ibid. Mark 11:17-18.

46   Ibid. Luke 19:45-48.

47   Ibid. Luke 20:1-8.

48   Ibid. Luke 20:19-26.

49 Ibid.

50 Ibid.

51 Ibid. Matt. 26:14-16.

52 *Harper's Bible Dictionary.* pp. 118-20.

53 *The Holy Bible, King James Version,* Matt. 27:37.

54 Ibid. Matt. 27:32.

55 Ibid. Matt. 27:57-66.

56 Ibid. Matt. 28:1-8.

57 Ibid. Matt. 28:11-20.

Chapter 6

1   West, E.W. (trans.). *Dinkard 7. Sacred Books of the East,* vol. 37. pp. 15-16.

2   Ibid. pp. 16-17.

3   Ibid. pp. 17-18.

4   Moulton, J.H. *The Treasure of the Magi.* p. 19.

5. Sivananda, Sri Swami. "Zoroaster". *Lives of Saints.* http://www.dlshq.org/saints/zoroaster.htm.

6   Gill, N.S. "Zoroaster." http://ancienthistory.about.com/od/monotheisticreligions/p/030910Zoroaster.htm.

7   Ibid.

8   Ibid.

9   *The Holy Bible, King James Version.*

10 From the Book of James, *New American Bible* (Roman Catholic). http://www.usccb.org/nab/bible.
    While considered Apocryphal by Bishop Ireaneous (180 AD), the narratives of this book has been accepted by the Vatican for the apparent omissions of the Gospels in the early life of Jesus and His mother, Mary. As with all Apocryphal Scripture, the veracity of the text should be questioned since it may be ill founded. (Fuller, Reginald C., Johnston, Leonard, Kearns, Conleth (eds.) *A New Catholic Commentary on the Holy Scripture*, 90h, p. 113.)

11 *The Holy Bible, King James Version.*

12 Ibid.

13 Ibid.

14 Ibid. Matt. 2:12-15.

15 *The Holy Bible, King James Version,* Matt. 4:1-11 and Luke 4:1-13.

16 Masani, Rustam. *Zoroastrianism: The Religion of the Good Life.* p. 41.

17 For further information of Zarathustra's healing abilities, look to Chapter 3. For more information of Jesus' abilities, look to Chapter 5.

18 *The Holy Bible, King James Version,* Matt. 10:1-8.

19 The Magi were said to have the gift of healing, although by them it should be considered a sign of the use of sorcery not spirituality. (*A New Catholic Commentary on Holy Scripture.* 713: d-g, p. 908.)

20 Anklesaria, Behramgore Tehmuras (trans.). *Greater Bundahishn.* http://www.avesta.org/pahlavi/grb27.htm.

21 *The Holy Bible, King James Version.*
    Author's Note: The Return (or Second Coming) of Jesus will be discussed in Chapter 9.

22 *The Holy Bible, King James Version,*1 Tim. 2:5; Rom. 1:4; John 16:24.

23 Darmesteter, James (trans.). *Avesta: Korda Avesta. Sacred Books of the East. American Edition.* http://www.avesta.org/ka/yt13sbe.htm.

24 *The Holy Bible, King James Version,* John 4:24.
    Boyce, Mary. *Textual Sources for the Study of Zoroastrianism. Yasna* 31:8, p. 38.

25 *Textual Sources for the Study of Zoroastrianism.* p. 154.

26 *The Holy Bible, King James Version*, Matt. REFERNCE?

27 *Zoroastrianism: The Religion of the Good Life.* p. 104.

28 *Textual Sources for the Study of Zoroastrianism. Yasna* 31:8, p. 38.

29 Cyrus II. "The First Charter of the Rights of Nations." http://www.farsinet.com/cyrus/.

30 *The Holy Bible, King James Version.*

31   *Textual Sources for the Study of Zoroastrianism.* p. 154.

32   Miller, Madeline S. and Miller, J. Lane (eds.) *Harper's Bible Dictionary.* pp. 157-58.

33   Grech, P. "Jesus Christ in History." *A New Catholic Commentary on Holy Scripture.* pp. 822-37.

Chapter 7

1   The theories concerning the length of ministry vary from eight months to three years. Most theologians and scholars believe His ministry included two Passovers; therefore it is suggested that His ministry was between thirteen and thirty-five months.

2   The only ancient mention of Jesus of Nazareth is in the official records of Herod Antipas, listing among the executed one Jesus of Nazareth. Historically one needs to use the New Testament for its record of the ministry of Jesus.

3   The historical influence of Zoroaster is well chronicled by historians from Greece, Cyria, Egypt and other Middle Eastern countries, as well as in Persian histories.

4   Miller, Madeline S. and Miller, J. Lane (eds.) *Harper's Bible Dictionary.* p. 123.

5   Ibid. p. 431.

6   Ibid. p. 431.

7   Ibid. pp. 481-82.

8   Ibid. p. 123.

9   *The Holy Bible, King James Version,* Esther 1:19 and Dan. 5:28.

10   Ibid. Ezra 1:7-11.

11   Ibid. 3 Kings 24:18-20.

12   Ibid.

13   *Harper's Bible Dictionary.* p. 123.

14   Ibid. p. 123.

15   Ibid. pp. 439-41.

16   Ibid. p. 647.

17   These authors' opinions from *Harper's Bible Dictionary.* pp. 337-39.

18   Ibid. p. 612.

19   Ibid. pp. 337-38.

20   Ibid. p. 612.

21   Ibid. p. 123.

22   *The Holy Bible, King James Version,* 2 Chron. 36:15-23.

23   *Harper's Bible Dictionary.* p. 127.
     Fuller, Reginald C., Johnston, Leonard, Kearns, Conleth (eds.) *A New Catholic Commentary on the Holy Scripture.* 314:a-j, pp. 386-88.

24   *The Holy Bible, King James Version,* Ezra 6:15.

25   Ibid. Ezra 5:3.

26   Ibid. Ezra 6:1-5.

27   Ibid. Ezra 6:6-12.

28   Lehderin, Linda. "The Behistun Inscription." http://www.livius.org/be-bm/behistun/behistun01.htm.

29   *Harper's Bible Dictionary.* p. 127.

30   **"Darius III."** *Encyclopedia Britannica.*

31   *Harper's Bible Dictionary.* pp. 529-34.

32   Ibid. p. 18.

33   Ibid. pp. 647-48.

34   "Fredrich Nietzsche." *Stanford Encyclopedia of Philosophy.* (Article rev. 2010). http://www.stanford.edu.

35   Translators, publication dates, and texts include: Max Muller (1879) *The Upanishads* (part 1 of 2); George Buhler (1879) *The Sacred Laws of the Aryas* (part 1 of 2); James Darmesteter (1880) *The Zend-Avesta* (part 1 of 3); E.w. West (1880) *The Pahlavi Texts* (part 1 of 5); Max Muller (1881) *The Dhammapada and the Sutta-Nipata*; T.W. Rhys David and Hermann Oldenberg (1881) *Vinaya Texts* (part 1of 3); T.W. Rhys David and Hermann Oldenberg (1882) *Vinaya Texts* (part 2 of 3); George Buhler (1882) *The*

Sacred Laws of the Aryas (part 2of 3); E.W. West (1882) *Pahlavi Texts* (part 2 of 5); James Darmesteter (1883) *The Zend-Avesta* (part 2 of 3); E.W. West (1884) *The Pahlavi Texts* (part 3 of 5); E.W. West (1892) *The Pahlavi Texts* (part 4 of 5); E.W. West (1895) *The Pahlavi Texts* (part 5 of 5).

36 As quoted on the back cover of *Thus Spoke Zarathustra*, Gateway ed.

37 "Fredrich Nietzsche." *Stanford Encyclopedia of Philosophy.* http://www.stanford.edu.

38 Ibid.

39 Ibid.

40 Nietzsche, Friedrich. *Thus Spoke Zarathustra.* p. 103.

41 Strauss, Ricard. *Also Sprach Zarathustra: The 2001 Overture.*

42 "Fredrich Nietzsche." *Stanford Encyclopedia of Philosophy.* http://www.stanford.edu.

43 Nietzsche, Friedrich. *Thus Spoke Zarathustra.* p. 6.

44 Ibid. p. 7.

45 Ibid. pp. 124-25.

46 "Fredrich Nietzsche." *Stanford Encyclopedia of Philosophy.* http://www.stanford.edu.

47 See Footnote 35.

48 "Fredrich Nietzsche." *Stanford Encyclopedia of Philosophy.* http://www.stanford.edu.

49 Ibid.

50 Ibid.

51 Kalish, Michael. "Friedrich Nietzsche's Influence on Hitler's *Mein Kampf*".

52 "Fredrich Nietzsche." *Stanford Encyclopedia of Philosophy.* http://www.stanford.edu.

53 Ibid.

54 Kalish, Michael. "Friedrich Nietzsche's Influence on Hitler's *Mein Kampf*".

55 Goodstein, Laurie. "Zoroastrians Keep the Faith, And Keep Dwindling." *The New York Times.* http://www.nytimes.com/2006/09/06/us/06faith.html?_r=1

56 Masani, Rustam. *Zoroastrianism: The Religion of the Good Life.* p. 49.

57 Ibid. pp. 93-94.

58 Boyce, Mary. *Textual Sources for the Study of Zoroastrianism.* pp. 133-34.

59 Boyce, Mary. *Zoroastrians, Their Religious Beliefs and Practices.* p. 1

60 "The Life of Thomas A. Edison."
    http://memory.loc.gov/ammem/edhtml/edbio.html.

61 Ibid.

62 Ibid.

63 Ibid.

64 Ibid.

65 Ibid.

66 Ibid.

67 Ibid.

68 Ibid.

69 Ibid.

70 Ibid.

71 Ibid.

72 "History Of Mazda." http://lifestyle.iloveindia.com/lounge/history-of-
    mazda-8927.html.

73 *The Holy Bible, King James Version,* Luke 3:21.

74 "History of the Crusades 1095-1291" *History World.* http://www.
    historyworld.net/wrldhis/PlainTextHistories.asp?groupid=1793&HistoryID=a
    b54&gtrack=pthc.

75 Ibid.

76 Ibid.

77 Trueman, Chris. "What Were the Crusades?" *History Learning Site.* http://
    www.historylearningsite.co.uk/cru1.htm.

Chapter 8

1   Dosick, Rabbi Wayne. *Living Judaism.* pp. 96, 104.

2   Ibid. p. 33.

3   Miller, Madeline S. and Miller, J. Lane (eds.) *Harper's Bible Dictionary.* pp. 157-59.

4   *Living Judaism.* pp. 96-97.

5   Ibid. p. 31.

6   Ibid. pp. 31-36.

7   Ibid. p. 33.

8   Ibid. pp. 96-97.

9   Ibid. pp. 33-35.

10   Ibid. pp. 232-37.

11   Ibid. pp. 229-32.

12   Ibid. p. 19.

13   Ibid. pp. 98-100.

14   Ibid. p. 43.

15   Ibid. p. 143-45.

16   See *The Holy Bible, King James Version,* Deut. 11:13.

17   *Living Judaism.* pp. 145-46.

18   Ibid. pp. 229-32.

19   Ibid. p. 229.

20   Ibid. pp. 61-62.

21   Ibid. p. 62.

22   Ibid. p. 62-63.

23   Ibid. p. 63.

24   Ibid. pp. 351-55.

25 Ibid. p. 188. For a total look at the Holocaust see pp. 181-94.

26 *The Holy Bible, King James Version,* Isa. 62.

27 Ibid. Exod. 13:15.

28 According to the *World Christian Encyclopedia*, there are over 33,000 denominations worldwide.   http://www.bringyou.to/apologetics/a106.html.

29 *The Holy Bible, King James Version,* Isa. 44:28.

30 Ibid. Isa. 45:1-5.

31 Ibid. Isa. 45:12-13.

Chapter 9

1 Heschel, Abraham Joshua. *Between God and Man: An Interpretation of Judaism.* pp. 51-52.

2 West., E.W. (trans.) *Dadistan-I Dinik* XIX:2. *Sacred Books of the East,* vol. 18. p. 44.

3 Mills, L.H. (trans.) *Yasna* XXXII:4. http://www.sacred-texts.com/zor/sbe31/sbe31010.htm

4 From Gaelic saying, made famous by President Grover Cleveland. http://www.famousquotes.com

5 New York State Department of Education. "Doc. A-421 Verbal Abuse." 6/29/2009.

6 "Norman Vincent Peale: Champion of Positive Thinking." http//normanvincentpeale.wwwhubs.com. Peale's book *The Power of Positive Thinking* was published in 1952.

Intermedia Publishing Group

Publishing That Works For You

Do you need a speaker?

Do you want Douglas Roper Krotz to speak to your group or event? Then contact Larry Davis at: (623) 337-8710 or email: ldavis@intermediapr.com or use the contact form at: www.intermediapr.com.

Whether you want to purchase bulk copies of *The Man Who Sent The Magi* or buy another book for a friend, get it now at: www.imprbooks.com.

If you have a book that you would like to publish, contact Terry Whalin, Publisher, at Intermedia Publishing Group, (623) 337-8710 or email: twhalin@intermediapub.com or use the contact form at: www.intermediapub.com.